The Chef's New Secret Cookbook

Louis Szathmáry

Illustrations by
Nancy Rodgers Peil

Henry Regnery Company • Chicago

Library of Congress Cataloging in Publication Data

Szathmáry, Louis
    Chef's new secret cookbook.

    Includes index.
    1. Cookery. I. Title.
TX715.S9868   641.5   75-13245
ISBN 0-8092-8354-9

Published by Henry Regnery Company
180 North Michigan Avenue, Chicago, Illinois 60601
Manufactured in the United States of America
Library of Congress Catalog Card Number: 75-13245
International Standard Book Number: 0-8092-8354-9

Published simultaneously in Canada by
Fitzhenry & Whiteside Limited
150 Lesmill Road
Don Mills, Ontario M3B 2T5
Canada

To Magda and Kirk, with love

Contents

1
Appetizers

Most scientists who study brain function agree that when you think about an event from the past, the first thing you remember is how it ended, then how it began, and slowly you recall what happened in between.

When people recall a meal, then, they are likely to remember first the dessert, then the first course—the appetizer. So it is very important how you start the meal.

As a rule, long, elaborate meals are the exception today. Three courses (or perhaps four at the most, with a salad being the fourth) are most common at evening meals and two or three courses at noon. Being very much aware of this trend, I have tried to think of "first course" or "appetizer" not only in selecting the recipes for this chapter but also in choosing the salads and soups. That is why no salad or salad-type dish is included among the appetizers. If a salad is what you are looking for, please turn to the chapter on salads and you will find a good selection.

Very few ingredients called for in this book are difficult to get, because I believe that proper methods and proper techniques, careful measuring and good combinations of textures and flavors are more important than exotic ingredients.

Of course, I know, because I keep in touch with thousands of homemakers, that the first course is often something we can purchase ready-to-serve, with no more involvement than transferring it from the original container to the service platter or plate. Demands on our time make it so. No less an authority than Auguste Escoffier recognized this fact a long time ago and suggested in his classic cookbook (which is the professional chefs' bible) that even in the finest hotel, restaurant, or private dining room, it is quite permissible to serve ready-to-eat items purchased in a grocery store or delicatessen, even in the original container.

As an example Escoffier suggested that fine Portuguese sardines should be served right in the can, with a paper doily and a silver plate underneath, and with fresh lemon and lightly buttered toast on the side. Caviar, Westphalian ham or Parma ham, smoked Scottish salmon, smoked sturgeon, anchovy rings, Greek, Italian, and Spanish olives, and hundreds of other items are always available as appetizers.

Instead of elaborating on this kind of starter for a meal, I prefer to select unusual ideas and methods which turn simple ingredients into great appetizers. The recipes in this section will tell you how I do it. But remember, to produce a successful first course, proper temperature, texture, and color are just as important for the appetizer itself as they are for the harmony of the whole meal.

Baked Green Peppers

8 servings

8 cubinella peppers, or 16 sweet banana peppers or light green peppers (sorry, for this dish bell peppers won't do)
1 cup oil

¼ cup vinegar mixed with ¾ cup water
1 tablespoon sugar
1 teaspoon salt
1 clove garlic

1.   Preheat oven to 400° F. Wash and wipe dry the peppers. Dip one or two fingers in the oil and gently coat the peppers.

2.   Place them in a large pan or on a cookie sheet and bake. Turn every 2 or 3 minutes until the peppers turn limp and brownish with pale bubbles. It will take 20 to 30 minutes for light green peppers or cubinellas, somewhat less with sweet banana peppers.

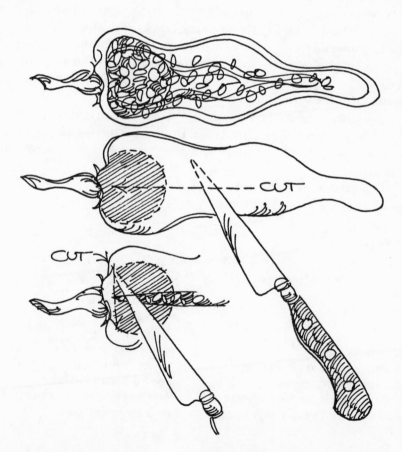

3.   Remove from the oven, let cool, peel, and slit up the side about a third of the way from the stem toward the tip. Carefully remove the seeds and the core, leaving on the stem and leaving the peppers whole.

4.   In a small saucepan boil the vinegar and water, sugar, and salt. When it comes to a rapid boil, pour it gently over the peppers.

5.   In a small bowl, mash the garlic with a few drops of the oil; then slowly add the remaining oil and stir until all the garlic is mashed. Place the peppers in a shallow dish, strain the garlic-oil through a fine sieve over them, and let them cool to room temperature. Cover the dish and chill the peppers overnight. Serve one pepper to a person with a thick slice of crusty bread. They are excellent with cocktails or with Slivovitz or Barack on the rocks.

CHEF'S SECRET: In Transylvania this is a favorite first course for festive dinners. It is usually made on the top of a wood stove, and the smoke coming through the cracks at the top of the range gives a special delicate flavor to the peppers. In the summer, if you roast the peppers in an aluminum foil pan on an outdoor grill before the fire dies down, you will have the same smoky tang.

If you wish, add a few drops of Tabasco to the vinegar, or slice in a hot pepper or just a part of it. Don't ever use hot peppers for the recipe proper, because you won't be able to control the "heat."

This dish may be kept for 2 or 3 weeks in the refrigerator as long as it is covered with oil.

Cheese-Filled Pecan Halves

60 to 80 pieces

2 ounces butter
4 ounces cream cheese
2 ounces Roquefort,
  Gorgonzola, or blue cheese
1 or 2 drops Tabasco (optional)

¼ teaspoon Worcestershire
  sauce (optional)
60 to 80 pecan halves
  (approximately 3 ounces)
2 or 3 large carrots

1. Leave butter and cheese for ½ hour or so at room temperature; then blend in electric mixer until fluffy. Add Tabasco and Worcestershire sauce if you wish.

2. Fill a pastry bag, fitted with a plain tube, with the cheese mixture. You may use a teaspoon if you have no pastry bag. Press a small dab of cheese mixture (the size of a walnut) onto each pecan half. Lay the pecan halves next to each other, cheese side up, on a waxed-paper-covered cookie sheet or shallow pan.

3. Peel the carrots and cut them with a sharp knife, on a bias, into discs about ⅛ inch thick.

4. When your guests begin to arrive, press a carrot slice on each pecan half so that the cheese spreads out evenly between the carrot and pecan. Arrange them on a doily-covered silver or glass tray, and serve with cocktails or wine.

CHEF'S SECRET: Years ago this was a popular dish to nibble on, but it was done without carrots—two pecan halves were pressed together with the cheese mixture in between. Now that pecan prices are up, the carrot helps two ways: it cuts expenses and cuts calories. Of course, this would not be an excuse for the change if the textures, colors, aromas, and taste did not go perfectly together.

If you cut on the correct bias, the carrot slices will be uniformly oval. Keep them for 5 minutes in ice water, then pat dry and put in a plastic bag in the refrigerator.

This hors d'oeuvre is especially good with sherry or with not too sweet, well-chilled white wine. If you wish you can try it with Kir (a popular aperitif in France).

Chef's Salt

1 cup

1 cup salt
1 tablespoon paprika
(Hungarian or Spanish)
1 teaspoon black pepper, freshly
ground

¼ teaspoon ground white
pepper
¼ teaspoon celery salt (not
garlic powder!)

Mix above ingredients well and keep in a jar. Use instead of salt.

Cottage Cheese Island

8 servings

1 pint large-curd cottage cheese
1 pint small-curd cottage
  cheese
1 pint yogurt
8 (or more) scallions with the
  green tops left on

1 teaspoon Chef's Salt (see
  index)
8 red radishes with the green
  tops left on
3 or 4 medium-sized tomatoes

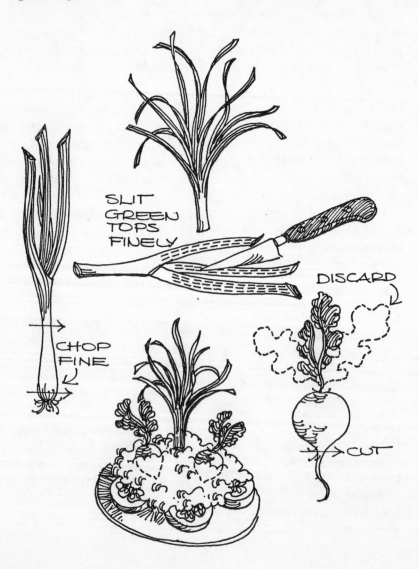

SLIT GREEN TOPS FINELY

DISCARD

CHOP FINE

CUT

1.   In a bowl, gently mix together the two kinds of cottage cheese and the yogurt. Refrigerate.

2.   Trim the scallions; discard the roots. Cut out the middle part of each (see illustration); discard tops of leaves. Chop the white part fine and mix with the cottage cheese and yogurt. Add Chef's Salt and return to the refrigerator.

3.   Carefully clean 8 radishes so that the middle 2 or 3 leaves remain. Cut off root ends, immerse in ice water, and chill.

4.   Slice the tomatoes to make 3 or 4 slices for each person.

5.   Just before serving, arrange the tomato slices on each salad plate. Spoon ⅛ of the cheese mixture on them, in the middle. Stick in the scallion to resemble a palm tree and the radish to resemble a small tropical plant. Serve with toasted rye bread.

CHEF'S SECRET: This is more of an idea than a recipe, but I like it very much because it serves some useful purposes. It is elegant and light as a first course for a formal dinner and a children's party alike. It can be made partially or totally from low-calorie dry cottage cheese or other types of diet cottage cheese for the one or two persons in the group who cannot eat the "real stuff."

And here's how I got this idea: Many years ago in New York I used to work in the executive dining room of a large corporation. One of the directors was a world-famous entertainer on a very strict diet. He was always concerned about keeping rigorously to his doctor's orders without letting people notice that he was on a diet. On the days when he ate with five or six others at a luncheon meeting, he would ask me to dream up something for him to eat that looked the same as what was on the others' plates. I had arrived in New York shortly before as a penniless immigrant, and I needed every cent I could make. So I appreciated his generous tips and little thank-you notes sent to me through his secretary.

I dreamed up this "island" for him. His was made from a skim-milk cottage cheese that tasted like plaster of Paris, with a couple teaspoons of skim milk, without any salt or chopped scallions, and with tomatoes sliced so thin you could read the newspaper through them. It was served with some kind of diet bread that tasted more like rubber sponge with sawdust than anything else. While the others enjoyed their good cottage cheese with fragrant rye bread, crisp scallions, and crunchy radishes, he chewed his imitation without anyone else knowing what was going on.

If you wish you can flavor the cottage cheese with prepared mustard, anchovy paste, or crushed caraway seeds. You can also add chopped walnuts or chopped salted peanuts, small bits of cold cuts or ham, or tiny pieces of cheese or grated Parmesan. The "looks" will sell the dish. The little palm trees, of course, can be used as decorations on many other dishes, such as cold potato salad, a ring mold of tuna salad, and so forth.

If radishes with green tops are not available, use radishes from the bag. In this case, make a hole in the leaf-end of the radish with a round wooden toothpick or with the tip of a small paring knife, and insert a couple of sprigs of curly parsley.

Beef Tartar

8 servings

8 ounces lean round or sirloin, free of fat
8 ounces lean tenderloin tip
1 egg, coddled
2 tablespoons very finely minced onion
1 tablespoon rinsed capers, chopped
1 teaspoon Chef's Salt (see index)

generous grinding of fresh black pepper
½ ounce Kirschwasser, vodka, or bourbon
German-type rye bread, pumpernickel, or cocktail rye, thinly sliced
unsalted butter
chopped onion or cleaned scallions

1. To make Beef Tartar is almost a religious ceremony. The classic way is to have the beef ground twice. Pile it up in the middle of a large platter, put an indentation in the top, and surround it with small containers (saucers from demitasse cups, for example, or other tiny dishes 2½ to 3½ inches in diameter).

2. On one container place the coddled egg (to coddle an egg, you slowly submerge it in boiling water for about 30 seconds, then remove and cool by placing it for a minute or so in cold water). On another small plate put the finely chopped onion.

(No, you cannot chop the onion the day before or even a few hours ahead; it must be chopped just before serving.) On other plates put the capers, the Chef's salt, and finally the freshly ground pepper. Have ready in a small glass the spirits of your choice.

3.   Break the egg into the indentation in the middle of the meat, sprinkle on the Chef's Salt and the pepper, and gently stir the spices into the egg with a fork.

4.   Add the onion, the capers, and the spirits. Work through the mixture with two forks until all the ingredients are well blended and the Beef Tartar is in the form of a ball in the middle of the large plate.

5.   Remove the small plates used for the ingredients and surround the beef with the bread. Place next to it the fresh butter and generous amounts of chopped onion or some cleaned scallions.

CHEF'S SECRET: If possible, grind the beef for this dish yourself, first cutting both meats into 2-inch-long and ½-inch-thick strips. Use the grinding plate with the largest holes, but grind it two or three times.

If tenderloin is not available, use all round or sirloin, but be sure it has no fat, not even marbling (that's the fatty tissue inside of the muscle that runs crisscross in the meat). As pleasant as the raw meat tastes if it is lean, that's how unpleasant it can taste if it is fat. The raw fat sticks to the roof of your mouth and coats it.

Eggplant Appetizer

8 servings

2 eggplants (approximately 1½ pounds total weight)
1 teaspoon Chef's Salt (see index)
½ teaspoon freshly ground black pepper
¼ cup oil
¼ teaspoon garlic salt
3 to 4 tablespoons vinegar (to taste)

½ teaspoon sugar
½ cup very finely minced onion, or ½ cup minus 2 tablespoons grated onion
Greek-style black olives, bell peppers, cherry tomatoes, for decoration
Greek bread and unsalted butter, or toasted, buttered bread triangles

1.   Preheat oven to 350°F. Split eggplants in half lengthwise, sprinkle the cut surfaces with Chef's Salt and black pepper, and rub with some of the oil. Bake for 75 to 90 minutes.

2.   Remove and let cool on the baking sheet until cool enough to handle.

3.   Peel the purple skin and discard it. With a stainless steel knife, first cube the eggplant into 1-inch cubes on a chopping board. Then chop fine with the stainless steel knife. Place in the bowl of an electric mixer, add remaining oil, garlic salt, vinegar, sugar, and minced onion.

4.   Beat first on slow, then on medium speed until smooth.

5.   Let the mixture stand overnight in the refrigerator. Cover the bowl securely with plastic wrap.

6.   Before serving, stir gently with a spoon or spatula, taste, and add a little more vinegar and salt if it is too bland or a small pinch of sugar if it is too tart. Transfer to a glass or silver bowl. Grind fresh black pepper on top and decorate with slices or rings of green pepper, black olives, and cherry tomatoes.

7.   Serve with flat bread (Greek, Lebanese, Turkish, etc.) and unsalted butter, or with lightly toasted, buttered bread triangles.

CHEF'S SECRET: Use about a teaspoon or so of oil to rub on each half of the eggplant—it protects the surface from evaporation. Eggplant contains a large amount of water, and if you don't protect the cut surface with the oil, as soon as the temperature of the eggplant reaches the boiling point for water it will start to evaporate. The evaporation point of oil is much higher, so even a very thin layer of oil will protect the eggplant and will keep the moisture inside, making it smoother and tastier.

Eggplant turns ugly blackish and blue from a carbon steel knife. That's why we emphasize the stainless steel knife. In the Mediterranean, where this dish is a favorite, wooden knives are used to chop the eggplant.

Holiday Rollmops

8 servings

16 pickled herring fillets, approximately 3½ to 4 inches long and about 1 to 1¼ inches wide (or 8 pickled herrings the same size)
8 scallions

1 large dill pickle
1 large carrot
1 tube anchovy paste
2 tablespoons mayonnaise
½ teaspoon paprika
buttered rye bread

1. Rinse the herring fillets, pat dry, and lay next to each other, skin side down, on a cutting board. Cut off the tails, if any. If you can't get fillets, then, with a paring knife, cut each herring in half along the backbone, remove the bone, and cut off the tails. Then rinse and proceed as above.

2. Cut off the roots of the scallions and cut each scallion into 1 ½-inch pieces. Cut both ends of each scallion piece with very close cross cuts about ¼ to ⅜ inch deep and drop the flared scallions into ice water. Both ends will open up, looking like small brushes. Lay a scallion on each herring fillet, at the tail end.

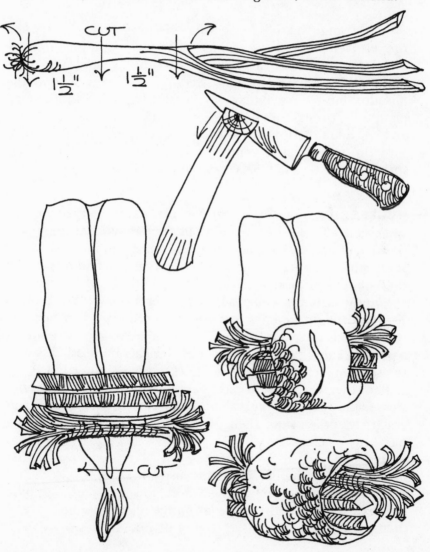

3.   Peel the pickle as you would a cucumber, and cut it into 16 pieces an inch long and approximately ¼ by ¼ inches thick.

4.   Peel the carrot and cut from the top part two pieces 1 ¼ inches long. From each of these cut 8 pieces 1 ¼ inches long and ¼ by ¼ inches thick.

5.   Squeeze from the tube a ½-inch-long strip of anchovy paste onto the herring, right next to the scallion. Press into the anchovy paste a piece of pickle and a piece of carrot, and roll it up starting at the tail. Each roll should have vivid green pickle, golden yellow carrot, and a snow white scallion visible at both ends.

6.   Arrange the rolls for serving as follows: Chop up very fine the leftover parts of the pickle. Grate through a medium-size grater the rest of the large carrot. Mix the two and pile in the middle of a serving platter. Arrange the rolls around the mixture. Put the mayonnaise in a pastry bag fitted with a small plain tube, or make a small cone-shaped bag from waxed paper and cut open the tip with kitchen scissors. After filling the bag with the mayonnaise, gently press it onto the rollmops and sprinkle with paprika. Serve with buttered rye bread.

CHEF'S SECRET: From something plain and inexpensive you can create a festive-looking and pungent appetizer without any cooking, simply by using a paring knife and a grater. If you have some extra herring left, you can chop that too, and mix it with the carrots and pickles.

You can flare the scallions in two different ways: With a sharp paring knife, make one cut right in the middle, then turn the scallion and cross your first cut. Then make cuts as you would cut a pie into 8 and perhaps 16 wedges. Repeat on the other end of the scallion. If scallions are too thick, peel off outer layers.

The other way is first to make parallel cuts starting on one end, close to the outside of the scallion. Keep cutting parallel until you reach the other side; then turn the scallion and repeat the parallel cuts crosswise.

If anchovy paste is too strong for your taste, use a little mayonnaise on the herring fillets instead.

If the herring you purchase is too pungent, sprinkle approximately ½ teaspoon sugar on the fillets after you spread them skin side down on the cutting board.

Mortadella Antipasto

8 servings

1 pound sliced mortadella or
   Italian-style bologna, or
   similar soft-textured pink
   sausage
1 or 2 Italian red onions
   (approximately 5 to 6 ounces
   total weight)
1 clove garlic
½ teaspoon salt

pinch of sugar
½ teaspoon freshly ground
   black pepper
¼ cup oil
¼ cup vinegar mixed with
   ¼ cup water
1 tablespoon rinsed capers
4 to 5 lettuce leaves

1. Cut sliced mortadella into ½-inch-wide strips (if the sausage has a skin, remove it before cutting). Peel and slice the onion thinly so that you will have different sizes of rings.

2. Rub the inside of a wooden salad bowl with the garlic clove; then mash it in the bottom of the bowl with a fork, together with the salt, sugar, and pepper, until it turns to a pulp.

3. To the bowl add drop by drop 1 tablespoon of the oil, stirring constantly. Pour in the rest of the oil in a thin stream; then stir in the vinegar-water mixture.

4. With 2 forks toss the mortadella into the mixture; then add capers and onion rings and toss again. Let stand about 30 minutes at room temperature, gently turning over 2 or 3 times so that the oil and vinegar clings to the ingredients.

5. Arrange lettuce leaves on a platter and pile on the antipasto. If you wish, surround it with radishes and scallions. You can also add a few cubes of Italian cheese. Serve with crusty rye bread and a robust red wine.

CHEF'S SECRET: Rubbing the bottom of the bowl and mashing the garlic with the salt, sugar, and black pepper will release all the oils from the garlic and turn it almost completely to liquid. Then, as you add the oil and mix, the oil will pick up the garlic flavor.

Coating the sausage with the oil and vinegar first will prevent the taste of the onion from affecting the sausage and making the whole dish taste like onions.

Pâté Maison

2 Pounds

1 cup finely minced onions
8 tablespoons lard, or chicken or duck fat
8 ounces chicken or duck livers
2 cups (approximately ¾ pound) cooked meat (chicken, beef, veal, pork, or a combination, but no lamb)

6 tablespoons unsalted butter at room temperature, mixed with:
4 tablespoons lard, or chicken or duck fat (no other shortening will do)
2 to 3 tablespoons brandy or cognac
2 teaspoons Pâté Spice (see recipe below)

1. Sauté onion in lard until very limp, but do not brown. Add livers, raise heat, and cook until the last trace of pink disappears from the thickest part of the thickest liver. Cool.

2. Grind the cooked meat three times, using the medium holes in the meat grinder. (Any roasted, broiled, boiled, baked, braised, or fried meat is good, especially chicken with skin, duck, turkey, pork, veal, or beef, but do not use lamb or mutton.)

3. Grind the livers and onions three times.

4. Beat the butter and lard together in an electric mixer; then, continuing to beat at low speed, blend in the ground liver and meat. Beat until fluffy; then add brandy or cognac and Pâté Spice.

5. Correct seasoning if necessary by adding more salt or Pâté Spice. Chill and serve with pickles and crusty bread.

CHEF'S SECRET: In this recipe the method is really more important than the ingredients. As you can see, you have a choice of lard, chicken fat ("schmaltz"), or duck fat. You have an option of chicken livers or duck livers or a mixture of the two. As for the cooked meat, it can be several different kinds. But please do not try to change the procedure. Do not combine the steps.

When you mix the butter with the lard or chicken or duck fat, note that I say, "No other shortening will do." Most any natural shortening will give the pâté its necessary fluffiness. Oil will not work, and man-made shortening will give the pâté a taste of tallow.

The amount of cognac or brandy may be adjusted, somewhat, but if you do not wish to use any alcohol in the pâté, you must add 2 or 3 tablespoons of some other liquid such as chicken broth or beef broth for proper consistency.

Pâté Spice
(Parisian Spice)

Herbs:

1½ teaspoons very finely crushed bay leaf

1½ teaspoons very finely crushed thyme

1½ teaspoons very finely crushed rosemary

1½ teaspoons very finely crushed basil

Spices:

2½ teaspoons cinnamon

1½ teaspoons mace

¾ teaspoon ground cloves

¼ teaspoon allspice

½ teaspoon ground white pepper

1 teaspoon Spanish or Hungarian paprika

¼ cup salt

1. Mix together the herbs in a spice mortar or crush them in a deep bowl with the bottom of a cup.
2. Sift the herbs through a fine sieve, two or three times, crushing again whatever remains in the sieve, until everything is sifted.
3. Mix with powdered spices and salt.
4. Store in a tightly closed jar.

Potted Shrimp

16 to 24 hors d'oeuvres

8 ounces cooked, ready-to-eat shrimp, or 12 ounces peeled and deveined ready-to-cook shrimp

8 ounces (two sticks) butter

juice of ½ lemon

½ teaspoon salt

¼ teaspoon black pepper

1. If necessary, cook shrimp according to package directions.
2. Cut cooked shrimp into small pieces; then chop until it resembles coarse bread crumbs or cooked rice.

3.   In a saucepan, melt butter. Add chopped shrimp, lemon juice, salt, and pepper, and stir over low heat until well blended. Pour into small casserole or cereal bowl. Let stand for 30 minutes; then refrigerate.

4.   Serve with warmed melba toast or good crackers, or, if nothing else is at hand, saltines. You can also trim white bread, cut into 4 small triangles, place on a cookie sheet, and toast in preheated 400° F. oven until the tips start to brown.

CHEF'S SECRET: This is a traditional English appetizer which goes beautifully with sherry, white wines, or other light aperitifs or even with liquor. It should be smooth enough to make it easy to spread, but coarse enough that the shrimp texture doesn't get lost. Be careful not to overheat the butter or it will have a peculiarly unpleasant taste. If there is too much butter for your taste, cut it down to 6 ounces.

Roquefort-Filled Hard-Boiled Eggs

8 servings

10 large eggs, hard-boiled
3 ounces Roquefort, blue,
   Gorgonzola, or similar
   cheese
⅛ cup heavy cream
3 ounces cream cheese

6 to 8 pitted green olives, finely
   minced
3 or 4 drops Tabasco
½ teaspoon Worcestershire
   sauce
16 rounds or ovals of toast

1.   Place eggs in an empty pot; add 1 tablespoon salt and water to cover plus one inch. Place over high heat and bring water to boil. When it starts to boil, lower heat so that the water just simmers. After 10 minutes, pour off the water and place the eggs under running cold water for a minute or two. Pour off the water, put the lid back on the pot, and shake the pot with the eggs in it, up and down, so that the shells break.

2.   Depending on the shape of toast you plan to use, halve the eggs crosswise or lengthwise and remove the yolks.

3.   Select the 4 least attractive halves and press them through a sieve together with all the yolks.

4.   In an electric mixer on medium speed, mix the crumbled Roquefort with the heavy cream and cream cheese. Slowly add the pressed egg yolks and whites, olives, Tabasco, and Worcestershire sauce, and mix until smooth. With a teaspoon or a pastry bag fitted with a star tube, pipe the filling into the egg halves.

5.   Spread the remaining filling on the toast pieces.

6.   Place an egg half on each toast piece. Serve two to a person as a first course or one to a person as an hors d'oeuvre.

CHEF'S SECRET: If you follow this method for cooking the eggs, I think you will have no difficulty peeling them. If the shell sticks to the egg, it is likely that the eggs are not fresh.

If you think this filling is too bland, you can increase the 3 ounces of cheese to 4 or 5 ounces and decrease the cream cheese accordingly. This will depend on the age, ripeness, and pungency of the cheese you use. Taste the filling and adjust accordingly.

Spanish Artichokes

8 servings

16 baby artichokes, 1¼ to 2
   inches in diameter
1 quart water
2 tablespoons vinegar
1 lemon
1 tablespoon salt

1 tablespoon sugar
1 or 2 bay leaves, crumbled
1 teaspoon black peppercorns,
   bruised
1 cup oil

1.   Select artichokes with the longest stems you can find, but if they don't have stems the dish will still be good. Wash the artichokes carefully and gently under running water and rinse out all sand from the inside. Pull off and discard dark leaves around stem. Cut artichokes on a bias so that when you place them on a serving dish with the cut side down, they will point their stems at the same angle (see illustration).

2.   Peel the stem and cut off only the very end. Put the artichokes into an empty pot. Add the quart of water, vinegar, ½ of the lemon sliced with the rind on, salt, sugar, bay leaves, and peppercorns.

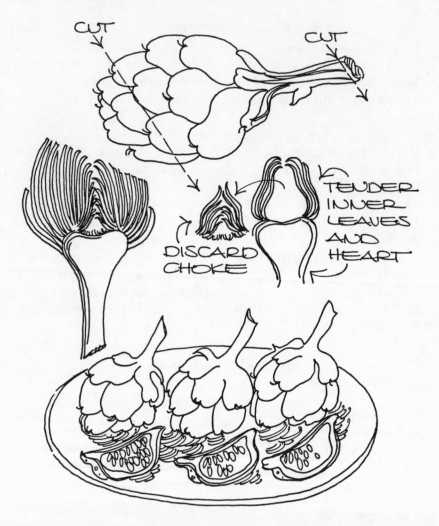

3.   Bring to a rapid boil and simmer for 15 minutes.

4.   Remove artichokes one by one and plunge into cold water. Remove to a towel or absorbent paper. Strain cooking liquid and discard. Keep the peppercorns, bay leaves, and lemon slices.

5.   Remove by hand the tiny inside purple leaves of the artichokes; then gently remove the silky inside (called the choke) and discard. Put the artichokes in a bowl, sprinkle on the juice from the second half of the lemon, spoon on the oil, and add the peppercorns, bay leaves, and lemon slices. Marinate for 2 hours; then chill.

6.   Remove from the refrigerator about one hour before serving time and keep at room temperature until the oil (which

was somewhat congealed in the refrigerator) warms up. Arrange the tiny artichokes on a glass or silver platter and offer them as an hors d'oeuvre or first course.

CHEF'S SECRET: I ate this type of small artichoke several times in Italy and Spain, and I always noticed how much the people who ate them enjoyed the stems. Finally I tasted a stem myself and found that it tasted just like the finest and most expensive part of the artichoke, the heart.

In certain restaurants the artichokes are cooked with much more vinegar, so that when you bite into them, hair starts to grow on your tongue. I personally don't like anything that sour, but, of course, if you wish, you can add more vinegar.

Stuffed Tomatoes with Sardines

8 servings

8 firm but not overripe
  tomatoes, 2 to 2½ inches in
  diameter
2 cans sardines
2 hard-boiled eggs, pressed
  through a fine sieve
1 tablespoon finely minced
  onion or scallions (optional)

1 tablespoon finely minced
  green olives
2 lemons
salt to taste
freshly ground black pepper
8 sprigs parsley and 8 black
  olives for decoration

1. Carefully cut off the stem end of each tomato, just enough so that it can stand flat. Then cut off the flower end, approximately ½ inch from the top (save the tops).

2. Remove the seeds and liquid from the tomatoes, then gently rinse under running water. (Be careful that the water does not hit the tomatoes with such force that it destroys the flesh.)

3. With a small spoon, remove the remaining flesh from the inside of the tomatoes and chop it fine.

4. In a bowl, mix the sardines with their oil, the chopped tomato, eggs, onions, and green olives. Squeeze in the juice of one lemon; add salt if needed, and a generous grinding of fresh black pepper. Mix.

5.   Fill the tomatoes, decorating the top of the filling with one black olive. Gently put back the top of the tomato, so that it is tilted a bit. Chill for one hour and decorate each with a sprig of fresh green parsley. Cut the other lemon in 8 wedges, and serve.

CHEF'S SECRET: If you wish you can peel the tomatoes, though I don't think it is necessary. To peel, put the tomatoes in boiling water for 15 to 20 seconds, remove, and plunge immediately into a bowl of water with ice cubes. Or, if you have a gas stove, insert a long fork into the stem end of the tomato and hold it for 30 seconds or so over the flame, turning it constantly. Then plunge it into ice water and peel.

Angels on Horseback

26 to 32 pieces

1 pint shucked oysters, drained
  (save liquid)
precooked half-slices of bacon
  (1 per oyster)

toast squares (¼ slice per
  oyster)

1.   Over a bowl, pour the pint of oysters into a sieve. Save all the liquid and count the oysters.
2.   Precook a half-slice of bacon for each oyster you have and make one toast square (¼ slice of bread) per oyster.
3.   Roll each oyster in a bacon slice. Be sure that the bacon overlaps beneath the oyster.
4.   Broil for 3 to 4 minutes as far as possible from the source of heat.
5.   Place each oyster on a toast square and brush it gently with the oyster liquid. Serve piping hot.

CHEF'S SECRET: The best and easiest way to cook bacon for this hors d'oeuvre is to cover a cookie sheet (the kind with a ½-inch rim) with aluminum foil. Place the bacon slices on the foil and chill for at least 2 hours. Then place the cookie sheet in a cold oven, set the temperature at 300° F., and turn on the oven. The bacon will cook slowly and evenly without shrinking or turning brittle in approximately 20 minutes.

Remove the bacon together with the fat and place in a large colander or sieve over a bowl. Collect the bacon drippings for other use. Pat the bacon dry on absorbent paper and wrap the slices around the oysters.

These are often served with Devils on Horseback, for which the recipe follows.

Devils on Horseback

24 hors d'oeuvres

24 large prunes
2 cups water
¼ cup sugar
½ cup sherry or port wine
24 pecan halves, almonds,
  or cashew nuts

24 precooked half-slices of
  bacon
24 toast squares (¼ slice of
  bread per prune)

1.   Cook prunes gently in a mixture of water, sugar, and sherry or port wine until they are half-done. Cool. If you buy pitted prunes, just press in a bowl, add sherry or port, and marinate for 1 hour.

2.   Stuff each prune with a nut.

3.   Wrap each prune in ½ slice precooked bacon and broil for 3 to 4 minutes as far as possible from the source of heat.

4.   Serve on toast squares and alternate with Angels on Horseback (see preceding recipe).

Cabbage Pie

8 servings

dough for 2-crust pie
melted lard or other shortening
  for brushing
4-pound head of cabbage,
  cored and finely chopped
½ cup shortening

1 tablespoon grated onion
2 teaspoons salt
1 teaspoon freshly ground
  black pepper
4 tablespoons sugar
1 egg

1.   Use a commercial pie-crust mix or your own. Roll out half of the dough and line a 9-inch pie pan. Brush with melted lard or other shortening. Set aside.

2.   Preheat oven to 325° F.

3.   Chop the cabbage so that the pieces are no bigger than oatmeal flakes.

4.   In a large, heavy skillet, melt ½ cup shortening, such as bacon drippings, lard, or oil. Add grated or finely minced onion.

5.   Add the cabbage and sprinkle on the salt, freshly ground black pepper, and sugar.

6.   Sauté gently over medium heat, stirring occasionally, until the mixture turns light gold and limp and loses about ½ of its volume. Keep stirring to avoid scorching. Add more fat if you think the mixture is drying out.

7.   Remove from heat and let cool until lukewarm. Pour into the pie shell. Roll out the rest of the dough for the top crust. Cover the cabbage with the dough and make a hole in the middle for the steam to escape.

8.   Brush top crust with a beaten egg and let dry. Brush again and let dry.

9.   Make designs by scratching the egg topping with a fork. Scrape the egg but don't pierce the dough. The design on cabbage pie is traditionally made by crisscrossing the top surface with wavy lines made by the tines of the fork.

10.   Bake 30 to 40 minutes or until the top and bottom crusts are done. Serve lukewarm.

CHEF'S SECRET: If you think you cannot chop the cabbage fine enough, grate it on the largest hole of a 4-sided grater. In this case don't take out the core; it is easier to grate if you hold it by the core. If you wish, you can use the same filling with commercially purchased strudel dough or filo leaf prepared according to package directions.

Potato Tidbits

48 to 60 pieces

8 ounces potatoes	1 egg
2 cups all-purpose flour	grated cheese, poppyseeds,
8 ounces soft butter	caraway seeds, or salt
1½ teaspoons salt	(optional)

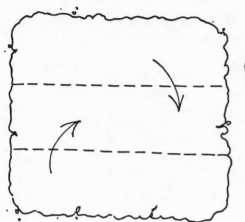 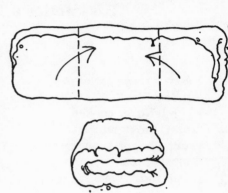

1. Peel, boil, cool, and mash potatoes.
2. On a pastry board or table top, mix the potatoes, flour, butter, and salt until the dough stays together. Refrigerate for 1 hour.
3. Preheat oven to 375°F.
4. Roll out the dough in a rectangle approximately 10 by 10 inches. Fold in three thirds, first folding the third farthest away from you to the middle, then the third closest to you over, then the right-side third over the middle third, and finishing with the left-side third. You can keep it like this, wrapped in plastic wrap or waxed paper, overnight in the refrigerator or until you want to use it.
5. Roll out the dough again to 10 by 10 inches and cut it into 1½-inch squares or, with a round cookie cutter, into 1½-inch diameter biscuits. Put them on a greased cookie sheet.
6. Brush with beaten egg. Sprinkle the top before baking, if you wish, with grated cheese, poppyseeds, caraway seeds, and salt. Bake for about 20 minutes or until golden brown.

CHEF'S SECRET: If you want higher biscuits, roll the dough only to a 5 or 6 inch square. When you first peel and then boil the potatoes, a certain amount of the starch in the potato will dissolve in the boiling water. Since the potato will be less starchy, it will blend better with the flour and butter.

Rissolettes à la Pompadour

20 to 24 pieces

1 recipe crêpe batter (see index)
1 cup leftover cooked beef, finely minced
½ cup chopped, sautéed mushrooms
½ cup sour cream

¼ cup fresh bread crumbs
½ teaspoon salt
¼ teaspoon freshly ground black pepper
2 eggs, beaten
1½ cups bread crumbs
oil for frying

1.   Prepare crêpes according to the recipe.

2.   Cut 4 crêpes into 2½-inch diameter circles with a cookie cutter or with the edge of a glass (approximately 20-24 rounds).

3.   Mix together cooked, finely minced beef, sautéed mushrooms, sour cream, and bread crumbs. Season well with salt and pepper. Place small dollop of mixture on each crêpe round. Fold in half and press edges or roll up like a jelly roll.

4.   Dip each filled piece into beaten egg and then in fresh bread crumbs.

5.   Fry in deep oil (300° F.) until golden brown. Drain on paper towel.

CHEF'S SECRET: Be sure the beef mixture is very cold before filling and frying. If you wish, add some extra sour cream on each serving.

Bread Crumbs

Commercially available bread crumbs are sometimes stale or rancid, which is nobody's fault. It is best to make your own bread crumbs.

Be sure to purchase a French or Italian type of bread and carefully read the list of ingredients. It should not contain any type of shortening. Flour, water, salt, and yeast are the ingredients of real Italian, French, or Vienna bread. Air dry the loaf two to three days, perhaps in a cheesecloth bag, then slice it thick. Roll to crumbs with a rolling pin, and sift. Or, if you wish, grate the slices on a four-sided kitchen grater.

Keep the crumbs in a container, but not air tight. And don't keep them too long. It is much less expensive to throw out ten cents worth of bread crumbs than one dollar's worth of Wiener Schnitzel.

Savory Puffs

80-100 puffs, depending on size

2 cups water
1 cup butter
¼ teaspoon salt
2 cups all-purpose flour
8 eggs, room temperature

Any one or all of the following:
2 cups coarsely grated or finely chopped real Cheddar, Swiss, or Gruyère cheese; or a combination of 1 cup finely minced or ground ham or any other smoked meat (chopped corned beef, chopped smoked tongue, etc.); or 2 cans sardines broken into small pieces after draining, mixed with 6 to 8 anchovy fillets finely minced

1.   Preheat oven to 425° F.
2.   In a saucepan, bring the water, butter, and salt to a boil. As soon as it boils, add the flour all at once. Remove from heat and stir vigorously with a wooden spoon until the dough forms a large ball that leaves the sides of the pan.
3.   Transfer the dough immediately to the pre-warmed bowl of an electric mixer. Don't use a wire whip; use a paddle or a dough hook. If you don't have either of these, forget the electric mixer and keep using the wooden spoon.
4.   Break one egg into a coffee cup. Check for freshness. Beat it gently with a fork. Add to the dough and stir in by hand or at the lowest possible speed of the electric mixer until the egg is completely blended. Repeat the same procedure seven more times, adding one beaten egg at a time. Be sure you don't add two eggs at one time, don't beat too fast, and don't stop beating before the egg disappears and the dough has the same consistency as before the addition—no yellow spots from the yolk, no shiny surfaces from the white. This is important.

5.   Gently fold in the cheese or other ingredients. Be sure you do not add more than two cups of other ingredients at once. If you add more, fold after each addition.

6.   Transfer the dough to a pastry bag without a tube. On a well-greased cookie sheet, form small puffs the size of a half dollar and approximately a half-inch high. Or, if you have no pastry bag, dip a teaspoon in corn oil and drop pieces about ¾ teaspoon-size on the cookie sheet. Bake for about 25 minutes until golden brown, and serve hot.

CHEF'S SECRET: In French they call these bite-sized puffs *bouchées,* and the longer ones, which look like unshelled peanuts, are called *Carolines.* There is no other way to make this simple dough except by following the instructions carefully, especially in adding the eggs.

For some reason it is hard for homemakers to purchase a good pastry bag and decent star tubes. If you want to obtain some, ask for a price list by writing to Chef Louis Price List, The Bakery Restaurant, 2218 North Lincoln Avenue, Chicago 60614. I will mail you a price list that will tell you, among other things, how you can order by mail two excellent pastry bags and six important tubes. A pastry bag is useful not only for this recipe but for many, many others. With proper care it will last for years and years.

If you want the puffs to look beautiful and shiny, separate an egg and add the white to the dough with the last whole egg. Then dip your finger in the remaining yolk and touch the top of each cream puff with yolk before baking. This will make the tops of the puffs a rich, shiny brown.

In the Burgundy region of France they use this dough to make just one large ring on a well-greased cookie sheet, about 8 to 9 inches in diameter, 2 inches wide, and 1 inch high. After baking they cut the rings in wedges and serve them with wine. The baking time for the ring will be 45 minutes to an hour, and the temperature should be lowered after 25 minutes from 425° to 400° F.

Spinach Crêpes

8 servings

8 unsweetened crêpes (see index)

1 12-ounce package frozen spinach

2 tablespoons butter

1 clove garlic

1 teaspoon salt

1 tablespoon flour

1 tablespoon cornstarch

1 cup milk

¼ teaspoon freshly ground black pepper

⅛ teaspoon nutmeg

3 to 4 tablespoons grated Parmesan cheese (mixed with 1 tablespoon fine dry bread crumbs, optional)

1. Prepare the 8 crêpes according to directions.

2. Preheat oven to 375° F. With a strong knife, cut the frozen spinach into pieces as small as possible. If it is too hard, thaw slightly before cutting. In a small saucepan, heat the butter and add the garlic mashed into a pulp with the salt.

3. Stir the flour and cornstarch into the milk with a wooden spoon. When the butter is hot, slowly stir in the milk and flour mixture. Add the chopped spinach all at once, stirring, and add pepper and nutmeg. Keep stirring until the mixture starts to bubble and comes to a boil. (It will take 10 to 15 minutes depending on the temperature of the spinach.) Remove from heat and keep stirring. If the mixture is too stiff, add 1 or 2 tablespoons milk; if it is too runny, add a tablespoon of bread crumbs and stir for a minute or so. It should have the consistency of soft mashed potatoes.

4. Divide the filling into 7 portions. Spread one portion on a crêpe placed in a round, well-buttered, oven-proof dish. Cover it with the second crêpe and spread another portion of filling on top. Be careful that the filling does not touch the edge of the crêpe. Repeat until all the filling is used. Cover the last spinach with a crêpe and warm in the oven for 10 to 12 minutes.

5. Sprinkle the top with grated cheese and put it under the broiler, 4 to 5 inches away from the source of heat, for about 30

seconds, until the cheese starts to brown. Remove, cut into pie-shaped wedges, and serve.

Variation: If you wish, divide the spinach filling into eight parts, spread each portion on one-half of a crêpe, and, starting with the filled half, roll it up jellyroll fashion. Tuck in the ends, lay in a row in a buttered rectangular or oval dish, and proceed as above. This will give you 8 individual portions.

CHEF'S SECRET: If you have a good food thermometer and you stick it into the frozen spinach, you will see that "frozen" can mean anything from +25° to -5° F., or even lower.

How thoroughly "frozen" the spinach is will determine how difficult it is for you to cut it. Be careful and don't try to cut it if it is too hard.

Do not defrost the spinach at room temperature. All the liquid will be released from the leaves, and you will have a green liquid and limp, chewy fibers. If you cut it up as suggested and add it immediately to the sauce, stirring constantly, the liquid seeping out from the leaves will be picked up by the flour and the starch in the sauce, and the spinach will keep its good taste and fresh appearance.

If you can get two pounds of fresh spinach, by all means use it instead of the frozen. Wash and rinse carefully. Be sure that it is free of all sand. Discard the wilted yellow leaves, take off the stems, and tear the spinach into postage-stamp-sized pieces. Steam by dropping the leaves into ½ cup of boiling water, cover the pot immediately over high heat, and shake the covered pot every 15 to 20 seconds for 3 or 4 minutes. Then chop the spinach very fine on a cutting board and add it to the white sauce as directed.

Try to master mashing the garlic with the salt into a pulp. Have a small cutting board, about 4 by 6 inches or 6 by 8 inches, which you use only for garlic and onions on one side and green parsley and other fresh herbs on the other side. Then you can be sure that other things you slice, cut, chop, or mince won't taste like garlic or onions.

To mash the garlic to a pulp, follow these directions: Peel the garlic clove and cut it into 1/16-inch slices with the tip of a paring knife. Cut the slices crosswise into slivers. Mix the slivers with the amount of salt called for in the recipe, and with the *flat side* of a knife, mash the garlic and salt by pressing firmly on the knife and at the same time moving it towards yourself, until the garlic turns to a pulp. Scrape up the pulp and form it into a small mound on the cutting board. Then crush it and mash it again. As the oils and juices ooze out from the garlic, they immediately form a solution with the salt, so the flavor will be distributed throughout the dish and you won't ever find small pieces of garlic stuck between your teeth.

The grated Parmesan you find in the stores is a good and reliable product, but you might try to find a piece of ungrated Parmesan or Romano, and a piece of real Swiss with the rind on, each a pound or pound and a half. Keep the two cheeses in the refrigerator, carefully wrapped—first in plain white paper, then in a plastic bag with a couple of holes in it. You can keep them this way for two or three months and grate only as much as you need. The flavor will be entirely different.

Real Swiss cheese may turn a bit green inside the holes, and a drop of clear liquid may also show there, but don't worry. Wipe off the liquid and scrape off the green mold. Neither will do any harm or affect the flavor.

Lecso-Franks in Chafing Dish

12 servings

1 large white onion cut in half and sliced
3 tablespoons lard or bacon drippings
2 large bell peppers cored, split, and cut in thin strips
1 or 2 fresh tomatoes, peeled
1½ cups tomato sauce

1 small clove garlic, mashed to a pulp with 1 teaspoon salt
1 tablespoon Spanish or Hungarian paprika
2 tablespoons sugar
12 good quality frankfurters, each cut in three pieces

1. Place onions and cold bacon drippings in a skillet and sauté over medium heat until limp and translucent.

2. Add green peppers, cover, and simmer over low heat for 5 to 6 minutes. Stir occasionally.

3. Add peeled tomatoes, tomato sauce, garlic pulp with salt, paprika, and sugar.

4. Stir, cover, and simmer over low heat for at least 30 minutes.

5. Add cut-up franks. Remove from heat and keep covered until serving time (at least 15 minutes).

CHEF'S SECRET: You may also use canned Vienna sausages for this recipe. The sauce may be made a day ahead or early in the morning. Standing will improve its taste. If you have leftover sauce, you can freeze it until the next party.

Cheese Fondue

2 servings

2½ cups Swiss cheese, shredded, approximately ½ pound
1½ tablespoons flour
1 garlic clove, crushed
1 cup dry white wine
salt and pepper to taste
dash of nutmeg

1 tablespoon Kirschwasser (cherry liqueur)
1 loaf French or other crusty bread
1 fondue dish with alcohol burner

1. Dredge the cheese with the flour.

2. Rub the inside of the fondue dish with the garlic; then discard the clove.

3. Pour the wine into the dish and place it on the range over very low heat to warm. When it begins to bubble, add the cheese, handful by handful, making sure each amount is completely absorbed and melted before adding more. Keep stirring until all the cheese is melted and is slightly bubbling.

4. Add a little salt, pepper, dash of nutmeg, and the Kirschwasser.

5. Remove the bubbling fondue from the heat. Place over the alcohol (or Sterno-type) burner and serve with bread cubes.

CHEF'S SECRET: Cube the bread into bite-sized pieces. Cut it so that almost every piece will have a portion of the crust.

If the fondue becomes too thick, add a little heated wine.

2
Soups

In ancient times, if you wanted to eat out you could find a meal only in hotels, inns, and other places where overnight accommodations were offered. Food selling was the privilege of the innkeeper. Later, widows began to sell food at roadside stands, and only in the seventeenth century did the first "restaurant" open.

The word *restaurant* derives from a Latin word meaning "to restore." What such places restored were strength, health, and vigor, and they did so primarily by selling soups. Since antiquity, people believed that soups were the quickest means of restoring one's energy, because soups, being liquids, were digested more quickly than solid food.

I don't know what the real physiological truth is, but I do know that soups are loved and consumed all over the world. The great cuisine of China boasts a tremendous variety of soups, as do the cuisines of Italy, Spain, and France. We know that Indians in North and South America prepared many soups in pre-Columbian times, and today they still make interesting native soups.

I have tried here to give a cross-section of soups that are favorites today—not too rich, not too thin, not too exotic or outlandish, but also not too common. I still feel that the most interesting soups are those that need a combination of several ingredients plus a dash of imagination. Some of the soups in the chapter are elaborate and take perhaps an hour or more to prepare (though during cooking time you need check only once in a while). Others are quick techniques or shortcuts to interesting results.

As a rule, in the recipes we mention canned broths and canned consommé as ingredients instead of stock. Of course, if you have the time, the patience, and the ingredients to make a stock, by all means do so! But let's face it: as classic as we *want* to be and as down-to-earth as we *have* to be, we should realize that good soup manufacturers hire the finest chefs to care for the taste, consistency, and color of their soups. They are perfectly acceptable for these recipes.

Nonetheless, at the beginning of the chapter we give two recipes, one for brown stock and one for white stock. If you have the time and the patience, start with them. More power to you and more joy to your taste buds.

I. Brown Stock

1 gallon

1 pound chicken backbones or chicken necks

2 to 3 pounds beef shank with bone in, cut into 1-inch slices

2 cups chopped carrots

1 cup chopped white or yellow turnip

1 large leek washed and split in half lengthwise, washed again, then sliced into ½-inch strips and washed again

½ cup chopped parsley root or parsnip

2 medium onions, with skin left on, cut crosswise at the root and stuck with a clove

2 pounds lean ground beef

5 quarts water

3 to 4 tablespoons salt

1 teaspoon black peppercorns, crushed or bruised

4 ribs celery tied with one bay leaf

1 clove garlic with skin on, split in half

4 to 5 sprigs parsley

1.   Place the chicken backbones and necks and the beef shank in a not-too-deep roasting pan and, depending on the size of the pan, place it over one or two burners of the stove top. Add half the carrots, turnip, leek, and parsley root, and one whole onion with the skin on. Keep turning the bones and the sliced shank so that they brown.

2.   Keep moving the vegetables around, preferably with a wooden spoon, until they start to brown; then remove from heat. Distribute the ground beef over the pan and pour 5 quarts of cold water over the mixture.

3.   Add salt, black peppercorns, celery ribs with bay leaf, garlic, parsley, and the second onion, and bake uncovered in a preheated 375° F. oven for approximately 3 hours. Remove, and strain the liquid.

4.   Put all bones, meat, vegetables, and remaining raw vegetables into a large (at least 3-gallon) soup pot. Add enough cold water to the cooking liquid to again have exactly 5 quarts. Pour the 5 quarts of liquid over the other ingredients, bring to a gentle boil, and then adjust heat to low and simmer for at least 4 hours, preferably longer.

5.   Just before removing from heat, add 2 cups cold water with one cup ice cubes in it. This will help bring all the fat to the top of the liquid. Skim as much fat as possible and let the stock

stand without stirring for about an hour. Then dip a kitchen towel in lukewarm water, soak it for a minute or two, squeeze it (not too dry), place it over a sieve or colander, and without disturbing the solids in the pot gently pour the liquid through the kitchen towel and colander into another container. Cool quickly and store. If you end up with less than a gallon, add enough water to make a gallon.

II. White Stock

3½ quarts

2 to 3 pounds beef shank, bone in, cut into 1-inch slices
3 to 4 pounds veal front, neck or breast, cut into small pieces
2 to 3 pounds chicken necks, wing tips, or chicken backs
1 cup chopped carrots
1 cup chopped turnip
1 leek washed, split lengthwise, washed again, cut crosswise into ½-inch pieces, and washed again

½ cup chopped parsley root or parsnip
1 medium onion, peeled and chopped
1 clove
1 bay leaf
2 or 3 sprigs parsley tied between 2 or 3 celery ribs
4 tablespoons salt
12 black peppercorns, bruised or crushed
5 quarts cold water

1.   Place all ingredients, including water, in a large stock pot. Bring to a boil; skim off the white scum from the top. Set heat very low and simmer for at least 4, preferably 6, hours.

2.   Remove from heat and pour into the stock 2 cups cold water with a cup of ice cubes to bring the grease to the top. Skim off the grease and let stock stand for about an hour on a wire rack.

3.   Skim off remaining fat. Place a colander in a clean, cold metal container. Line the colander with a moist but not wet kitchen towel and ladle the stock through it into the container. Cool and use immediately or store for later use.

CHEF'S SECRET: These two recipes for stocks are basic and, of course, can be improved if you add herbs or spices of your choice. If you want the brown stock to be darker, simply add a tablespoon or so of Kitchen Bouquet or Gravy Master. Or grate a

2-inch length of carrot into a small pan, add 1 tablespoon shortening and 1 tablespoon sugar, and cook over high heat until carrots and sugar start to brown. Remove, add 2 or 3 tablespoons hot water or hot stock, and strain the carrot caramel juice into the stock.

If you want the white stock to be golden yellow like chicken stock, follow the same procedure, omitting the sugar and heating only the carrots in the shortening.

Both stocks can be frozen in an ice cube tray. Pack each cube individually in aluminum foil or plastic and then put them in a plastic bag or container. Do not keep frozen longer than a month.

Beef Borscht with Cabbage

8 servings

1 pound lean chuck
2 pounds beef bones
4 tablespoons shortening
1 cup chopped onion
1 chopped carrot
1 parsley root or parsnip (sliced into discs)
4 to 5 stalks celery (cut into small pieces)
1 teaspoon marjoram
½ teaspoon tarragon
¼ teaspoon chervil (optional)
1 small head (1 ½ to 2 pounds) cabbage, cut into finger-wide pieces
1 one-pound and 11-ounce can sauerkraut
2 tablespoons cornstarch
2 tablespoons flour
1 pint sour cream
1 pint buttermilk or milk

1. Wash the meat and check it for small pieces of bone. Carefully clean the cut ends of the beef bones and discard the small splintered pieces.

2. In a soup pot over high heat melt the shortening. When it is very hot, add the chopped onions, stir, and when they are translucent, add the carrots, parsnip (or parsley root), and celery.

3. While stirring, add the meat, marjoram, tarragon, and chervil. Cover with water and cook over high heat until it starts to boil; adjust to simmer and cook for approximately 1½ hours. Add the cabbage.

4.   Drain the sauerkraut and save the liquid. Gently rinse the sauerkraut and add it to the soup with 2 quarts of water. Cover and bring to a boil over medium heat (it will take approximately 30 minutes).

5.   Remove beef chuck and bones. Mix cornstarch and flour with ½ cup cold water and pour into the boiling soup, stirring constantly until the soup thickens. Discard the bones. Cut the beef chuck into small, finger-sized strips and put them back into the soup.

6.   Simmer over low heat for 5 more minutes. Mix sour cream and buttermilk or milk, add a bit of the hot soup, and stir until the mixture warms. Remove the soup from the heat and stir in the warm mixture. Let stand for 5 minutes, covered. Serve, offering some of the sauerkraut juice so that your guests can add as much or as little tartness as they like in their beef borscht.

CHEF'S SECRET: If you learn this basic beef borscht you can make your own combination by adding preboiled potatoes, beets, raw potatoes, wax beans, or green beans instead of or along with the cabbage and sauerkraut. If you don't like sauerkraut, simply add more cabbage and ¼ cup or so of vinegar.

Note that you do not add salt to this soup. The sauerkraut is pickled with salt, and I think the amount of sauerkraut used gives the soup enough salt. But, if you wish to add more salt, go ahead.

Depending on the kind of sauerkraut you use, you may feel that something is missing in the soup. A half-teaspoon of sugar may do the trick.

To make this soup into a real meal in a pot, in the last 5 minutes of cooking add two all-beef franks per person.

Oven Baked Beef and Vegetable Soup

8 servings

4 pounds beef shank, beef chuck, or other bone-in inexpensive cut
2 large marrow bones

1 package fresh soup vegetables, cleaned and diced
1 clove garlic or ½ teaspoon garlic salt (not garlic powder)

1 bay leaf
2 cups cubed potatoes
2 10-ounce cans consommé and
  6 cans water
1 tablespoon salt
6 to 8 black peppercorns,
  bruised

½ teaspoon celery salt
1 package frozen mixed
  vegetables
½ cup fresh chopped parsley or
  1 tablespoon dried parsley
flakes

1.   Wash the meat and remove small pieces of bone.

2.   In the bottom of a soup pot place the beef and marrow bones. Add the fresh soup vegetables and all other ingredients except the frozen mixed vegetables and parsley.

3.   Preheat oven to 225° F. Cover the soup pot and bring to a rolling boil over very high heat. Place the pot in the oven and reduce the heat to 200° F. Bake for 6 hours.

4.   Add frozen vegetables to the soup, cover, and return to the oven for 10 to 15 minutes. Remove.

5.   Skim fat, lift out the meat and remove the bones. Discard bones. Place meat in a soup tureen or casserole. With a slotted spoon remove all vegetables and add to meat in tureen. Let the liquid stand undisturbed for 5 minutes, then ladle it over meat and vegetables, leaving the last 2 to 3 ladles in the pot. The remaining liquid will be thick and full of small meat particles, and this will make an excellent sauce base. Sprinkle with the parsley, and serve with crusty white toast or crackers.

CHEF'S SECRET: This is an ideal dinner or supper dish on a day when you plan to spend 5 to 6 hours away from home. Be sure that the lid fits very securely on the pot; otherwise too much liquid will evaporate.

If you find that the soup loses too much liquid, don't hesitate to add some warm water; but let the soup stand for at least 15 minutes under cover in the oven so that it has a chance to recover its heat.

You can make the same soup with beef soup bones and a 3½- to 4-pound fowl or stewing hen instead of the 4 pounds of beef. Of course, in this case, replace the consommé with chicken broth.

Transylvanian Beef Soup

8 servings

1 pound stew meat (chuck or similar, cut up)

2 slices bacon cut into small strips, or 3 tablespoons shortening

2 cups sliced onion

1 pound fresh green beans, cleaned and cut on a bias; or 12-ounce package frozen green beans, French cut; or the same amount of wax beans; or 1 16-ounce can green beans (liquid discarded and beans rinsed in cold water)

2 quarts water

1 cup milk

2 tablespoons flour

1 tablespoon cornstarch

1 teaspoon tarragon

½ teaspoon chervil

1 teaspoon salt
pepper to taste

1 pint sour cream

2 large onions, chopped and marinated in ¼ cup white vinegar, ¾ cup water, 1 tablespoon sugar, ½ teaspoon salt, and a generous grinding of fresh black pepper

1. With a very sharp knife, cut the meat into matchstick-sized pieces. (When it is all cut it should resemble meat-colored spaghetti.)

2. In a large soup pot over high heat, fry the bacon or heat the shortening of your choice. Gradually add the slivered meat, stirring constantly.

3. Add sliced onions and continue frying.

4. If you use fresh beans, add them immediately. If you use frozen or canned beans, don't add them yet. As soon as the meat is fried and the onions are limp, add 2 cups of water. Continue cooking.

5. In a small bowl, whisk together the milk and 1 cup water with the flour, cornstarch, tarragon, and chervil. Stir this mixture until no lumps show, and pour it into the boiling soup, stirring constantly. Keep stirring and, as it thickens, add the remaining water, salt, and pepper.

6. Simmer over very low heat 1½ to 2 hours.

7. If you use frozen beans, add them 15 minutes before serving time. If you use canned beans, add 10 minutes before serving time.

8. Put the sour cream into a large soup tureen, add to it a few spoonfuls of the soup, and stir until the sour cream heats

through. Add the rest of the soup. Serve with garlic toast and offer the marinated raw onions and more sour cream if you wish.

CHEF'S SECRET: This soup from my native Transylvania is one of the most delightful beef soups you have ever tasted. The meat almost vanishes, but the beef flavor permeates the soup.

If you add the hot soup to the sour cream in small amounts, it won't curdle or get lumpy.

The garlic toast that is traditionally served with this soup is made somewhat differently. Use a firm-textured rye, whole wheat, or pumpernickel bread and toast it under the broiler—or, even better, on a large toasting fork over the stove burner (either electric or gas will do the job). Toast it a bit more than you usually would. Peel a couple of cloves of fresh garlic and rub the dry toast generously on both sides. Brush or spread melted butter, duck fat, bacon drippings, lard, or oil on the garlic toast and reheat it in a 300° F. oven before serving.

Instead of garlic toast, you can boil one medium-sized potato per person, peel, and place in each soup plate. Or serve the soup with corn bread as we used to eat it in Transylvania.

You can serve the onions as a small side dish, or you can spoon some of them, including the marinade, right into the soup.

After you discard the liquid from the canned beans, rinse them thoroughly with cold water; then chill them in the refrigerator for an hour or so or keep them in ice water for 10 minutes. They will lose a lot of their canned taste.

You can try the same soup using 1 quart of loosely packed sliced cabbage, or the same amount of sliced iceberg lettuce. If you make it with cabbage, add the cabbage together with the meat. If you use lettuce, do not add it until the last 10 minutes of cooking.

Hamburger Soup

8 servings

1 pound ground beef
2 eggs
2 slices white bread, trimmed
   and torn into small pieces

1 teaspoon sugar
2 tablespoons finely minced
   onion or scallions
1 cup diced potato

1 teaspoon salt
¼ teaspoon black pepper
2 tablespoons shortening,
    preferably a mixture of 1
    tablespoon oil and 1
    tablespoon bacon drippings,
    lard, or butter

1 cup diced carrot
1 cup celery, sliced
2 10¾ ounce cans beef con-
    sommé, plus 6 cans water; or
    8 to 10 cups stock or stock
    plus water
2 teaspoons salt

1.   Mix the ground beef, eggs, and bread together with the salt and black pepper. With your hands, form 16 tiny hamburgers.

2.   Line a cookie sheet with waxed paper or plastic. Lay out the 16 hamburgers and place in the freezer to chill.

3.   Heat the shortening in a frying pan, and when it is very hot add the sugar, onions, potatoes, carrots, and celery, and keep stirring with a spatula over high heat until they all turn brown on the edges and start to caramelize. Remove all vegetables to a soup pot.

4.   In the same pan, fry the hamburgers on both sides over very high heat. Do not add any more shortening.

5.   Add fried hamburgers to the vegetables. Then add the consommé and water, or stock, bring to a gentle boil, adjust the heat, and simmer the soup for 45 minutes to an hour.

If you wish, add 4 ounces of elbow macaroni or other pasta according to package directions. Or in the last 5 minutes add a cup of frozen green peas or green beans.

CHEF'S SECRET: The name of this soup "sells" it to children, but it is really not for children only.

Serve it with toasted hamburger buns and let your guests put "the works" on the buns — thick slices of raw onions, ketchup, mustard, and so forth.

Tyrolean Meat Soup

8 servings

2 pounds beef bones
1 pound smoked pork, picnic or
    shoulder, or smoked
    spareribs

1 parsley root or parsnip cut the
    same way
1 rib celery
1 bay leaf

3 quarts water
1 medium onion with skin on
2 cloves garlic split in half
1 carrot, cleaned and cut into 4
   or 5 large pieces

6 to 8 black peppercorns,
   bruised
salt to taste

Place all ingredients in a large soup pot and bring to a full boil over medium heat. Lower heat and simmer 3 hours; do not let it boil. While the soup is cooking, make Tyrolean dumplings.

Tyrolean Dumplings:

2 hard rolls or 4 or 5 slices of
   crusty Vienna bread, cut into
   ¼-inch cubes (4 cups) and
   toasted on a cookie sheet in a
   low oven
1 egg
1 cup milk
1 cup water
1 tablespoon minced onion,
   sautéed in 1 tablespoon
   bacon drippings or other
   shortening

1 tablespoon finely minced
   green parsley
½ teaspoon salt
½ teaspoon ground black
   pepper
1 cup sifted all-purpose flour
4 ounces chopped ham or
   luncheon meat cut into ¼-
   inch cubes
2 quarts water with 2
   tablespoons salt

1.   Put toasted bread cubes in a large bowl.

2.   Beat egg with milk and water in a small bowl. Add sautéed onion, parsley, salt, and pepper. Mix and pour over bread cubes.

3.   Sprinkle flour over the surface of the cubes and with wet hands mix all the ingredients quickly. Let stand about 15 minutes. Divide into eight portions. With wet hands, pat each portion flat. In the middle of each place one-eighth of the chopped ham formed into a ball. Repeat with the other seven portions. Let the dumplings stand on a lightly floured surface for about ½ hour.

4.   Meanwhile, bring to a boil the water and salt. When it comes to a full boil, reshape the dumplings with wet hands, if necessary, and plunge dumplings gently, one by one, into the boiling water. Wait until the water starts to boil again, adjust the heat, and simmer gently for 15 to 20 minutes. Plunge dumplings into ice water for about a minute to stop the cooking. Place them in a small bowl in a warm place until you are ready to serve the soup.

5.   To serve, strain the soup through a fine sieve into a soup tureen and add the dumplings. Serve the smoked pork and cut vegetables on a warm plate next to the soup. Discard garlic and peppercorns.

CHEF'S SECRET: This is an interesting and tasty soup. It can be a meal in itself if served with crusty Vienna bread and either a large green salad or a large bowl of hot leaf spinach.

You may add the chopped ham to the other ingredients in the dumplings and mix thoroughly so that the ham is all the way through instead of in the middle; or you can form the whole amount into a loaf, roll it into lightly greased aluminum foil, and seal the ends. It will make a roll approximately 6 to 7 inches long and 2 inches in diameter. Place it in an empty pot, gently pour on boiling water, and boil for 30 minutes. Remove, let cool in the foil, and slice it with a sharp knife.

Fresh Asparagus Soup

8 servings

1½ to 2 pounds fresh asparagus
2 tablespoons shortening
⅓ cup chopped onions
1 small carrot, scraped
1 cup chopped celery
Tie securely in a piece
   of cheesecloth or gauze:
   ½ teaspoon black peppercorns; 1 very small clove garlic;
   2-3 sprigs fresh parsley;
   1 teaspoon dried tarragon
2 quarts veal or chicken stock,
   or enough canned chicken
   broth diluted to make 2 quarts

salt, as needed (approximately
   1 tablespoon altogether)
4 tablespoons butter
8 tablespoons flour
2 cups milk
1 cup half-and-half
1 cup sour cream at room
   temperature
2 tablespoons chopped fresh
   parsley

1.   Wash the asparagus and cut off approximately ¼-inch from the bottom end and discard. Lay down 6-8 pieces of asparagus so that the heads, or tips are all together. Cut off the tips. Set aside and cut off a 1-inch length right under each head. Make a separate batch from these pieces. Cut the rest of the asparagus into small discs down to the white part. Keep the hard

bottom part, giving you 4 piles. Repeat these steps with all of the asparagus.

2.   In a large soup pot, melt the 2 tablespoons shortening. Add the chopped onions and cook over medium heat, stirring constantly until the onions start to turn yellow. Add carrot and celery and cook for another 2 minutes, continuing to stir. Add the third pile of asparagus (the one right next to the hard-bottom parts). Cover the soup pot, adjust the heat to very low, and simmer.

3.   In another pot, add the bottom parts of the asparagus, the cheesecloth bag with the spices, and pour in the veal or chicken stock. Add some salt, as needed (this will depend on the saltiness of the stock used). Bring to a boil, then simmer.

4.   In a small saucepan, melt the butter. Mix the flour into the milk with a wire whip. Slowly, stirring constantly with a wire whip, add the flour-milk mixture to the hot butter and keep stirring. If you add it slowly enough, it will thicken immediately. When you finish, it will be just like a white sauce of medium consistency. Remove it from heat and stir in half-and-half.

5.   Strain the broth, in which the hard parts of the asparagus have simmered, through a fine sieve into the pot with the onion, carrot, celery, and asparagus. Discard spice bag and hard stalks. Add the white sauce, stir, and simmer over low heat.

6.   Put the second part of the asparagus (from directly under the tips) into an electric blender and blend until liquefied. Set aside.

7.   Add the first pile, the asparagus tips, to the soup and gently simmer over low heat for 10 minutes. Taste; add salt if needed.

8.   In a soup tureen, stir together the liquefied asparagus and the sour cream. Add to it one ladle of the hot soup, then a second one. When the asparagus-sour cream mixture heats through, add the rest of the soup, garnish with parsley, and serve.

CHEF'S SECRET: On first reading this sounds very complicated and involved, but if you read the recipe a second time, before you start to prepare it, you will realize it is a simple soup to fix. The uncooked asparagus juice and the barely cooked tips will give such an intensive taste as to make this incomparable to any other asparagus soup.

To further intensify the asparagus taste, add a teaspoon of sugar.

Chef Tony's Onion Soup

8 servings

1 pound onions (peeled weight)
1 tablespoon flour
1 tablespoon Hungarian or
   Spanish paprika
pinch of white pepper
pinch of freshly ground black
   pepper
1 clove garlic
½ teaspoon salt
¼ pound butter
3 cups chicken broth ⎫
3 cups beef consommé ⎬ or 9 cups homemade stock
3 cups water ⎭

Croutons:
½ loaf thin French bread
4 tablespoons grated Parmesan
   cheese
4 tablespoons grated cheese
(cheddar, Swiss, American,
   or any cheese of your choice)
4 tablespoons melted butter

1. Cut onions in half and slice into very thin slices.
2. On a large dish, separate the layers of sliced onions. Combine the flour, paprika, white pepper, and black pepper, and sprinkle the mixture over the onions.
3. Crush the garlic, mix with salt, and press with the flat surface of the tip of a knife until the garlic turns to pulp. Distribute over the onions.
4. In a large pot, melt butter and sauté onions over medium heat, covered, for about 10 minutes, stirring 2 to 3 times.
5. Add chicken broth, beef consommé, and water. Bring to a boil. Adjust heat to low and simmer, covered, for 30 minutes, stirring once or twice.
6. Remove from heat and let stand, covered, for at least 1 hour. Reheat before serving with croutons.

Croutons

1. Slice the half-loaf of thin French bread into 8 diagonal slices.
2. Distribute cheese mixture on one side of each slice.
3. Sprinkle with melted butter and bake in a preheated 400° F. oven for 8 to 10 minutes or until top turns brown. Serve with soup.

CHEF'S SECRET: It is important that you slice the onions very thinly. The thinner the slices, the better the soup, because more flavor will come out.

As you know, flour, onions, and even paprika have natural sugars which caramelize during the sautéing process. That is what turns the flour and the onions brown. As the heat releases the volatile oils of the onions, they will mix easily with the butter and will be picked up readily by the flour. The mixture will retain its good onion taste and won't have the unpleasant taste of plain boiled onion water. That is why it is so important to sauté.

Cold Beet Borscht with Black Caviar

8 servings

½ cup chopped scallions or leeks
½ cup chopped carrot
½ cup sliced onion
1 cup chopped celery
4 tablespoons shortening
2 cups chopped red beets, canned

2 10½-ounce cans chicken broth
1 can water, and the same amount of beet juice from the canned beets
1 pint sour cream
8 teaspoons black caviar

1. In a covered soup pan over low heat, sauté all the chopped raw vegetables in the shortening for 15 to 20 minutes. Add beets and sauté for another 5 minutes. Add chicken broth, water, and beet juice. Simmer for 15 minutes, strain, and let the liquid cool.

2. Purée the vegetables in a blender and add to the cooled liquid. Chill for 3 or 4 hours, then gently fold in ½ pint of the sour cream.

3. From 6 cups of the liquid fill 8 champagne or wine glasses almost to the top with the chilled borscht. Place on the top a dab of sour cream and top it with a teaspoon of caviar. Serve with dry rye toast triangles or with rye crackers.

CHEF'S SECRET: This is a favorite soup of Everett Kovler, who eats it with a very fine imported black caviar. I tried it with a much cheaper caviar, and to be honest, it didn't taste as good. Whatever caviar you serve it with, be sure to rinse the caviar in a sieve under running lukewarm tap water to wash off the excess salt used to preserve it.

Corn Chowder

8 servings

2 pounds raw turkey wings
1 cup carrots, peeled and cut
  into ½-inch cubes
2 tablespoons minced onion
1 small turnip, peeled and cut
  into ½-inch cubes
½ cup chopped celery
2 small potatoes, peeled and cut
  into ½-inch cubes
1 tablespoon chopped parsley
2 tablespoons butter

1 tablespoon Chef's Salt (see
  index)
pinch of sugar
1 tablespoon finely grated
  carrot
½ teaspoon Hungarian paprika
10 cups water
2 ears fresh or frozen corn on
  the cob
2 tablespoons flour
2 cups milk or half-and-half

1. Cut the turkey wings into pieces 1½ to 2 inches long,
leaving the bones in.

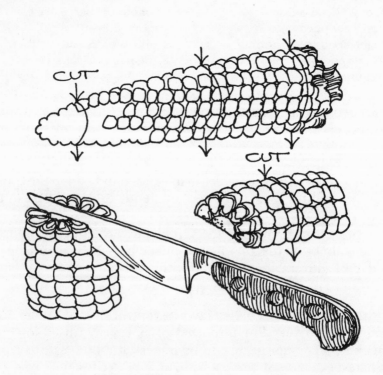

2.   Combine the chopped vegetables, parsley, butter, and Chef's Salt in a large soup pot. Place over medium to high heat and start to brown the vegetables, stirring frequently.

3.   When the edges of the vegetables start to turn brown, add the pieces of turkey. Add a light sprinkling of sugar to improve the caramelization, and add the tablespoon of grated carrot.

4.   Add paprika. Keep stirring, and when the bits on the bottom of the pot start to turn brown, add the water. Continue to stir until all the small bits are loosened from the bottom of the pot.

5.   Cover, reduce the heat to low, and simmer for 1 hour.

6.   Cut each ear of corn in half crosswise, split each half lengthwise, cutting through the cob, and then cut crosswise again into approximately one-inch pieces. Add to the soup and continue to simmer for another hour.

7.   Remove from heat. Remove the pieces of turkey and let them cool; then remove and discard the bones and skin. Return the pieces of meat to the soup.

8.   Approximately 1 hour before serving, adjust the liquid so that you have 2½ to 3 quarts, place over medium heat, and bring to a boil again.

9.   Mix the flour into the milk or half-and-half; then stir the mixture into the soup. Simmer over low heat for approximately 20 minutes. Remove and keep warm until serving time.

CHEF'S SECRET: If you make this chowder on a day when you serve roast turkey, the raw, cut-up second wing joints and wing tips of the turkey along with the neck will be enough for a chowder for 8. In this case, add to the chowder those juices from the roasting pan that you did not need for the giblet gravy.

The recipe says, "Adjust the liquid so that you have 2½ to 3 quarts." How do you do this? Very simple. When you start with 10 cups water, just measure with the handle of a wooden spoon how far the water level is from the top of the soup pot. Then, when you get to the point where you want to adjust the liquid back to the original level, place the same wooden spoon into the pot and slowly pour water until it reaches the mark on the spoon handle. The amount will be exactly 10 cups.

Cream of Kohlrabi Soup

8 servings

1 to 1 ½ pounds fresh kohlrabi
4 tablespoons butter
½ cup finely minced onion
1 tablespoon sugar
1 carrot
1 parsley root
4 to 5 peppercorns
½ bay leaf
salt to taste

2 10-ounce cans chicken broth and 2 cans water
½ cup coarsely chopped flat-leaf parsley
3 tablespoons flour
3 tablespoons cornstarch
1 pint milk
1 cup sour cream or heavy cream

1.   Wash and pare kohlrabi. Cut into ½-inch cubes.

2.   In a heavy pot, melt the butter and sauté the onions until translucent. Add the sugar and kohlrabi. Cover and cook over medium heat for 2 to 3 minutes. Turn the heat to low and simmer for 15 to 20 minutes.

3.   Scrape, wash, and chop the carrot and parsley root. The pieces should be a little smaller than the kohlrabi pieces. Add to the kohlrabi with the peppercorns, bay leaf, and a very little salt. Cover and simmer again for 15 to 20 minutes.

4.   Add the two cans of chicken broth and two cans of water, along with half of the chopped parsley. Bring to a boil.

5.   Dissolve the flour and cornstarch in the milk. With a large spoon, stirring the soup constantly, pour in the milk mixture. Turn the heat to low, cover, and simmer for another 20 to 25 minutes. Correct the seasoning by adding more salt if it is needed.

6.   Combine the remaining parsley with the sour cream or heavy cream. Pour this into a soup tureen and ladle the soup over it.

If you like a thicker soup, simply add more flour and cornstarch, mixing it first with a little cold water or cold milk.

CHEF'S SECRET: If you have time, you can make the soup with 1 pound of veal bones cooked in 6 to 8 cups of water with a little salt, black pepper, and a bay leaf. Use this instead of the canned broth and water mixture.

Cream of Potato Soup

8 servings

4 tablespoons shortening, preferably lard, bacon drippings, or a mixture of lard and oil
4 cups potatoes, peeled and cut into ½-inch cubes
½ cup chopped flat-leaf parsley
1 cup finely minced onion
1 bay leaf
1 ½ teaspoons salt

½ teaspoon freshly ground black pepper
5 cups water, chicken stock, or chicken broth
2 cups light cream or half-and-half
4 tablespoons flour
1 cup sour cream (optional)
additional chopped parsley for decoration

1.   In a large soup pot, melt the shortening and sauté the potatoes with parsley, chopped onion, bay leaf, salt, and pepper over medium heat.

2.   Cook, covered, over low heat for 15 to 20 minutes.

3.   Add the stock (or water or broth) and continue cooking.

4.   Mix the light cream with the flour and stir into the soup. Keep stirring while pouring so that no lumps form.

5.   Simmer the soup for at least 30 minutes.

6.   Serve with additional cream (or egg yolk and cream mixture, as in other cream soups) or, just before serving, stir in sour cream. Sprinkle the top with additional chopped parsley or with chopped chives.

CHEF'S SECRET: This soup is the basic form of a large family of soups you can create by adding different ingredients. In some parts of my native Hungary dried marjoram is added to the soup; in other parts a few bruised caraway seeds are sautéed together with the onion. During Lent it is made with oil, and for each person a whole egg is broken into the soup—carefully, so that the yolk doesn't break—five or six minutes before serving. If you want to, try this: Break the eggs one by one into a cup. Have the soup just below boiling point. Carefully plunge the eggs, one by one, into the soup, stirring gently while you do it.

Polish or Hungarian sausage may be added to the soup, or the soup may be started by boiling a ham hock and using the stock from it instead of the chicken broth (omit the salt in this case).

Sauerkraut Soup

8 servings

1-pound can sauerkraut
1 quart finely sliced or
   shredded cabbage
2 quarts water
1 pound smoked pork neck-
   bone or smoked pork hock
½ pound Hungarian or Polish
   sausage
4 ounces bacon

½ cup finely minced onion
2 tablespoons flour
1 tablespoon cornstarch
1 tablespoon Hungarian or
   Spanish paprika
½ teaspoon freshly ground
   black pepper
2 cups sour cream

1. Rinse and press out sauerkraut. Save the juice.
2. Mix sauerkraut with cabbage. Place in a large soup pot.
3. Add water and smoked pork. Cover, bring to a gentle boil over medium heat, and cook for 1½ to 2 hours.
4. Remove pork. Pick off all the meat and put it back into the soup, discarding the bones. Slice the sausage into ¼-inch slices and add to the soup. Continue to cook.
5. Cut the bacon into small pieces and fry it in a small frying pan until the small bits turn brown and crisp. Remove the bits and add to the soup. Sauté onions in the bacon fat until limp and translucent. Remove from heat and add flour, cornstarch, paprika, and pepper. Stir and return to heat until it starts to bubble around the edges. Remove from heat and slowly add 2 to 2½ cups of soup liquid. With a small wire whisk stir it until smooth; then add to the soup. Bring to a boil, adjust heat to low, and simmer the soup for 15 to 20 minutes.
6. Heat the sour cream by adding small amounts of the soup to it; then add it to the soup. Serve with salt sticks or garlic bread. In a separate small bowl, serve the sauerkraut juice if someone wishes to add it to the soup.

CHEF'S SECRET: This recipe has no salt as an ingredient because as a rule the sauerkraut, sausage, and smoked neck bones or hocks are salty enough. If you like the soup saltier, add some before serving.

This soup improves a good deal if it is cooked one or two days ahead to the point when the sour cream would be added, then reheated in a 250° F. oven for about 3 hours before adding the sour cream. If you really want all the flavor possible, withstand the temptation to eat it immediately and take the trouble to heat it up two days in a row and eat it on the third day.

Wax Bean Soup

8 servings

½ of a medium-sized onion, finely minced
2 tablespoons chopped flat-leaf parsley
3 tablespoons butter
1 pound fresh wax beans, cleaned and cut up
½ teaspoon white pepper
1 clove garlic, crushed with ¼ teaspoon salt

1 bay leaf
2 cups chicken stock or canned chicken broth
4 cups water
2 cups milk
2 tablespoons flour
1 tablespoon cornstarch
parsley and sour cream for garnish

1.   In a heavy aluminum pot, sauté onion and parsley in butter until onion turns transparent.

2.   Add cut wax beans, white pepper, garlic-salt mixture, bay leaf, chicken stock, and water.

3.   Cover and cook until beans are tender, approximately 45 minutes.

4.   Thicken soup with a mixture of milk, flour, and cornstarch, stirring constantly while adding it to the soup.

5.   Serve garnished with fresh chopped parsley and sour cream. You may add ½ cup vinegar for a tangy soup.

CHEF'S SECRET: A cold, thick soup can be made from this recipe by using an extra tablespoon each of flour and starch. When the soup is ready, let it cool, stir in the sour cream, chill, and serve it on a hot day with a half-lemon per serving to squeeze into it.

If you cut the beans, cut them on a diagonal. It is even better simply to break them by hand if the beans are fresh and snap when you break them. Of course, you can substitute fresh green beans for the wax beans, but the taste is somewhat different.

Avgholemono, or Egg Lemon Soup

8 servings

1 package soup greens (remove
   potatoes and use only the skin
   from the onion)
1 tablespoon salt
3 to 4 black peppercorns
1 bay leaf
2 quarts water

1½ pounds chicken wings
1 10½-ounce can chicken with
   rice soup
2 whole eggs
½ cup heavy cream
1 large lemon
freshly chopped dill (optional)

1.   Place the washed, cut-up greens, along with the skin from the onion, in a large pot. Add the salt, peppercorns, bay leaf, water, and chicken wings.

2.   Strain the chicken soup into the pot, reserving the rice for later use.

3.   Bring the soup to a boil, reduce heat to low, and simmer for approximately 1½ hours.

4.   Strain the stock from the vegetables. Remove the chicken wings and save them for another use. Remove and discard the bay leaf and onion skin. Purée the vegetables with the rice, adding as much stock as needed, in a food mill or blender. Stir the purée into the remaining stock.

5.   In a mixing bowl, beat the eggs with a wire whip until they are frothy. Then beat in the heavy cream. Gently add about 1 cup of the warm soup to the beaten egg mixture (to warm the mixture so that it will not separate); then add the egg mixture to the soup, beating it with a wire whip.

6.   From one end of the lemon, slice about 6 to 8 very thin slices. Grate the peel and squeeze the juice from the remaining part of the lemon into the soup.

7.   Reheat the soup over low heat just to the boiling point, beating constantly with a whip to make it frothy. Be careful not to bring it to a boil or it will curdle. Serve, floating the lemon slices on top. You may add additional lemon juice to taste, if you wish, and a little freshly chopped dill.

CHEF'S SECRET: This amount of soup will generally be too much for 8 persons. To prepare an excellent luncheon dish for the next day, debone the chicken wings and place the meat in a flat casserole dish. Soften two packages unflavored gelatin in ¼ cup of water. Bring ½ cup of water to a boil and stir in the softened gelatin. Combine the gelatin with two cups of the lemon soup. Pour over the deboned chicken, garnish with olives, and refrigerate until set or overnight. Slice and serve on a bed of lettuce leaves.

Serbian Chicken Soup

8 servings

1 frying chicken, 2¼ to 2½ pounds
1 pound chicken back bones, necks, or wing tips
4 tablespoons butter mixed with 4 tablespoons corn oil
1 cup carrots sliced into discs
½ cup parsley root or parsnip, sliced into discs
1 cup celery, sliced
½ cup finely chopped onion
1 bay leaf
8 to 10 black peppercorns, bruised
1 tablespoon salt

½ cup bell pepper or green pepper, chopped
1 medium or 2 small tomatoes (total weight approximately 8 ounces)
8 tablespoons flour
1½ to 2 teaspoons Hungarian paprika (to taste)
juice of 1 lemon
freshly ground black pepper
2 egg yolks
1 cup sour cream
½ cup finely chopped flat-leaf parsley

1. Cut the chicken into serving pieces, place them in a heavy soup pot together with the bones and necks, and add 2½ quarts water. Bring to a quick boil over high heat, adjust heat to medium, simmer for 3 minutes, and then skim off the foam from the top.

2. In a small sauté pan, add 2 tablespoons butter mixed with 2 tablespoons corn oil and sauté the carrots, parsley root, celery, and onion until they start to turn brown.

3. Add the bay leaf, peppercorns, and salt, and pour the sautéed vegetables into the soup pot. Cover and gently simmer for 20 to 25 minutes.

4. Add green pepper and 5 minutes later the tomatoes, diced in one-inch pieces.

5.   In the same sauté pan you used for the vegetables, add the remaining butter and oil. Heat slowly and stir in the flour to make a roux. When it starts to turn light yellow (approximately 3 to 4 minutes), keep stirring with a wooden spoon and add the paprika.

6.   Remove from heat 1 minute after the addition of the paprika, and immediately pour in 1½ to 2 cups cold water. Keep stirring with the wooden spoon so that the roux will be very smooth.

7.   Add the diluted roux to the soup, stirring constantly. Correct the seasoning with a little more salt, the juice of a lemon, and some freshly ground black pepper.

8.   Simmer very slowly over low heat for another 10 minutes; then remove from heat and keep covered for at least 15 minutes.

9.   In a large soup tureen, stir the egg yolks with the sour cream until smooth. Add to it in small amounts about 2 cups of hot soup, stirring constantly so that it won't curdle. Then ladle the rest of the soup into the tureen.

10.   Sprinkle generously with parsley and serve.

CHEF'S SECRET: The mixture of oil and butter with flour and paprika is an East European relative of the classic French roux. As a rule I am against making a roux, because I find it in most cases unnecessary. But this soup is different. Its authentic flavor is derived partially from the golden yellow roux.

If your store doesn't carry Italian or flat-leaf parsley, just ask the produce manager to get you some. He can do so with no difficulty. Parsley root is often sold with parsley greens (the flat-leaf variety) on it. If you buy a large bunch of parsley root, don't throw away the stems and leaves. Wash them thoroughly with cold water, drop the whole bunch for 3 seconds in boiling water, and plunge immediately into ice water. Remove the greens and shake them, leaving a little water on them, and roll very tightly into a piece of aluminum foil, long enough to cover the greens at least twice, all over. You can freeze the parsley, and it will be easy to cut in its frozen state with a sharp knife. The important thing is to put the unused portion back into the freezer immediately.

Ten-Minute Chicken Soup

8 servings

2 whole chicken breasts, or 4 halved chicken breasts, total weight 20 to 24 ounces
2 10-ounce cans chicken broth, plus 6 cans water
2 chicken bouillon cubes
1 teaspoon Chef's Salt (see index)

2 stalks celery
1 carrot
1 scallion (or ¼ cup onion sliced thin)
2 tablespoons butter
1 teaspoon sugar
½ cup instant rice

1. Remove the skin and bones from the chicken breasts. Put skin and bones in a small pot with 1 cup water and start cooking them on low heat. Reserve the meat.

2. In a soup pot, heat the chicken broth, water, bouillon cubes, and Chef's Salt over medium heat.

3. Cut the chicken breasts into matchstick-sized pieces, across the grain of the flesh.

4. Chop the celery, carrot, and scallion into pieces of approximately the same size as the chicken pieces.

5. Heat the butter with the sugar in a heavy frying pan or sauté pan with a lid. When it is very hot, add the chicken and vegetables. Stir it for a minute over high heat, then carefully add 2 cups of the chicken broth. Cover and cook vigorously for 10 minutes.

6. Add precooked rice prepared according to package directions.

7. Strain the stock from the skin and bones and add to the soup. Correct seasoning and serve.

CHEF'S SECRET: This is a kind of emergency soup. When I demonstrate it on television, it takes me 9 minutes from beginning to end, starting with the raw materials and serving the hot soup for four people in the ninth minute. Of course, it takes longer for 8 servings — 15 minutes. So figure 30 minutes when you try it for the first time.

Instead of cutting the vegetables into matchstick size you can grate them through the largest hole of a grater. Instead of rice you can add fine noodles, which will cook in 3 to 4 minutes.

Ujházy Chicken Soup

8 servings

3 medium carrots, scraped and split lengthwise in fourths

2 cups scraped, coarsely chopped parsley root

1 bunch flat-leaf parsley, tied with a bay leaf to a medium sized leek split lengthwise from the end almost down to the bottom

1 medium onion with the skin left on, studded with a clove

1 teaspoon marjoram

1 teaspoon tarragon

1 clove garlic mashed to a pulp with 1½ teaspoons salt

½ teaspoon black peppercorns, slightly bruised

½ teaspoon white peppercorns, slightly bruised

1 tablespoon salt

1 stewing hen, about 4 to 5 pounds, cut up, with giblets, neck, and heart

2 fryers, about 2 pounds each, split in half

1 teaspoon sugar

1 tablespoon butter

2 to 3 tablespoons finely grated carrot

8 ounces very thin (angel hair) noodles, barely cooked, rinsed, and kept in cold water

Liver Dumplings:

8 ounces chicken livers

½ cup bread crumbs

2 tablespoons flour

2 heaping tablespoons finely minced onion

1 teaspoon shortening

1 egg

1 tablespoon finely chopped parsley

freshly ground black pepper to taste

1 clove of garlic mashed to a pulp with 1½ teaspoons salt

1.   Place all the vegetables and spices in a large soup pot. Cover with the cut-up hen and the giblets, neck, and heart.

2.   Pour in enough water to cover, or approximately 4 quarts. Cook gently for 1½ hours.

3.   Add the chicken halves and enough additional water to cover. Bring to a boil again. Cook gently for another 30 minutes, or until the chicken halves are tender.

4.   Remove the chicken halves with a slotted spoon and keep them warm.

5.   To prepare the liver dumplings, blend all the ingredients

in an electric blender until completely smooth. Let the mixture stand for at least 15 minutes.

6.   Strain approximately 1 quart of the soup broth into a saucepan. Bring to a boil. Using a teaspoon, drop small portions of the liver mixture into the boiling soup, forming almond-sized dumplings. Cook until they are firm, approximately 3 to 5 minutes. Keep the dumplings warm and completely covered with soup.

7.   In another small saucepan, heat the sugar over medium heat until it begins to brown at the edges. Add the butter. When the mixture starts to foam, stir in the freshly grated carrots and remove from the heat. Add 2 to 3 spoonfuls of soup. Keep stirring until the mixture turns a bright orange color.

8.   Strain all the soup through a fine sieve. Keep the cooked stewing hen and vegetables for other use. Add the carrot mixture to the clear soup by straining through a fine sieve also.

9.   To serve, place in each soup plate a good cupful of cooked noodles, a chicken quarter, and a few liver dumplings. Ladle in some soup, and serve with crusty white bread and mustard sauce.

CHEF'S SECRET: This Hungarian soup was named for a nineteenth-century Hungarian actor who, according to legend, ate it at noon every day of his life.

If you don't have a pot large enough to cook the chicken, place the chicken halves, slightly overlapping, in a roasting pan with a tight-fitting cover. After 1½ hours, pour the soup on the chicken, cover the roasting pan, and place it in a 350° F. oven for about 45 minutes.

If the noodles were cooked in the soup, they would ruin its clarity and would make serving difficult. Cook the noodles only *al dente* and keep them in cold water. They will be firm, won't stick together, and will immediately heat through when the hot soup is poured over them.

Be sure to give the guests a knife and fork with the soup, and small butter dishes containing mustard sauce. After a few spoonfuls of soup, your guests can cut the chicken and put some mustard sauce on each bite.

Hungarian Halászlé Soup

8 servings

1 to 1½ pounds whitefish, filleted (save head and bones)
1½ pounds pike, filleted (save head and bones)
1 pound perch, filleted
1 pound smelts
2 cups finely chopped onion
1 tablespoon Chef's Salt (see index)
1 whole onion with skin on, plus skin and peelings of the chopped onion

2 tablespoons butter
1 tablespoon oil
1 tomato, cored and cut into small pieces
7 tablespoons Hungarian paprika
1 bell pepper or other green pepper, cored, split in half, and thinly sliced
freshly ground black pepper to taste

1. Ask for whitefish and pike with the heads on. After weighing and cleaning, keep the heads, tails, fins, and bones, and put them in a pot with the smelts. Add ½ cup of the onion and the Chef's Salt.

2. Add 3 quarts of cold water. Split the whole onion in half and add it to the pot with the peelings and skin from the other onions. Cover and simmer over slow heat for approximately 2 hours.

3. Strain and discard all ingredients except the liquid.

4. In the bottom of a large soup pot with a tight-fitting lid, put 1 tablespoon of the butter, the oil, the remaining chopped onion, and 1 cup water. Place over medium heat, cover, and cook 20 to 25 minutes, stirring occasionally until the onions cook to a pulp. If they start to brown during this process, add more water, a couple of tablespoons at a time.

5. Add the whitefish, pike, and perch, cut into slices about 1½ inches wide. Add the tomato and 6 tablespoons of the paprika. Pour the hot liquid over the fish, bring to a vigorous boil for 2 minutes, lower the heat, and simmer for 20 minutes.

6. Remove from the heat and let stand uncovered.

7. In a small saucepan melt the remaining 1 tablespoon paprika in the remaining 1 tablespoon butter, stirring constantly until it turns vivid red.

8. Transfer the soup from the pot, very gently, without

breaking the fish, into a tureen. Pour the paprika-butter mixture over the top of the soup.

9. Arrange green pepper slices on top. Taste for saltiness and add salt if necessary. Add freshly ground black pepper and serve with crusty Vienna bread.

CHEF'S SECRET: When you cut up the fish, be sure that you lay it down with the skin on the cutting board, flesh up. Don't forget that the skin is nature's protection against the teeth of other fish; the outside skin is extremely tough and dulls the edge of the best knife in a few minutes. If you cut the skin from the inside, through the flesh, you won't have the same difficulty, and the pieces will be even and straight.

The onions prepared this way will cook to a thick substance that will add considerably to the body of the soup. You cannot stir this soup while it is cooking or you will break the pieces of fish. You will have to swish it—move the pot clockwise and counterclockwise *and* up and down.

You can substitute for Hungarian paprika a good grade of Spanish or Bulgarian paprika, but if possible try for the "real stuff." It is available in all better food chains, or you may order from: Hungarian Enterprises, 11802 Buckeye Road, Cleveland, Ohio 44120.

Lamb Tarragon Soup

8 servings

3 pounds lamb (breast or neck)
4 ounces bacon, chopped
1 cup minced onion
1 clove garlic
1 carrot, chopped
1 parsley root, chopped
few sprigs parsley tied with 1
  bay leaf
1 tablespoon dried tarragon or
  2 to 3 tablespoons freshly
  chopped tarragon

2 tablespoons Chef's Salt (see
  index)
½ cup vinegar
3 quarts water
6 to 10 black peppercorns
1 cup sour cream
2 egg yolks

1.   Trim the fat from the lamb, if any, and render it with the bacon pieces in a small sauté pan.

2.   Strain the fat into a large soup pot over moderate heat. Add onion and simmer until it begins to brown. Add the garlic, carrot, and parsley root, and saute until they start to brown. Cut the lamb into bite-sized pieces and add to the pot. Increase heat to high and stir until the meat turns whitish. Add remaining ingredients, except sour cream and egg yolks, reduce heat to low, cover, and simmer for 3 to 3½ hours, stirring once in a while. Correct seasoning.

3.   Combine sour cream and egg yolks in a soup tureen. Ladle some soup into the tureen, stir to warm up sour cream and egg, add the remaining soup, and serve.

CHEF'S SECRET: If your butcher can't supply you with lamb trimmings, buy the front and neck of a baby lamb, or inquire at a Greek or Latin butcher shop. They usually have baby lamb on hand.

If you can't get fresh tarragon, look for tarragon vinegar of the type that has a sprig of tarragon in the bottle. It won't be perfect, but it will certainly be better than no fresh tarragon at all.

When fresh tarragon is available, wash and rinse the bunches, tie the stems, and dip each bunch for 2 or 3 seconds into boiling water. Then remove and dip immediately into ice water with plenty of ice cubes in it. Shake to dry, roll tight in aluminum foil, and keep frozen. It will be usable for 6 to 8 months. Use it straight out of the freezer, chopping only as much as you need at the last minute. Refreeze the rest immediately. Of course, you can do the same with other fresh greens.

Cold Cantaloupe Soup

8 servings

4 pounds (peeled weight) ripe,
   firm cantaloupe
1 cup sugar
¼ cup cognac or brandy

¼ teaspoon salt
pinch white pepper
2 whole cloves
¼ teaspoon cinnamon

1 tablespoon maraschino
  cherry juice from a jar, with
  4 or 5 maraschino cherries
  chopped fine
1 quart water

2 cups half-and-half or light
  cream
2 cups white wine
1 lemon, thinly sliced

1.   Cube about one-fourth of the melon. Place in a glass dish, add half the sugar and all the brandy, maraschino cherry juice, and chopped cherries. Cover and chill at least 1 hour.

2.   Cut up the rest of the melon, place in a saucepan, add remaining sugar, salt, pepper, cloves, and cinnamon, and gently cook in the water for about 20 minutes. Chill and press through a sieve, or strain and run through a blender without the liquid.

3.   Stir the light cream and the wine into the cold cooked melon juice and blended pulp. Add more sugar and salt, if needed. Mix with the melon cubes and serve, topped with thinly sliced lemon.

CHEF'S SECRET: When shopping for melons (cantaloupes, honeydew, or similar types), look for even-shaped not lopsided melons. Compare same size fruits and always choose the heavier one. (If two melons each are about 16 inches around, but one weighs a few ounces more, it probably has thicker flesh and a smaller cavity than the other.)

To check ripeness, gently press the flower end of the melon with two thumbs and sniff at the same place. If the flower end is somewhat softer than the stem end, and if you can smell the melon aroma, you will probably have a good melon.

Purchase melons a day before you use them, and do not refrigerate but keep in a paper bag in a sunny, warm place. Then cut, peel, arrange, and chill for an hour. Keeping the melon at room temperature will help it ripen and grow sweeter.

If you first mix the ice cold soup with the cream, then slowly add the ice cold wine, the soup won't curdle.

If you don't like the flavor of maraschino, omit the maraschino liquid and cherries and add 2 tablespoons orange liqueur.

If you wish, you can offer freshly toasted almonds with the soup, or toast strips lightly brushed with butter and sprinkled with mild grated Swiss cheese. It sounds curious, but it is a wonderful combination.

Cold Watermelon Soup

8 servings

watermelon, about 5 pounds
1¼ cups sugar

2 cups red wine, preferably
    Spanish Sangria or similar
juice of ½ lemon
½ lemon sliced thin

1.   Carefully remove the seedless middle part of the melon. Cut it into even ¾-inch cubes, sprinkle with 2 or 3 tablespoons of sugar, cover, and chill.

2.   Remove as many seeds as you can from the rest of the melon and press the melon flesh through a colander or sieve. Discard the seeds.

3.   Mix the melon juice with the red wine. Add the rest of the sugar, squeeze in the lemon juice, add the chilled melon cubes, and chill for 3 hours or more.

4.   Serve in chilled soup cups or glasses and float ½ slice lemon on each serving.

CHEF'S SECRET: This soup is a European favorite. When it is made from half a watermelon, you can leave the shell intact, cut the edge zigzag, and serve the soup right in the melon.

If you wish, freeze the melon juice without adding the wine. Just mix with the sugar and lemon juice and freeze until it becomes slushy. Then add it to the chilled wine and melon cubes. This way it will stay cold longer.

3
$\mathcal{M}eats$

If we can believe our statisticians, per capita beef consumption in the United States is not only the greatest in the world but is also the fastest growing among all foodstuffs. In the early 1950's the average American consumed around 50 pounds of beef per year; he now eats more than *160* pounds per year.

As I travel around the country and talk to groups of homemakers and students of home economics, restaurant management, and related subjects, most of the questions asked me are about frozen meats and methods of freezing. So I think it is important to explain a few important points about freezing and dispel some fallacies and misinformation.

To begin with, what you think is a freezer standing in the corner of your kitchen, in or next to the refrigerator, is, I am sorry to say, not a freezer but a "frozen food holding cabinet." In other words, it was designed to keep frozen foods (which were purchased frozen, taken home frozen and placed into this cabinet immediately) frozen. It was not meant to freeze unfrozen foods.

Of course, you can freeze unfrozen food in this cabinet, but not *properly*. What's the difference between proper and improper freezing? Heaven and hell. To freeze beef properly you need a temperature of at least 20° below zero and a movement of air something like a wind blowing 20 miles an hour or more. As we all know from our friendly TV weatherman, the temperature and velocity of the wind together are responsible for the "chill factor." When the temperature of the air is near the freezing point and no wind blows, the liquid in the atmosphere starts to fall in the form of snow, and the flakes are large and soft. When the temperature falls toward zero and the wind starts to blow, the snowflakes turn into snow crystals, their size decreases, and their hardness increases. Under a magnifying glass they won't show as many sharp edges as snow that falls during warmer weather.

When the temperature drops, the liquid enclosed in the cells of beef behaves just like the liquid trapped in the clouds: it turns into solid crystals. If the temperature is relatively high, the crystal-forming process inside the meat cells is relatively slow, and the ice crystals are large. They will pierce and cut the cell walls of the beef (or any other meat), and when you defrost this slowly frozen meat, the holes in the cell walls will release a tremendous amount of the juices and the protein walls will collapse and turn into a spongelike, fibrous, dry, chewy substance.

But if the same meat is processed in a frozen-food processing plant, the very low temperature and the high velocity of air movement will produce such a tremendous chill factor that the liquid enclosed in the cells of the beef will freeze extremely fast into considerably smaller crystals, and they won't have a chance to pierce the walls of the cells. Therefore, during defrosting or cooking no juices will ooze out, and the taste, texture, and chewability will all be much better. They all contribute to what we call tenderness.

If you have a good thermometer, put it on the top shelf of your freezer, close the door, and check the temperature five minutes later. Then do the same thing on the bottom shelf. You will be amazed at the difference in temperature between the top and bottom shelves—as much as 15 to 25 degrees.

I don't say that you shouldn't buy steaks on sale for the freezer because I know the temptation is too great. Instead, I'll try to suggest the best way to handle the meat for freezing. Here are the basic rules:

1. Don't buy roasts or large pieces for home freezing in a frozen food cabinet.

2. Don't put any meat, as you purchase it, immediately into the freezer, and especially not on the top or middle shelf.

3. Don't buy more ground beef than you are sure you will eat within 60 days, and don't freeze it in bulk. Make it into patties.

4. Don't buy meat thicker than two inches.

5.   Don't ever freeze meat as one unit that you will not use at one time. Cut the meat into meal-sized or preferably portion-sized pieces, and then proceed as follows:

Empty the bottom shelf in the freezer by transferring the food there to the next shelf up. Lay a cookie sheet on the floor of the freezer. Close the door and don't open it for at least 30 minutes. (Be sure that all this is done around the middle of the defrosting cycle, if there is one.)

Brush the surface of each piece of meat with fresh corn oil, place the meat in the *refrigerator,* and chill it for 30 minutes or more. Remove from the refrigerator piece by piece and lay them on the cold cookie sheet in the bottom of the freezer. Close the freezer door again for an hour.

Meanwhile, prepare a piece of aluminum foil or plastic and a piece of freezer wrap for each unit of meat.Remove the pieces of meat very quickly, one by one, from the freezer, wrap each in foil or plastic, and immediately replace it in the freezer. When you are through wrapping, wait another 30 minutes or so, then remove pieces one by one from the freezer and wrap each piece again in the freezer paper.

Now remove the cookie sheet, place the meat on the bottom shelf, and put the cookie sheet on top of it. Then pile on top of the cookie sheet all the frozen food from the second and third lowest shelves. This is the most important step. Don't forget, cold air moves down, not up. In order to freeze the unfrozen meat faster, you must put frozen food on *top* of it!

The next big question is how to defrost the frozen meat. After more than two decades of experimenting, I find that the best way to defrost portion-sized pieces of frozen beef—steaks, Swiss steaks, braising pieces, stew meat—is to place them in a shallow dish, cover with oil, and refrigerate overnight. If you must defrost them faster, let the meat stand on one narrow edge so that the air circulates around it. Or, if you wish, place it on a rack. The most important thing is that the bottom surface be exposed to the air just like the top surface. Don't forget, hot air always rises. For the same reason, keep turning the meat while you defrost it.

If you think my suggestions may not be worth the extra trouble, you can try them out with two identical pieces of meat. Handle one the way you usually do, and handle the other piece according to my suggestions. You will taste the difference.

Beef Roast

8 servings

1 cup coarsely chopped carrots
1 cup coarsely chopped celery
1 cup coarsely chopped onion
½ cup coarsely chopped turnip, rutabaga, parsnip, or parsley root
2 cloves garlic
6 teaspoons Chef's Salt (see index)

4 tablespoons oil, lard, or other natural shortening
2 tablespoons Kitchen Bouquet (optional)
1 cup oil or other shortening
4 to 5-pound beef roast
1 cup red wine mixed with 1 cup beef consommé, or 2 cups beef consommé

1.   Put the chopped vegetables, garlic, and 2 teaspoons Chef's Salt into a roasting pan. Add 2 cups of water. Preheat oven to 350° F.

2.   Rub the roast with the 4 tablespoons shortening, 4 teaspoons Chef's Salt, and Kitchen Bouquet. On top of the stove, heat a heavy skillet large enough to hold the roast. Place ½ cup of the oil or other shortening in the empty pan as it heats. When the shortening starts to smoke, gently ease in the meat. Press it to the frying pan for 2 to 3 minutes until the surface turns brown. Remove, let the shortening heat up again, and repeat until all sides of the meat are seared brown and crusty. Discard fat.

3.   Place the meat on a double sheet of aluminum foil large enough to wrap so that the folds are on the top of the meat. Bring up the two ends and the two sides of the aluminum foil. Be sure that there is no crease on the bottom. Lace the meat with the mixture of wine and consommé, or with the consommé if you are not using wine. Close the foil and place the meat on top of the vegetables in the roasting pan. Cover and roast for 75 to 90 minutes, or until a meat thermometer (the type you stick into the meat for a few seconds until it registers) registers 100° internal temperature. Remove meat from the oven. Carefully lift the cover so as not to burn yourself with the steam. Open the aluminum foil and pour the accumulated liquid from the foil onto the vegetables in the pan. Let the beef stand at room temperature on a tray or cookie sheet for approximately 1 hour.

4.   While the meat is cooling, drain the pan juices through a sieve and empty into a chilled pot. Add a handful of ice cubes to bring the fat to the top so you can remove it easily.

5. Remove the garlic and run the vegetables through an electric blender, or press them by hand through a sieve. Add to the cooking liquid, let stand for a few minutes, and again remove the fat from the top.

6. If you like a thick gravy, mix 2 tablespoons flour with 1 tablespoon cornstarch and ½ cup water for each pint of liquid. Bring the cooking liquid with the puréed vegetables to a boil and stir in the flour-cornstarch-water mixture. Let it cook over low heat for 5 to 10 minutes. Set aside.

7. If you want just juice, then simply strain the pan liquid and discard the vegetables or keep them for other use (they are excellent to serve around the beef or on an extra plate; or you can mash and mix them into 2 cups mashed potatoes, place in a well-buttered shallow casserole, sprinkle the top with some paprika, bake for 20 to 25 minutes, and serve with the beef).

8. Approximately 30 minutes before serving, heat the other ½ cup shortening in a small pan over high heat to the smoking point. Place the roast on a cookie sheet with sides and pour the fat over it. Place the meat in a preheated 450 to 475 degree oven; turn every 5 minutes. For medium-rare, bake 20 minutes; for medium, 30 minutes. Remove and let stand at least 15 minutes before slicing with a very sharp knife.

CHEF'S SECRET: In this method the beef is exposed to the heat three times. First the surface is crusted and seared in hot fat. Second, it is moist-roasted in a covered pan with the double protection of the aluminum foil. Finally, it is dry-roasted at very high temperature. In this way the beef will be all pink on the inside and crusty and tender on the outside. If you prefer your beef rare, simply cut the second moist-roasting time by 20 to 25 minutes and the dry-roasting time to 15 minutes. If you want it well-done, increase the moist-roasting time to 2 hours and keep the meat warm until serving. Omit the dry-roasting.

To remove the garlic easily from the vegetable mixture, stick a toothpick in each garlic clove before you place it among the vegetables. You can use this method of handling garlic in any soup, meat, sauce or other recipe which requires whole cloves of garlic to be removed after cooking.

Roast à la Hotel Adlon

8 servings

8- to 10-pound boned prime rib roast, or a 5- to 6-pound rib eye covered with a thin coating of beef fat

8 ounces Westphalian ham or country ham, raw, in one piece, not sliced

3 tablespoons Chef's Salt (see index)

2 envelopes unflavored gelatin

1 cup chopped carrots

1 cup chopped onions

½ cup chopped celery

½ cup chopped turnip, parsnip, or parsley root

2 to 3 sprigs parsley

1 tablespoon rinsed capers

1 clove garlic

2 cups white wine

For the sauce:

1 quart of the roasting liquid

1 tablespoon cornstarch and 1 tablespoon flour diluted in 1 cup dry white wine or fruity, not sweet, white wine

1 teaspoon rinsed capers, chopped

1 black truffle, chopped fine, or 4 to 5 pitted black olives brought to a boil in ½ cup of white wine, cooled, rinsed, and chopped

1 ounce cognac, brandy, or strong whiskey

1 tablespoon rinsed whole capers

1.   Ask the butcher to debone the prime ribs and cut the coat of fat from the top. Or if you buy rib eye, ask for half of a rib eye, lip off, covered with a square piece of surface fat from the sirloin or rib.

2.   Cut the ham into 2-inch-long pieces as thick as a matchstick. Lay the pieces on a piece of aluminum foil and freeze.

3.   Sharpen the end of a wooden kitchen spoon. Pierce the outside of the rib eye with the kitchen spoon approximately 2 to 2½ inches deep, aiming toward the center of the beef, making about 6 holes around one circumference, and about 7 rows around. You should end up with about 42 holes and as many matchstick pieces of ham.

4.   After you have made the holes, remove the ham from the freezer and stick the pieces into the holes.

5.   Chop the remaining ham and save it for the sauce. Preheat oven to 375° F.

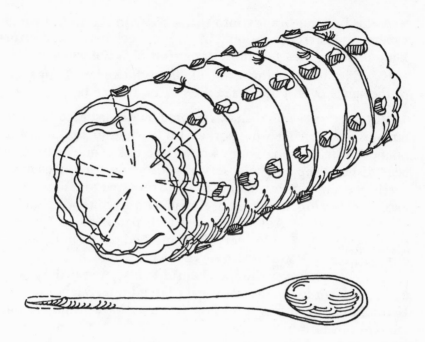

6.   Rub the surface of the roast with 3 tablespoons Chef's Salt mixed with the gelatin. Roll the whole roast into the blanket of fat and tie with butcher's string. The ties should be an inch apart from one another. Make a knot and cut the string each time you go around, or run the string spirally from one end to the other and then back.

7.   Place the carrots, onions, celery, turnips, parsley, capers, and garlic in a roasting pan with a good cover. Mix wine with enough water to almost cover the vegetables. Place the roast on top of the vegetables, cover the pan, and roast for approximately 2 hours for medium rare.

8.   Remove the roast, cut off the string, discard the fat blanket. Let stand for 30 to 45 minutes.

9.   For the sauce, drain the pan juice into a dish, add a handful of ice cubes, stir, and skim the fat that accumulates on the top. Bring pan juice to a boil, add the mixture of cornstarch, flour, and wine and cook until it comes to a boil. Simmer for a few minutes. Add the chopped ham and rinsed and chopped capers and continue to simmer. Place the finely chopped black truffle or the chopped olives in a small pan over high heat. Pour on the cognac and ignite it with a match. Pour the truffle or olives

with the flaming brandy into the sauce, add the rinsed whole capers, and correct seasoning by adding perhaps a small sprinkling of sugar or a few more spoonfuls of white wine.

10.   Slice the beef into even, medium-thick slices. Pour some of the sauce over it and offer the rest in a sauce boat.

CHEF'S SECRET: This dish was created by August Escoffier, the famous French chef who worked for a while in Berlin at the famous Hotel Adlon. To my knowledge this is one of the few beef dishes prepared and served with white wine. Germany excels in white wine but has not much to show in reds. That's why Escoffier developed a great beef dish with a white wine sauce.

As a rule, Beef Adlon is served with pan-fried or hashed-brown potatoes or with a very finely mashed potato or creamed puréed potato. You can also serve it with rice or noodles.

If you have leftover chopped ham after inserting all the pieces in the beef, stir it into the sauce at the last minute. But be careful. If the ham you use is too salty, you may have to adjust the amount of salt in the sauce.

The gelatin mixed with the Chef's Salt will help the beef coagulate as it cools and will prevent the juices from oozing out.

Don't worry if the holes you make in the beef are larger than the ham pieces. The meat has a natural gelatinous substance that will surround the ham pieces as they cook and hold them tight so they won't fall out and no juice will run out of the meat.

Beef Roulade

8 servings

1 ham steak, 8 ounces
8 ounces slab or thick-sliced
    bacon
2 large kosher pickles
4 pounds round or butt cut into
    1-inch thick, 2-pound slices
2 tablespoons Chef's Salt (see
    index)
2 tablespoons prepared
    mustard

1 bay leaf
1 clove garlic
10 to 12 black peppercorns
1 cup sliced onion
3 tablespoons Kitchen Bouquet
1 can onion soup
2⅓ cups Italian plum or pear
    tomatoes

2 tablespoons finely minced
onion
1 envelope unflavored gelatin
1 cup chopped celery tops
1 cup coarsely cut carrots

8-ounce can tomato sauce with
peppers
2 tablespoons cornstarch
1 tablespoon flour
½ cup water or red wine
(optional)

1. Preheat oven to 375° F.

2. Cut ham, bacon, and pickles into even, pencil-thick strips. Set aside.

3. Pound with a mallet the two slices of beef, gently but firmly moving the mallet so that it doesn't hit the meat directly but with a down and out movement.

4. Sprinkle the beaten sides with half the Chef's Salt. Turn the pieces over and sprinkle the other sides with the remaining Chef's Salt.

5. On each piece of meat spread half the mustard and sprinkle 1 tablespoon of minced onion. Then gently pound the meat all over with the mallet with the same movement as described above, so that the meat spreads out. If you do this correctly, the meat will double in size.

6. Sprinkle the gelatin around a 2-inch outside border of the pieces of meat.

7. Starting in front of you, lay strips of ham, bacon, and pickle alternately on top of the meat until you use half the amount you have. Roll up meat jellyroll fashion. Be sure that the outer edge is on the bottom. Repeat with the second piece of meat.

8. In a roasting pan, lay the celery tops on the bottom of the pan with the scraped and coarsely cut carrot and the bay leaf, garlic, peppercorns, and the onion. Rub the outside of the two meat rolls with the Kitchen Bouquet and place the rolls on the vegetables.

9. Pour the onion soup and the tomatoes into the pan. Cover and bake for 1 hour 45 minutes to 2 hours, basting the meat occasionally.

10. Remove the rolls to a warm platter. Strain juices through a colander, discard the peppercorns, bay leaf, and garlic. Put the remaining vegetables in an electric blender with a few tablespoons of juice and purée them.

11. Mix the puréed vegetables, the tomato sauce, and about 3

cups of cooking liquid together in a saucepan over medium heat. Stir the cornstarch and flour together into ½ cup cold water (or red wine if you wish). When the vegetable mixture boils, stir in the cornstarch and flour mixture with a wire whip.

12.   Place the roulades back in the roasting pan. Ladle the sauce over them. Cover and keep in a 200°F. oven until ready to serve.

CHEF'S SECRET: This is an excellent dish for a festive occasion if you can get the proper meat. In most supermarkets you must ask for special service in the meat department and explain to the butcher what you want. It is important that the two pieces of beef are solid and without a seam running through (which during pounding would divide the piece into smaller ones). If this happens, simply make 3 or 4 smaller rolls.

Do not pound the meat too hard; striking it gently but repeatedly with the mallet will give better results. If you wish, omit the mustard and replace it with anchovy paste.

Beef Wellington

8 servings

5- to 6-pound trimmed beef
    tenderloin
4 cups flour
1 teaspoon salt
10 tablespoons butter, chilled
10 tablespoons lard, chilled
1 egg yolk
10 tablespoons cold water
1 pound (approximate) ground
    beef from the edible
    tenderloin trimmings

½ pound Pâté Maison (see
    index)
1 to 1½ teaspoons Pâté Spice
    (see index)
pinch of salt
pinch of freshly ground black
    pepper
Chef's Salt (see index)
¼ cup corn oil
1 cup flour for dusting
1 egg mixed with 1 tablespoon
    cold water

1.   Remove fat surrounding the tenderloin; then remove the tough silvery surface which is called the "silverskin." The best way to do this is to loosen the skin at the tail end with the point of

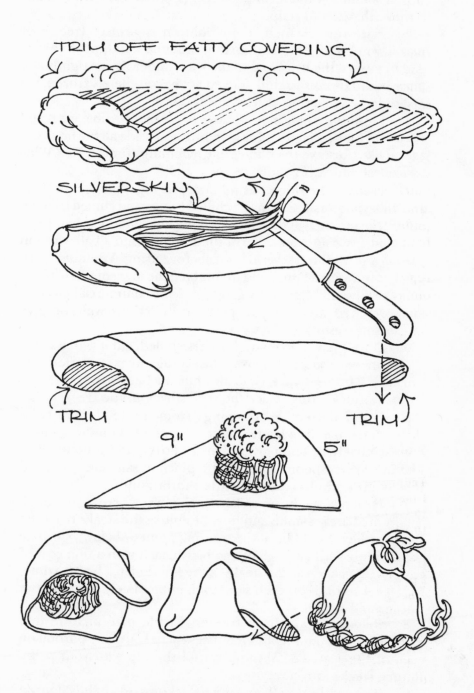

TRIM OFF FATTY COVERING

SILVERSKIN

TRIM

TRIM

9"

5"

a sharp knife. Pulling and cutting toward the "head end," remove the skin in strips.

2.   Place the "cleaned" tenderloin on a sheet of freezer or plastic wrap and, holding it firmly with one hand, push the tail end in toward the head end to form a cylinder. Wrap tightly and place in the freezer to chill. It need not be completely frozen, but it should be chilled to at least 26° to 28° F.

3.   From the trimmings, remove every bit of edible meat and cut it into half-inch cubes for grinding. Put aside all the fat to use as you like. Reserve the non-edible trimmings for the Red Wine Sauce (see index for sauce recipe).

4.   Prepare the dough as follows: Sift together 4 cups flour and 1 teaspoon salt. Cut in the chilled butter and chilled lard (no other shortening will do), working quickly. Then work in 1 egg yolk and the cold water. Form the mixture into a ball, wrap in plastic, and chill for several hours before using. You must work quickly and with a light hand to combine the ingredients without overworking the dough. (A good grade of commercial piecrust mix prepared according to package directions will also give satisfactory results.)

5.   Once the whole tenderloin has chilled, cut it with a sharp knife into equal portions. From the average steer tenderloin you can cut 8 5-ounce steaks. (Use the ends for Beef Stroganoff. See index.) After cutting, place the steaks back in the freezer.

6.   Grind the edible trimmings from the tenderloin twice through the medium blade of a meat grinder. You should have approximately 1 pound ground meat. To this add ½ pound Pâté Maison, 1½ teaspoons Pâté Spice, a pinch of salt, and a pinch of freshly ground black pepper. Mix thoroughly.

7.   Heat a large, heavy skillet to the point where a drop of oil will immediately smoke and burn. Remove the steaks from the freezer (they should be at the freezing point or below), sprinkle them lightly with Chef's Salt and brush each with a thin coat of corn oil. Quickly sear the steaks in the hot skillet, a few at a time, for 3 or 4 seconds on each side; then immediately return to the freezer and rechill.

8.   Remove steaks from freezer. Divide pâté mixture into eight equal portions, about 3 ounces each. Place one portion on each of the seared steaks and round the top with your palm. Return steaks to freezer.

9.   Roll out the dough to ⅛-inch thickness on a lightly floured

pastry board. Beat the egg with cold water and brush the surface of the dough with the eggwash. Cut the dough into triangles about 9 by 9 by 5 inches. Place steak close to the narrow corner, so that the bottom is completely on the dough, and pull the long end over the steak, completely covering it and pressing the dough firmly together to form a seal around the bottom rim. Your first Wellington may look clumsy and hopeless, but don't give up.

10.   With a knife, trim pastry to about ¾ inch from base of steak. Pick up the pastry-covered steak in one hand, and with the other make a pinched rim around the base, as you would edge a pie.

11.   From the leftover dough, cut eight triangles, ¾ by 1½ inches, pinch together the short end of each triangle so that it looks like a leaf, and then score veins into the leaf with a knife.

12.   Brush the Wellingtons with the eggwash again, place the leaves on top, and return them to the freezer. At this point the Wellingtons are best kept on a well-floured tray; but if they will be stored overnight or longer, they must be tightly covered.

13.   To finish for serving: Preheat oven to 475°F. Bake the prepared Wellingtons on a cookie sheet until a meat thermometer registers as follows:

> 115° for rare
> 120° for medium-rare
> 130° for medium
> 140° for medium-well

14.   After 5 minutes baking time, brush each Wellington again with eggwash and continue to brush every 5 minutes.

CHEF'S SECRET: If your butcher can supply a fully trimmed tenderloin 2½ to 2¾ pounds, approximately 11 to 12 inches in length and 2½ to 3 inches in diameter, plus 1 pound of ground beef for the pâté and another pound of scraps or ground meat for the sauce, you can begin the preparation by wrapping the trimmed tenderloin in the aluminum foil to chill.

Don't skip the eggwash basting every 5 minutes while baking, because it has a much more important purpose than beautifying the Wellingtons. The cold eggwash cools off the pastry while the meat keeps cooking. This way, even if you like the beef done to medium-well (which we really don't recommend), the pastry won't burn or dry out.

Not knowing your oven and how correct its temperature is, I am reluctant to give specific baking times for the Wellingtons. Our experience shows that in a preheated, accurate 475° F. oven, 8 Wellingtons on a cookie sheet bake to rare (115° internal temperature) in 12 to 13 minutes; to medium-rare in 15 minutes; to medium in 18 minutes; and to medium-well in about 20 minutes at most.

Meat is so expensive that I feel you should invest in a good professional meat thermometer that is a scientific instrument rather than a gadget. If you wish to purchase one, send for my price list (see index), which will tell you where a good thermometer can be obtained.

French Provincial Pepper Steak

8 servings

For the Sauce:

1 teaspoon sugar
2 slices bacon
1 cup chopped onions (½-inch squares)
1 medium green bell pepper, cored, cut into ½-inch squares
1 medium red bell pepper, or 1 small can (about 2 ounces) whole pimientos, cut into ½-inch squares

1 tomato, not too ripe, peeled and seeds removed, cut into ½-inch pieces
1 cup Burgundy or similar red wine
10½-ounce can beef consommé
1 tablespoon flour and 1 tablespoon cornstarch mixed with 4 tablespoons cold water
8 ounces small fresh mushrooms
salt and pepper to taste

1. In a saucepan wiped completely dry, over high heat, brown the sugar. As it starts to brown, add the bacon cut into ½-inch pieces. As the fat from the bacon is rendered, add onions and sauté quickly, then add green peppers, red peppers, and tomatoes and set the heat low. (If you use canned pimiento, don't add until after you add the mushrooms [see step 3] because it will fall apart.)

2. In a small pot, bring to a boil the wine and consommé.

When it boils, stir in the flour-cornstarch-water mixture. Let it come to a boil again and then simmer.

3.   Wipe mushrooms with a damp cloth and cut each into 2 to 3 pieces, depending on size. Add to the onion-bell pepper mixture.

4.   After sautéeing the vegetable mixture for 8 to 10 minutes, add it to the sauce and simmer for an additional 10 to 15 minutes. Correct seasoning. The amount of salt you have to add will depend on ·the saltiness of the consommé used.

For the Steak:

8 12-ounce boneless strip sirloin steaks, each closely trimmed on the fat side

4 tablespoons Kitchen Bouquet (optional)

2 tablespoons Chef's Salt (see index)

8 tablespoons whole black peppercorns gently bruised in a kitchen towel with a blunt object

1½ cups corn oil

1.   Brush steaks with Kitchen Bouquet.

2.   Mix Chef's Salt with crushed peppercorns. Press this mixture gently but firmly into the surface of the steaks. Place the steaks in a shallow dish and pour the oil over them. Refrigerate for at least 4 hours.

3.   Remove half the oil from the steaks and pour it into a heavy skillet over moderately high heat.

4.   When the oil starts to smoke, place 4 of the steaks in the pan. Remove after about 30 seconds. Let the oil heat up again and when it starts to smoke, return the steaks to the pan on the uncooked sides. Cook for approximately 2 minutes, then turn and cook on the other side for the same time. Remove to a warm place.

5.   Add the remaining oil to the pan and repeat as above with the remaining steaks.

6.   Let the steaks stand on a warm platter for not longer than 10 minutes, then reheat the pan and finish pan frying—3 minutes per side for rare, 5 minutes per side for medium-rare, or 6 minutes per side for medium. Have the sauce ready at serving temperature. Arrange the steaks on a hot serving platter with sauce to cover about one-third of each. Serve the rest of the sauce in a sauce boat.

CHEF'S SECRET: I am sure you have often seen, in restaurants and homes, steaks that are beautiful on one side and pale on the other. This happens regardless of how the steaks are prepared—on the grill over charcoal, or pan-fried, or even under the broiler. The reason for this is that people do not realize that after the steak touches the surface of whatever utensil you use, a tremendous amount of heat is lost. If you remove the steak after a few seconds and wait until the utensil recovers the heat, the other side of the meat will also brown quickly. This is why it is so important to follow the instructions here closely.

Steaks as we know them are American in origin. For hundreds of years they were never prepared in any other way than pan-fried. That is why I feel that pan-frying is the ideal way to prepare a good steak. I am convinced that after you try this method you will never prepare a good steak any other way again.

Pepper Steak Parisien
(Contre-Filet au Poivre Vert)

8 servings

8 well-trimmed sirloin steaks, each 12 to 16 ounces and ¾ to 1 inch thick, or 8 tenderloin steaks, each 6 to 8 ounces
1 tablespoon Chef's Salt (see index)

Sauce:

1 cup canned consommé, or 1 beef bouillon cube dissolved in 1 cup hot water
1 tablespoon flour and 1 tablespoon cornstarch stirred into a paste with ½ cup red wine and 2 tablespoons cold water, or with the same amount of red wine only
1 cup sour cream
3 to 4 tablespoons milk, light cream, or cream

2 tablespoons corn oil
1 tablespoon Kitchen Bouquet
3 to 4 tablespoons corn oil mixed with lard, or butter mixed with oil or lard for pan-frying

1 tablespoon canned green peppercorns, rinsed and chopped
1½ to 2 teaspoons green peppercorns, rinsed and soaked for at least 15 minutes in cold water, then drained and patted dry
1 teaspoon or more Kitchen Bouquet

1. Sprinkle both sides of steaks evenly with Chef's Salt. With a brush, brush both sides with a mixture of corn oil and Kitchen Bouquet. Pan fry steaks in the shortening in a large, heavy aluminum or cast-iron skillet. For medium rare, fry 3 to 4 minutes on each side. Keep steaks warm on a serving platter.

2. In a small pan, bring the consommé to a rolling boil. With a wire whip, stir in the mixture of flour, cornstarch, and red wine, and bring to a second boil. The sauce will be very thick. Keep stirring constantly while it cooks, 4 to 5 minutes. Remove from heat. It will resemble a thick pudding.

3. Put 2 to 3 tablespoons of this hot sauce into the sour cream and gently fold it in to warm the sour cream. Then add sour cream to the rest of the sauce. If too thick, add a few tablespoons milk, light cream, or cream. Simmer 10 minutes.

4. Add the rinsed finely chopped green peppercorns. Stir thoroughly. Let stand for at least 15, but preferably 30, minutes in a warm place in a covered saucepan placed in a larger pan filled halfway with hot, not boiling, water.

5. Just before serving, add the 1½ to 2 teaspoons whole green peppercorns and the Kitchen Bouquet to the sauce, and serve immediately.

CHEF'S SECRET: Because of a disagreement over canning practices, until a short while ago it was impossible to bring green peppercorns from Madagascar—the only place where they are processed—to the United States. But now they are available in many stores throughout the country. If you cannot get any, write to me, Chef Louis, at The Bakery, 2218 North Lincoln Avenue, Chicago 60614, and I will tell you where to get them.

Black pepper, white pepper, and green pepper are all berries grown on the pepper bush. The bush, native to India and to some territories in the Polynesian Islands and Madagascar, has tiny white flowers in clusters, and the flowers turn into the peppercorn or berry. If they are harvested green and dried in the sun, they turn black. This is the black pepper with which we are most familiar. If the berries are left on the bush until they turn completely ripe, they will be ivory white. This is what we know as white pepper or white Montauk pepper. If the berries are picked green, but instead of being sun dried are immediately canned in a brine, they are called green peppercorns.

Green peppercorns are used liberally in the *haute cuisine* of

France, mainly for flavoring sauces for beef, duck, pork, veal, and many other meats. The green peppercorn's characteristic flavor is a tantalizing pungency without a bite. Unfortunately, when cooked they always turn very bitter; therefore you should never bring to a boil a sauce or a dish containing green peppercorns. If you use a leftover the next day or later on, be careful to heat just to the serving point, not to the boiling point.

Spanish Steak

8 servings

8 8-ounce boneless strip
  sirloin steaks
2 teaspoons salt
½ teaspoon black pepper
½ teaspoon cumin

½ teaspoon cardamom
1 teaspoon chili powder
8 ounces chorizo sausage
8 tablespoons oil

1. With a mallet, pound the steaks until they are almost double in size. Cut edges to prevent shrinking. Mix and divide the spices among the 8 steaks and rub into the surface. Keep pounding until steaks are about 3 times or more their original size.

2. Open and discard casing of chorizo and fry the sausage

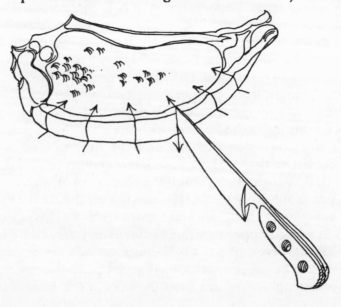

for 5 to 6 minutes. Pour off and retain the fat and the scraped chorizo bits from the frying pan.

3.   Add to the pan the oil and about 4 tablespoons of the fat from the chorizo. Heat to smoking point and pan-fry the steaks about 2 to 3 minutes to a side.

4.   Serve with rice and beans (canned Spanish style) puréed, or use a can of red kidney beans, pressed through a sieve and flavored with salt and pepper. Sprinkle chorizo on steak and rice and beans. Also, if you wish, sprinkle the steaks and rice with some fresh Cilantro (Mexican parsley) or coriander leaf.

5.   Decorate with sliced tomatoes. Serve tortillas instead of bread.

CHEF'S SECRET: It is important to make cuts along the edges of the steaks, especially the edge where the fat cover coats the sirloin. This prevents the meat from shrinking or curling up, and if the steak stays flat, the whole surface cooks evenly.

If you can't get any chorizo, which is Spanish-style sausage, buy the same amount of Italian sausage, remove it from the skin and add some chili powder, Spanish paprika, and a light sprinkling of cumin and cardamom before frying it. The taste will be very close to the Spanish. If no Italian sausage is available, your next choice is American sausage mixed with the same spices and perhaps some garlic powder.

Cilantro is a fragrant, flat-leaf Mexican parsley which is sold in all Latin neighborhoods. Unfortunately it resists drying, so if you can't get it fresh you can't get it at all. But if it is available, definitely try it. Its fragrance is incomparable.

Beef Stroganoff

8 servings

2 tablespoons onions, minced very fine
1 tablespoon butter
1 tablespoon oil
1 cup beef consommé
2 tablespoons flour
1½ pounds thinly sliced beef tenderloin

2 teaspoons Chef's Salt (see index)
3 tablespoons lard
½ cup red wine or beef consommé

1 teaspoon tomato purée or 1 tablespoon tomato juice	1 to 1½ cups thinly sliced mushrooms
1 teaspoon Chef's Salt	1 tablespoon butter
½ teaspoon black pepper	2 cups sour cream
1 bay leaf, washed (optional)	8 firm white mushroom caps, approximately same size

1.   Sauté onions in 1 tablespoon butter and 1 tablespoon oil over medium heat until the onions turn limp and translucent, about 3 minutes.

2.   Add ½ cup of the consommé, stir, and continue cooking for another 3 minutes.

3.   Meanwhile, mix the flour, tomato purée or tomato juice, 1 teaspoon Chef's Salt, and black pepper into the remaining ½ cup of consommé. Stir until smooth and pour it over the onions. If you wish, add the bay leaf and let the sauce simmer over low heat for at least 15 minutes. Stir occasionally to prevent scorching. Remove the bay leaf after 10 to 15 minutes of simmering.

4.   Sprinkle the meat with 2 teaspoons Chef's Salt and divide it into three even portions. Place in a large heavy skillet 1 tablespoon lard. When it heats to the smoking point, add ⅓ of the meat and sauté for a minute or so, turning constantly. Remove to a serving platter. Repeat with the second tablespoon lard and the second portion of meat, then with the third.

5.   After cooking the meat, pour the ½ cup red wine or consommé into the pan and with a spatula loosen all the bits and pieces stuck to the bottom of the pan. Strain the liquid into the sauce. If you wish, sauté the thinly sliced mushrooms in the same pan with 1 tablespoon butter, or simply sauté them with the last part of the meat in step 4. If you like the sliced tenderloin medium or medium well, cook it longer according to your taste.

6.   Dilute the sour cream with 2 tablespoons of the hot sauce; then add the sour cream to the rest of the sauce. This method prevents the sauce from curdling. Ladle the hot sauce over the meat.

7.   If you wish, cut the 8 mushrooms according to the illustration, and sauté them in a very small amount of fat in a hot pan, stems up. In this way the surface of the mushrooms will brown but the carved design will remain white. Place the decorated mushroom caps on top of the sauce and serve the Stroganoff with Alsatian noodles, plain noodles, or rice.

CHEF'S SECRET: It is best to a make the Stroganoff from tenderloin tails or tenderloin tips. Buy them already trimmed or trim them yourself. Roll each piece tightly, wrap in aluminum foil, and place in the freezer for an hour or so. Then cut on a diagonal into very thin slices, preferably less than ¼ inch.

If you prefer to make medallions of Stroganoff, then cut ½-inch-thick medallions and sauté them on low heat for 2 to 2½ minutes on each side. Arrange them just as you would tomatoes, placing on each portion one mushroom cap.

The bay leaf, which is optional, gives an authentic taste to the Stroganoff sauce, but if you don't remove it after 10 to 15 minutes of simmering, it will overpower the sauce. I suggest you wash the bay leaf before you add it. Its taste and fragrance will be much better if you wash it in tepid water, rubbing the surfaces with your fingers.

SUGGESTIONS FOR CARVING THE MUSHROOM CAPS: Classic French cuisine uses the term *turning* to describe the preparation of the mushroom caps. It is done by pressing a small, very sharp paring knife at an angle to the top of the mushroom and guiding it with the thumb while turning the mushroom. If you follow the illustrations, and try it a few times, the mushrooms will look very pretty.

Transylvanian Mitite

8 servings

2 pounds ground beef
½ cup onion, minced very fine
1 clove garlic, crushed with 1½
  teaspoons salt
1 teaspoon freshly ground
  black pepper

2 eggs
4 tablespoons matzo meal or
  bread crumbs
5 to 6 ice cubes

1. In a bowl, work together the meat, onion, garlic, salt, pepper, eggs, and matzo meal with the ice cubes until it becomes a firm, dough-like mixture.

2. Cover with plastic or aluminum foil and chill in refrigerator for several hours.

3. One hour before serving, form the meat into an oblong piece ¾ to 1 inch thick. With a wet knife, divide into 24 pieces. Each will be about the size of a thumb. With wet hands, roll little sausage-like rolls.

4. Let the pieces stand at room temperature and, a few minutes before serving, fry them in a heavy, hot skillet in a very small amount of oil—just enough so that they won't stick to the pan.

5. Serve with big heaps of freshly chopped sweet onions and prepared mustard. The dish goes well with mashed potatoes, rice, or string beans.

CHEF'S SECRET: The ice cubes will add moisture to the meat so that when you fry the mitite the added water will evaporate instead of the juices from the meat itself. The matzo meal or bread crumbs pick up the moisture in the meat as it heats up, keeping the mitite juicy.

Beef Stew à la Bully Hill

8 servings

2 pounds beef chuck, cut into
  1-inch cubes

3 cups finely chopped onion
4 tablespoons flour

2 tablespoons Chef's Salt (see index)
1 tablespoon Hungarian paprika
¼ teaspoon black pepper
1 tablespoon Kitchen Bouquet
¾ cup shortening, preferably lard

2 tablespoons cornstarch
2 cups beef stock
3 cups Bully Hill red wine
3 tablespoons tomato paste
½ teaspoon sugar
4 whole cloves
1 bay leaf
½ teaspoon thyme

1.   Season the meat with the Chef's Salt mixed with paprika and black pepper. Sprinkle Kitchen Bouquet over meat and toss to coat evenly.

2.   In a large, heavy saucepan, heat shortening to the smoking point. Brown the meat in it, turning with a spatula so that it browns on all sides.

3.   Add onions and cook over low heat until they turn limp.

4.   Sprinkle flour mixed with cornstarch over meat and onions, and cook for 5 minutes, stirring constantly, to keep the mixture from sticking to the pan.

5.   Add beef stock, wine, tomato paste, and sugar and stir.

6.   Add remaining spices, cover, and simmer over low heat for 2½ hours, or until meat is tender. (If you wish, 1 cup pre-cooked, sliced carrot and 12 to 16 pre-cooked small whole onions can be added just before serving.)

CHEF'S SECRET: This recipe has been in the Taylor winegrowing family of New York State for four generations. If you make it with another kind of red wine, ½ teaspoon sugar may not be enough; add more.

This is a thick stew, designed to be eaten with bread dipped into the glorious red wine gravy.

Baked Pork Chops with Stuffed Butter Squash

4 servings

4 center-cut pork chops, approximately 4 ounces each
2 teaspoons Chef's Salt (see index)
4 white butter squashes
1 quart boiling water with 1 tablespoon salt

2 tablespoons shortening
8-ounce can tomato sauce
8-ounce can tomato sauce with green peppers
16-ounce can corned beef hash
1 large fresh tomato

1. Preheat oven to 350° F. Trim pork chops if necessary. Sprinkle both sides with Chef's Salt.

2. Cut off approximately ⅓ from top of butter squash, remove the soft inside with a spoon, and blanch the squash and top in salted boiling water for 5 minutes. Discard water.

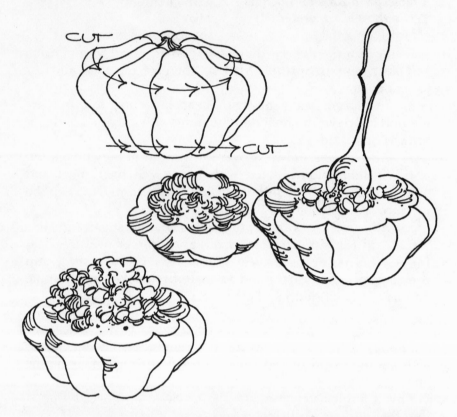

3. Let squash cool upside down until lukewarm and easy to handle.

4. Heat shortening in a heavy skillet and quickly sauté pork chops on both sides for 2 to 3 minutes until golden brown. Keep warm.

5. Brush the bottom of an ovenproof casserole with oil; arrange the squash and pork chops in it.

6. Mix the two tomato sauces together and pour over the chops, leaving about 8 tablespoons for the four butter squashes. Stuff each butter squash with a fourth of the hash. Pour 2 tablespoons sauce mixture on the hash in each squash; then replace the top.

7. Cover the ovenproof casserole with aluminum foil or its own cover and bake 30 minutes.

8. Remove cover. Cut tomato into four thick slices and place each slice on a pork chop. Remove the tops from the squash, place them alongside, and bake the dish for another 10 minutes. Replace the tops and serve at once.

CHEF'S SECRET: As you can see by the illustration, butter squash is a very pretty vegetable. Because its taste resembles fresh asparagus, it is sometimes called asparagus squash.

If you wish, you can make an entirely different dish by altering this recipe slightly. Replace the two small cans of tomato sauce with 2 cups sour cream and the whole tomato with 4 sliced mushrooms. Fluffy rice, pasta, or mashed potatoes are excellent with this dish.

Hungarian Pork Chops

8 servings

8 rib pork chops, ½ inch thick, 6 to 7 ounces each
1½ tablespoons Chef's Salt (see index)
3 tablespoons flour
4 slices bacon, chopped

2 cups sliced onions
2 cups bell peppers, coarsely chopped
2 cups sliced mushrooms
½ cup tomato juice
4 to 6 drops Tabasco

1. Preheat oven to 350°F. Tenderize the chops by hitting them lightly on both sides a few times with a mallet. Sprinkle with Chef's Salt and stack the chops in two piles. Press gently and let them stand for ½ hour; then tenderize them again with the mallet. After they have enlarged to about 1½ times their original size, sprinkle with flour evenly on both sides.

2. In a heavy skillet, render the bacon until the bits turn dark brown. Remove the bits. Fry the chops over very high heat in the bacon fat until they are rosy brown on both sides.

3. Set the chops aside. Add the onions and peppers to the skillet. Cover, lower the heat, and cook for 10 minutes. Add mushrooms and cook for another 5 minutes. Stir in tomato juice, add Tabasco, and correct the seasoning by adding sugar or salt if needed.

4.   Place pork chops in a baking pan and cover with the cooked vegetables. Cover the pan with aluminum foil or with its own lid and bake until the chops are done, approximately 45 minutes. Serve around or over a bed of parsley rice or with mashed potatoes.

CHEF'S SECRET: When the onions, peppers, and mushrooms are cooked over low heat under a lid, they will turn limp and soft. Eventually, as they are mixed with the tomato juice, they will lose their identity and turn into a thick sauce.

If you can purchase sweet Hungarian yellow peppers or sweet banana peppers, substitute one of these for a part or all of the bell peppers.

If you wish, you can stretch this dish by frying one frankfurter for each person and serving it on top of each pork chop.

Pork Chops with Mushrooms

8 servings

8 center-cut pork chops, 6 to 8
  ounces each
2 teaspoons Chef's Salt (see
  index)
1 tablespoon caraway seeds,
  bruised
5 tablespoons flour
4 tablespoons butter
4 tablespoons oil

Sauce:

4 tablespoons butter
1 pound mushrooms, sliced
4 tablespoons chopped flat-leaf
  parsley
½ teaspoon salt
¼ teaspoon black pepper
⅔ cup light cream or half-and-
  half

1.   Trim the pork chops if necessary. Mix Chef's Salt, caraway seeds, and flour, and sprinkle the chops. With the flat side of a mallet, hit the chops on both sides once or twice to flatten them a bit.

2.   In a large heavy skillet, heat the butter and oil to the smoking point. Sauté the chops 4 at a time. When one side browns, remove the chops to a plate. Allow the shortening to heat up again; then brown the other 4 chops on one side. Remove the second batch of chops and return the first 4 chops to the skillet. Sauté the other side; then place *under* each chop one

that is fried on only one side. You will have 8 chops in the skillet. Cover, lower, the heat to high, and cook for 10 minutes. Add mushrooms and cook for another 5 minutes. Stir in tomato juice, add Tabasco, and correct the seasoning by adding sugar or salt if needed.

3.   Meanwhile, make the sauce. In a small skillet heat the 4 tablespoons butter. When it is hot, add at once the mushrooms, parsley, salt, and pepper. Sauté over medium heat, turning frequently until the mushrooms start to get limp. Immediately stir in the cream and remove from the heat.

4.   Arrange the pork chops on a serving dish. Spoon the mushroom sauce over the chops. Serve immediately with fluffy rice or noodles.

CHEF'S SECRET: You probably don't have a skillet large enough to hold 8 pork chops at once, but nearly everybody has one that can accommodate 4. That is why I suggested the double-deck frying of the chops. When both sides of all 8 chops are brown, it doesn't make much difference if they overlap while the cooking is finished under cover over slow heat.

If you wish, after removing all chops to the serving dish you may sprinkle a tablespoon of flour into the large skillet, stir it, add the sautéed mushrooms with the cream, and stir for a while, scraping the bottom. This way the mushroom sauce will have some brown and black specks of flour. It won't look as pretty, but it will taste much better.

Stuffed Pork Chops with Fresh Cauliflower

8 servings

8 boneless pork chops, ½ to ¾ inch thick, approximately 4 ounces each

2-ounce can liver pâté

2 tablespoons Hungarian paprika

2 teaspoons salt

¼ teaspoon freshly ground black pepper

⅛ teaspoon garlic salt

2 tablespoons lard

1 head cauliflower, approximately 2½ to 3 pounds, with boiling salted water for cooking

1 cup sour cream

½ cup fresh bread crumbs, sautéed in 2 tablespoons butter until golden brown

freshly chopped green parsley

4 black olives, split in half

1.   Trim each chop, removing as much of the fat as possible. Cut a pocket in each by inserting a sharp knife into the side of the chop, then moving the knife clockwise inside the chop, in a half-moon shape, being careful not to get too close to the edges at any point.

2.   Insert your finger in the cut and gently move it around to open up the pocket. Stuff each chop with pâté; then press together the edges. Combine paprika, salt, pepper, and garlic salt. Rub each chop on both sides with the mixture.

3.   Mince trimmings, place in a large skillet over low heat, slowly render the fat from the trimmings, and add lard. Fry chops over medium heat, turning several times until nicely browned on each side, approximately 20 to 25 minutes.

4.   Meanwhile, wash cauliflower and trim away discolored leaves from core end. Cut a deep X in the core to help it cook faster. Place in a large pot, core side up, and pour boiling salted water over it.

5.   Place over high heat and bring to a boil again; then reduce heat and cook gently until cauliflower is easily pierced with a toothpick but not overcooked. Drain and invert onto a serving dish.

6.   With a wire whip, gently stir sour cream until it is smooth and has the consistency of a thick sauce. Pour sour cream over cauliflower. Sprinkle browned bread crumbs and chopped parsley on top, arrange pork chops around it, decorate with black olives, and serve immediately.

CHEF'S SECRET: This is a beautiful dish with an interesting color combination—festive yet inexpensive.

The crosscut in the stem of the cauliflower reduces cooking time by at least half. Be sure that you cook the cauliflower with the bottom side up so that you can invert the cauliflower to a serving platter without damaging.

If you wish, instead of the pâté you may use a good quality liverwurst to stuff the pork chops.

Soul Food Casserole

8 servings

8 to 10-ounce piece slab bacon
or boiling bacon
2 cups chopped onion
1 cup chopped green peppers (2
to 3 bell peppers, depending
on size)
2 to 3 chopped tomatoes, 10 to
12 ounces total
2 or 3 ham hocks, 9 to 10 ounces
each; or 1 or 2 larger ones

1 cup catsup
1 cup barbecue sauce
16-ounce can black-eyed peas
16-ounce can butter beans
16-ounce can lima beans
16-ounce can Great Northern
beans
¼ cup maple syrup
½ cup brown sugar, well
packed

1. Cut bacon into four or five pieces. Slice one of the pieces, approximately 2 ounces, into very thin slices, and place the slices in a large pot over high heat to render the fat.

2. Lower heat. Add 1 cup of the onions and all the green peppers and tomatoes. Stir for 3 or 4 minutes.

3. Add remaining pieces of bacon, ham hocks, remaining onion, catsup, barbecue sauce, and enough water to cover the ham hocks. Simmer 1½ to 2 hours, or until meat can be easily removed from the bones.

4. Lift out ham hocks and cool. Remove meat from bones and put it back in the pot. Discard bones (or save them for soup). Preheat oven to 300° F.

5. Open the four kinds of canned beans. Rinse each for two or three minutes under cold running water, holding your hand over the strainer and moving it back and forth so the water won't bruise the beans.

6. Skim off excess fat from the liquid in the pot. Add beans, pour maple syrup on top, and bake the casserole for at least 45 minutes.

7. Sprinkle brown sugar on top and place the casserole under a hot broiler until brown sugar melts and bubbles and starts to caramelize.

CHEF'S SECRET: This recipe is as authentically "soul food" as it can be. Ouida Lindsey, author and TV personality, served it to me in her home, then came to my test kitchen and cooked it with me three times until we had it right.

You can never know until the dish is ready how fatty the ham hocks are inside. So you may have to do a lot of skimming to remove all the fat on top of the pot. If you tilt the casserole and put an inverted saucer under one edge, letting it stand like this for 2 to 3 minutes, all the fat will accumulate on one side and it will be easy to skim off. Or place the top third of the liquid, with some of the beans in it, in a tall, narrow container and set it in the freezer for a few minutes. Let the fat coagulate, discard it, and pour the juices and beans back into the casserole.

As with many casserole dishes, this one is better if it is cooked a day ahead. Cool at room temperature, refrigerate overnight, and reheat in a 300° F. oven for 2 hours.

If you do this, omit step 7, and skim the fat off after refrigeration.

Don't forget to offer Tabasco with this dish—the hotter the better.

Transylvanian Szekely Tokany

8 servings

2½ to 3 pounds beef (preferably boneless chuck, not too lean)
½ pound sliced bacon
2 tablespoons oil or butter
2 to 2½ cups chopped onion
2 cloves garlic mashed to a pulp with 1 teaspoon Chef's Salt (see index)
1 teaspoon marjoram

1 teaspoon salt
½ teaspoon freshly ground black pepper
¼ teaspoon thyme
1 cup dry white wine
½ cup tomato paste, or 1 cup and 3 tablespoons tomato juice
1½ to 2 cups chopped green peppers

1. Cut beef into finger-sized pieces. Discard hard tendons and gristle, but don't discard fat.
2. Cut bacon into thin strips or chop into ½-inch squares.
3. Cook bacon with oil or butter over medium heat until brown and crisp. Strain shortening into the pot in which you will

cook the meat. Add onion and sauté over medium heat until limp and translucent. Add beef, garlic crushed with Chef's Salt, marjoram, salt, pepper, and thyme.

4. Cover pot and cook over high heat, stirring every 5 minutes until all liquid has evaporated and meat starts to fry with the onions. This will take approximately 30 minutes. Be careful—you must keep turning and scraping the meat. For the correct flavor it is important that all the liquid evaporate.

5. Now add white wine, tomato paste or tomato juice, green pepper, and enough water to cover meat. Adjust heat to low, cover, and cook gently, stirring occasionally until some of the liquid evaporates and the meat is tender (approximately 1 hour). Stir it at least once every 10 minutes.

6. Serve with Puliszka (see index).

CHEF'S SECRET: This dish requires care in preparation. You must stay with the meat all the time, but the reward is a tantalizing flavor. When the meat cooks with the spices it gets a slightly caramelized taste; then when it cooks with the wine, tomato paste, and green peppers, it develops an incomparable gravy.

If you wish, you can add, before serving, 1 to 1½ cups sour cream. First mix some of the hot gravy from the meat into the sour cream; then stir the warmed mixture into the meat. Instead of Puliszka, a corn dish that is a Transylvanian version of American spoon bread, you may serve the beef with mashed potatoes, rice, or noodles.

Pork Cakes

8 servings

4 cups dry bread cubes
⅔ cup milk
⅔ cup chicken broth or water
½ cup finely minced onion
2 tablespoons lard or oil
2 pounds lean ground pork
1 egg beaten with 1 tablespoon water
pinch marjoram
¼ teaspoon ground white pepper
1 tablespoon chopped parsley
1 clove garlic
1 teaspoon Chef's Salt (see index)
2 cups bread crumbs
½ to ⅔ cup lard
3 cups sliced onions

1.   Soak the bread cubes in a mixture of the milk and broth.

2.   Sauté onions in 2 tablespoons lard or oil for 5 minutes; then add to the same bowl with the bread cubes. Add pork, beaten egg, marjoram, white pepper, parsley, and garlic mashed to a pulp with the Chef's Salt. Wet your hands and mix until it becomes fluffy. Correct seasoning and chill in the refrigerator for about an hour.

3.   Divide the mixture into 16 equal portions. With wet palms, form from each portion a half-inch-thick cake. Roll in bread crumbs, cover with a paper towel, and chill. Half an hour before serving time, heat approximately ½ to ⅔ cup of lard in a skillet until it is very hot. Fry the chilled pork cakes, 4 to 6 at a time depending on the size of the skillet, turning them 2 to 3 times until they are dark brown and crusty. Repeat until all cakes are fried; then in the same pan sauté sliced onion rings or half rings over medium heat until translucent with slightly brown edges. Drain the onion rings on absorbent paper. Place several onion rings on each pork cake. Serve with lentils, beans, split peas, or mashed potatoes.

CHEF'S SECRET: Don't overheat the shortening to fry the pork cakes, because the outside will burn and the inside will be raw. On the other hand, if the shortening is not hot enough, instead of frying the pork cakes it will soak into them. This is why the pork cakes should be chilled before frying. The temperature difference between chilled pork cakes and medium shortening will be as great as between room temperature and smoking hot shortening.

Paprikash Krumpli
(Paprika Potatoes)

8 servings

⅔ cup bacon drippings or lard, or a mixture of the two, or 1 cup finely chopped bacon

1 pound onions, peeled and finely chopped

1 bell pepper cut into ¼- by 1-inch strips

approximately 4 ounces Hungarian sausage per person if used as a main dish,

6 tablespoons Hungarian
paprika

3 pounds medium-sized
potatoes, peeled and
quartered

2 teaspoons salt

1 peeled fresh tomato,
chopped, or ½ cup tomato
juice

or 1 to 2 ounces if used as a
side dish

chopped green parsley
(optional)

1.   In a large, heavy-bottomed saucepan, melt the shortening over medium heat.

2.   Add the onions and cook until they start to sizzle and turn yellow.

3.   Add 5 tablespoons of the paprika. Stir quickly and immediately fold in the potatoes. Add the salt. Stir for about 2 minutes, or until all the potatoes are coated with paprika and onions.

4.   Pour in enough water to barely cover the potatoes. Stir again to loosen the onions and paprika from the bottom of the pan. Bring to a rapid boil, uncovered, over high heat.

5.   Add fresh tomato, bell pepper, and sausage; then cover and reduce heat to very low, or, if you cannot reduce the heat quickly enough, remove from heat for a few minutes and then return to low heat. Simmer under cover until potatoes are barely done.

6.   Remove sausage and let it cool enough to be able to handle it; then cut it into slices. Put the sausage back into the pot and stir it in. When some of the potatoes begin to get overcooked, so the juice thickens somewhat, the dish is ready to serve.

7.   Sprinkle the top with the remaining 1 tablespoon of paprika and, if you wish, decorate with chopped green parsley.

CHEF'S SECRET: In certain parts of Hungary they add sour cream, but then the name changes from Paprikash Krumpli to Krumpli Paprikash. The dish is commonly served with a green salad, with a dressing made from vinegar, salt, pepper, a little sugar, and oil, diluted with water, or with a fresh cabbage salad or dill pickles. If used as a side dish, with roast pork or meat loaf, less sausage is added.

Layered Potatoes

6 servings

3 pounds medium-sized
  potatoes
6 eggs
1 teaspoon salt
1 pound Hungarian- or Polish-
  Style sausage, ring bologna,
  or hot dogs

2 cups sour cream
2 cups buttermilk
¼ cup butter
salt and pepper to taste
1 cup grated American cheese
  (optional)

1.   Scrub potatoes but don't peel. Place in cold water to cover over medium heat. Cover and bring to a rolling boil. Boil 5 to 6 minutes; remove. Pour off water, replace lid, and let potatoes stand covered for at least an hour.

2.   Place eggs in a saucepan with enough cold water to reach about one inch above the eggs. Sprinkle a teaspoon of salt into the water, bring to a boil, and gently simmer for 10 minutes.

3.   Drain and cool at once under cold running water for at least 5 minutes. Break the egg shells under the water by hitting the eggs gently against one another, and peel.

4.   Cook the sausage or use it as it comes, depending on the variety. If you get real Hungarian or Polish smoked sausage, you don't have to cook or heat it. Whatever sausage you use, slice it on the diagonal into even, thin, oval slices.

5.   Mix sour cream with buttermilk. Brush the inside of a three-quart ovenproof casserole with some of the butter. Preheat oven to 300° F.

6.   Peel potatoes and slice enough thin slices to cover the bottom of the casserole. Slice enough eggs (1 or 1½) to distribute evenly over the potato slices. Cover with another layer of potatoes, then about ¼ of the sausage. When you have used half the ingredients, cover with a layer of potatoes and sprinkle with salt and pepper. Spoon on top a bit less than half the sour cream-buttermilk mixture.

7.   Continue with layers of potatoes, eggs, and sausages until all ingredients are used. The top layer should be potatoes. Gently press down all the layers, then dot the top with butter and spoon about half the remaining sour cream-buttermilk mixture on top.

8.   Cover and bake 30 minutes.

9. Remove cover; spoon remaining sour cream-buttermilk mixture on top. You may sprinkle with the grated cheese if you wish, or with paprika. Bake 15 minutes more. Serve piping hot with a big mixed green salad, sliced tomatoes, or chilled kosher dill pickles. In Hungary, a slice of dark bread is usually served with the casserole.

CHEF'S SECRET: If you wish, cook the potatoes a day ahead and keep them in their jackets in the refrigerator overnight. To make peeling easier, place the cold boiled potatoes in a container of hot tap water for about 10 minutes.

To remove the skin from the sausage, wash the sausage with warm water. Then cut it along its length with a very sharp knife. Ease the tip of the knife underneath the skin, cut it, and peel along the cut.

Truffled Pork Tenderloin

8 servings

1 pork tenderloin, cleaned and trimmed (approximately 20 to 24 ounces trimmed weight)
1 small can black truffles
1 tablespoon Chef's Salt (see index)
4 teaspoons unflavored gelatin
½ cup carrots, coarsely chopped
½ cup celery tops, coarsely chopped
½ cup onions with skins, coarsely chopped
1 quart water
salt to taste
¼ teaspoon white pepper
2 tablespoons fresh lemon juice
4 drops yellow food coloring (optional)

1. Preheat oven to 350° F. Cut the tail end of the pork tenderloin so that it is about the same thickness from end to end. With the point of a sharp knife, carefully cut a hole from each end of the tenderloin toward the middle, being careful to make the hole meet at the center. Insert your forefingers into each end to open the hole and to make sure it goes completely through.
2. Slice truffles into ¼-inch by ¼-inch sticks, laying them the length of the tenderloin to make sure there will be enough for

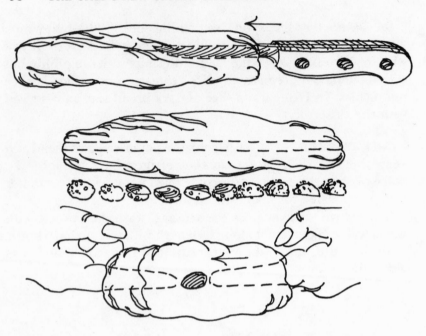

stuffing. Again, insert the forefinger of your left hand into one end of the tenderloin so that it goes approximately to the middle of the loin. Working from the opposite end, insert the pieces of truffles so that the first one touches the forefinger of the left hand, the next touches the first piece, and so on. After one end is filled, repeat from the opposite end.

3.   Rub the tenderloin's outer surface with ½ tablespoon Chef's Salt and sprinkle with about ½ teaspoon of gelatin. Roll the tenderloin tightly in a piece of aluminum foil that is approximately 18 by 18 inches.

4.   Place carrots, celery tops, and onions in the bottom of a small roasting pan. Add water and sprinkle remaining Chef's Salt in the water. Lay foil-wrapped tenderloin on the vegetables, cover, and roast for 45 minutes. Remove from oven and let cool for 15 to 20 minutes; then open the foil and place the pan back in the oven for an additional 25 minutes.

5.   Remove tenderloin from foil and set aside to cool for a few minutes. With a wet kitchen towel, straighten the piece of baking foil, sprinkle it with ½ teaspoon gelatin, and reroll the tenderloin in the foil. Be sure to roll it tightly and evenly, gently pressing it as you wrap. Chill for at least 4 hours before you slice it.

6.   Strain pan juices through a sieve and skim fat from the surface. Place two or three ice cubes in the center of a wet kitchen towel, gathering the towel together and twisting it to secure the ice cubes in a ball; gently move it over the surface of the liquid, submerging it slightly. The fat will firm up and adhere to the ice in the wet cloth. Strain the juice again through a wet cloth; it should be very clear.

7.   Correct seasoning of the juices by adding some salt, white pepper, and lemon juice. For each cup of clear liquid you have (about 3 cups) dilute 1 teaspoon gelatin in 2 tablespoons water; let stand for a couple of minutes, then stir into strained pan juices. Simmer the mixture over low heat for 15 to 20 minutes, being careful that it doesn't boil. Remove and cool to room temperature. Add yellow food coloring if you wish. Pour into a flat container and chill.

8.   To serve, carefully hand-slice the truffled cold pork tenderloin and arrange it in a row in the middle of a small silver platter. Remove the firm aspic to a cutting board and chop finely. Put the chopped aspic in a pastry bag with a plain ⅓-inch pastry tube and pipe it around the slices of truffled tenderloin. Serve with very thin dry toast, fresh butter, and tart, tiny pickles.

CHEF'S SECRET: As the tenderloin is cooked, it will shrink and may even change shape a bit. That's why I suggest that after it cools off, you straighten out the foil, sprinkle some gelatin on the foil, and roll up the tenderloin again. This second packaging will straighten the tenderloin so that after the final cooling it will be an even tubular shape with a gelatin coating already on it.

If you wish, you may add some applejack or French apple brandy (Calvados) to the liquid from which you make the aspic.

If you have some leftover truffle, wrap it in aluminum foil with the liquid from the can and place it in the freezer. The liquid will make an excellent addition to a sauce, and the leftover truffle can be used in many ways. The best way to keep it for more than a few days is to put it into a small plastic container such as the kind a pharmacist uses for pills. Pour in the canned liquid and fill it up with enough port wine or sherry to cover. The alcohol won't freeze solid, but it will protect the very expensive truffle.

Pig's Feet Parisienne

4 servings

2 quarts water
4 whole pig's feet, split lengthwise
1 cup sliced onions
1 clove garlic, chopped
12 black peppercorns
2 tablespoons salt
1 bay leaf
6 or 7 sprigs parsley
½ cup chopped carrots

2 tablespoons French mustard
¼ teaspoon freshly ground
black pepper
1 cup flour (approximately)
2 eggs beaten with 2 tablespoons water
2 to 3 cups fresh sifted bread
crumbs
2 cups shortening
1 lemon, cut in four wedges

1.   In a large pot over medium heat, bring water to a boil. Tie each split foot with a string so that it won't fall apart. Plunge pig's feet into the water. Add onions, garlic, peppercorns, salt, bay leaf, 2 or 3 sprigs of the parsley, and carrots and return to a boil. Adjust heat and simmer for 1½ hours, or until fork penetrates very easily, without resistance. Remove from heat and let stand until lukewarm. Lift out pig's feet carefully; they will be very soft now and not easy to handle. Cut the string, remove the bones, and discard. Spread some of the mustard on the inside of the foot, sprinkle with pepper, and place the two halves together. Press gently between two trays or boards. Chill for 3 or 4 hours.

2.   Dust pig's feet with flour. Dip in egg wash, then in bread crumbs. Cover completely and press so that the crumbs adhere.

3.   In a heavy skillet, heat the shortening (preferably a mixture of 1 cup butter and 1 cup lard) until a bread crumb dropped into it will immediately spring to the surface and dance. Fry pig's feet until golden brown, turning very carefully. Serve with lemon and remaining parsley sprigs and offer fresh mayonnaise (see index).

CHEF'S SECRET: Around the famous old central market in Paris, several restaurants specialized in this dish. Perhaps the most famous among them was Pie de Cochon. It is now gone, as is Les Halles. But my favorite place prepared the pig's feet better than either of those restaurants. That was the place where I watched as they brushed the mustard inside the feet and sprinkled them with the freshly crushed black pepper. This made the great difference.

If you really want to splurge, stuff the pig's feet with black truffle before preparing it for frying.

Because of the gelatin in the skin and bones, the liquid in which the pig's feet were cooked will make a wonderful base for soup. Mix it with beef extract or consommé.

Mayonnaise

2 cups

2 large or 3 medium egg yolks	2 tablespoons plus 2 teaspoons white vinegar
⅔ teaspoon salt	1½ cups corn oil
small pinch white pepper	4 teaspoons lemon juice
few grains cayenne pepper	1-2 tablespoons boiling water
4 teaspoons sugar	

1. Carefully place the egg yolks in a mixing bowl and add the salt, white pepper, cayenne pepper, sugar, and vinegar. Using an electric mixer, a must for this recipe, beat the yolks and seasonings at the highest possible speed for 2 to 3 minutes, or until the mixture turns pale yellow and liquid.

2. Adjust the speed to medium and add the oil—first drop by drop, then in a thin stream.

3. When all of the oil is mixed into the yolks, set the mixer on low speed and add the lemon juice and boiling water. Store the mayonnaise in the refrigerator in a plastic or glass container.

CHEF'S SECRET: Mayonnaise is a more than 100-year-old formula, and there is very little variation in its preparation, but certain points must be stressed.

All utensils, especially the mixing bowl and beaters, must be absolutely clean and free of grease and moisture. Therefore, rinse them with a boiling mixture of 3 cups water and 1 cup vinegar. Then rinse under a large amount of cold running water and dry with a fresh, clean kitchen towel. If the bowl or the beaters are not completely dry, the mayonnaise will not be perfect.

Sometimes the mayonnaise breaks down despite the best care in preparation. To reconstitute, just use the absolutely clean and dry mixer and start to beat the mayonnaise on the lowest speed. Slowly increase the speed to medium and add ⅓-½ cup oil, pouring in a very thin stream. The very best way to assure a thin stream is to pour the oil from a spouted container, held approximately 15-18 inches from the top of the mixing bowl.

CHAMPAGNE MAYONNAISE

Add 3 tablespoons champagne for each cup of mayonnaise and omit the boiling water.

GREEN MAYONNAISE

Chop very fine 1 cup coarsely chopped green parsley and place it in a wet kitchen towel. Gather towel so that the parsley resembles a ball. Squeeze the parsley juice into a small dish. Add 2-3 tablespoons to 1 cup mayonnaise.

Veal Cutlets à la Nelson

4 servings

1 cup finely minced onions
¼ cup butter
4 boneless veal cutlets, 4 ounces each
½ teaspoon Chef's Salt (see index)
½ cup finely minced or sliced mushrooms
1 cup cooked rice
2 eggs beaten with 2 tablespoons water

1 cup flour
2 cups bread crumbs
½ cup butter mixed with ½ cup oil

Sauce:

½ cup butter
1 cup Madeira wine
2 tablespoons sour cream
½ teaspoon Chef's Salt

1.   Preheat oven to 325° F. Sauté onions in the ¼ cup butter under cover over low heat.

2.   Pound the veal cutlets very thin with a mallet. Be careful not to make holes in them. Sprinkle with Chef's Salt.

3.   When the onions are soft and pale yellow, add mushrooms, stir for a minute or so, and then add cooked rice. Stir, remove from heat, and empty into a bowl. Cool and put the mixture through a meat grinder or, if no meat grinder is available, chop fine with a food chopper or sharp knife.

4.   Place the cutlets next to each other and spread ¼ of the mixture on each cutlet. Fold cutlets in half. Brush edges with some of the beaten egg and press together. When all 4 cutlets have been prepared, bread them as follows: dip in flour, shake off excess, dip in beaten eggs, then cover with bread crumbs and gently pat the bread crumbs into the surface of the veal. Shake off excess.

5.   In a heavy skillet, heat the butter mixed with oil. Sauté each side of the cutlets until light brown. Remove, place on a baking sheet, and bake 20 minutes.

6.   While cutlets are finishing in the oven, prepare the sauce. Heat the butter in a skillet, add Madeira wine, bring to a boil over medium heat, and boil until it reduces to half. Remove from the heat, swirl in sour cream with a wire whip, and season with ½ teaspoon Chef's Salt. Keep warm.

7.   To serve, arrange the cutlets on a warm platter and pour half the sauce over them. Serve the remaining sauce in a sauceboat.

CHEF'S SECRET: Because this dish has a rice filling, it is best to serve it with only a plain hot vegetable and a large salad.

Veal Tarragon

8 servings

2 cups minced onions	1 cup white wine
4 tablespoons butter	⅓ cup vinegar
1 clove garlic, mashed with 2 teaspoons salt	3 tablespoons chopped flat-leaf parsley
2 pounds cubed veal	½ pound mushrooms
1 bay leaf	1½ cups milk
2 teaspoons tarragon	4 tablespoons flour
2 teaspoons sugar	1 cup sour cream

1.   Sauté onions in butter until transparent.

2.   Mash the garlic and salt together with the flat surface of a knife until it turns into a pulp. Add to the onions; then add veal,

bay leaf, tarragon, sugar, white wine, vinegar, and 2 tablespoons chopped parsley. Adjust heat to medium.

3.   Cover and cook until veal is tender, 30 to 40 minutes.

4.   Add mushrooms and cook 2 to 3 minutes.

5.   Mix milk and flour. Stir mixture into the veal. Correct seasoning if necessary.

6.   Just before serving, mix the sour cream into the sauce and add remaining parsley.

7.   Serve with noodles or gnocchi.

CHEF'S SECRET: Adding some of the parsley while cooking and the rest at the last minute will serve two purposes. The part added during cooking will give out all its flavor and aroma, but it will turn brownish-gray and won't even be recognizable. The parsley added just before serving will give a beautiful green color accent and, as it warms through on the surface of the sauce, its oils will intensify and give a pleasant aroma to the dish.

Gnocchi is Italian for small dumplings, spaetzles, and several similar products.

Veal Casserole with
Spinach and Mozzarella Cheese

4 servings

2 10-ounce packages frozen
    chopped spinach
4 veal shoulder chops
2 teaspoons Chef's Salt (see
    index)
garlic salt to taste
2 tablespoons flour

2 tablespoons butter
2 tablespoons oil
juice of ½ lemon, combined
    with 2 to 3 tablespoons water
8 ounces sliced mozzarella
    cheese

1.   Defrost frozen spinach to room temperature. Sprinkle the chops with Chef's Salt and garlic salt; then pound with a mallet. Sprinkle both sides with some of the flour and press the flour into the chops with the palm of your hand. Mix half the butter and all the oil in the skillet over medium heat. Brown the chops on both sides. Remove and set aside. Preheat oven to 325° F.

2.   Pour the lemon juice mixture into the pan and scrape

loose the browned particles. Add the defrosted spinach and heat through. Distribute half the spinach evenly in the bottom of an ovenproof casserole that has been brushed with the second tablespoon of butter.

3.   Add the browned chops and distribute the remaining half of the spinach over them. Cover the spinach with the sliced mozzarella and bake 45 minutes, under cover. Remove cover and bake another 10 to 15 minutes, or until mozzarella starts to brown. Skim the fat from the surface, near the edges of the casserole. Serve with hot garlic bread and a green salad.

CHEF'S SECRET: It is important that you first sprinkle the spices on the chops and then pound them with the mallet. This works the spices into the fibers of the meat.

Veal should never be cooked over high heat. That's why I suggest that even the browning be over medium heat instead of high, as it would be for pork, beef, or lamb.

Veal Cutlets Normandy

8 servings

8 veal cutlets, 4 to 6 ounces each
2 teaspoons Chef's Salt (see index)
¼ cup flour
6 tablespoons butter
4 tablespoons oil
5 ounces fresh mushrooms

2 red apples
1½ cups heavy cream
3 to 4 tablespoons applejack or Calvados (optional)
½ cup chicken broth or veal stock

1.   Sprinkle the cutlets with Chef's Salt, then pound with a mallet, gently but firmly, until evenly thin. Dust both sides with a little flour.

2.   In a sauté pan, melt the butter and oil and heat to smoking point. Fry the veal slices very quickly, 2 to 3 at a time, and immediately remove to a dish and keep warm.

3.   Wash and slice the mushrooms. In the same pan, sauté over medium heat for 4 to 5 minutes, tossing once in a while. Remove mushrooms and keep them warm with the veal.

4.   Core the apples, but do not peel, and cut them into quarters. Cut each quarter into 3 slices, like orange segments.

Sauté over medium heat for about 5 minutes, being careful not to break the slices. Remove and keep warm with veal and mushrooms.

5.   If necessary, add 1 more tablespoon oil and butter to the frying pan. Scrape the bottom of the pan to loosen particles.

6.   Add remaining flour not used in dusting the cutlets. Over medium heat, using a wire whip, slowly stir the cream into the pan. Add 2 tablespoons of the apple brandy and gently bring to a boil. Add a few tablespoons of chicken broth or stock.

7.   Arrange the apple slices and mushrooms over the veal on a serving platter. Heat remaining apple brandy in a small saucepan, ignite it, and pour it over the veal. Spoon on the sauce and serve immediately with French bread and butter or garlic butter.

CHEF'S SECRET: Applejack is New Jersey's contribution to American gastronomy. It is a fine, unique brandy made from apples and has a definite flavor and aroma of ripe, pungent apples. Calvados is apple brandy from that part of France called Normandy, where apple growing and apple products play a great role in the local cuisine.

Veal in Cream Sauce with Fresh Vegetables

8 servings

2½ pounds cubed veal
2 quarts water with 1 teaspoon salt
4 tablespoons oil
6 tablespoons butter
½ cup finely chopped onion
10½-ounce can beef consommé
½ cup freshly chopped parsley
¾ teaspoon salt
¼ teaspoon pepper
1 teaspoon sugar
1 cup fresh green peas (or canned or frozen)

1 cup fresh carrots, lightly scraped and cut into ¾-inch pieces
1 pound fresh asparagus, tips removed and stem ends cut into ¾-inch diagonal pieces
8 ounces fresh button mushrooms
2 tablespoons cornstarch
2 tablespoons flour
2 cups cream
2 egg yolks

1.   Blanch the veal cubes in the salted water. Drain.

2.   Heat the oil and butter in a large pan. Add onions and sauté until they start to turn yellow. Add blanched veal cubes and brown lightly. Pour in beef consommé; add parsley, salt, pepper, and sugar. Cover and simmer for 45 minutes. Add peas, carrots, and asparagus (but not asparagus tips) and continue cooking until veal is tender, approximately 20 more minutes.

3.   Add fresh mushrooms and cook for 2 to 3 minutes.

4.   Meanwhile, bring a small amount of lightly salted water to a boil and quickly cook the asparagus tips (which should be tied into small bunches). Immediately rinse them in cold water to stop the cooking.

5.   Once the veal is tender, strain the pan juices into a small saucepan. Mix the cornstarch and flour into 1 cup of the cream. Mix the egg yolks with the other cup of cream. Place pan juices over medium heat and bring to boiling point. Slowly add the flour-cornstarch-cream mixture, stirring constantly with a wire whisk. Once the mixture thickens, blend a little of the hot mixture into the egg yolk-cream mixture to warm; then pour the egg yolk-cream mixture into the sauce. Immediately remove from the heat and stir until the sauce is smooth and well blended.

6.   Just before serving, arrange the veal, asparagus tips, and vegetables in a serving casserole. Pour hot sauce over the top. Serve with buttered rice.

CHEF'S SECRET: This is a "classic" dish in the French nineteenth-century manner. Blanching means placing the meat in cold water to cover with a very small amount of salt in it (½ teaspoon to a quart) and then bringing it gently to the boiling point. Drain and cool immediately in cold water. This process firms up the veal cubes and keeps them in nice shape during the cooking time when they are browned and then cooked until tender.

To tie the asparagus tips into small bunches, use a soft cotton yarn, not too thin, which won't cut into the tender asparagus but will be firm enough to hold it. Don't put more than 4 or 5 medium or 6 to 8 thin heads of asparagus in a bunch.

Veal Marengo

8 servings

2- to 2½-pound boneless veal
  leg, sliced approximately
  ½-inch thick
1 clove garlic mashed with 1
  teaspoon Chef's Salt (see
  index)
½ cup flour
8 ounces fresh mushrooms
the green part of one bunch
  fresh scallions
2 large ripe tomatoes

2 cups tomato juice
10½-ounce can chicken broth
  (or ½ can chicken broth and
  ½ cup white wine)
8 tablespoons butter
4 tablespoons corn oil
1 cup coarsely chopped bell
  pepper
24 medium-sized pitted black
  olives

1.   With a mallet, pound the veal gently but firmly on both sides. Sprinkle each piece with garlic and Chef's Salt and dust with flour on both sides. Do not lay slices on top of one another.

2.   Wash the mushrooms quickly in a sieve under running lukewarm water. Shake dry and cut into pieces.

3.   Cut the scallions into pieces about the size of the olives. Peel the tomatoes and coarsely chop them. Have ready the tomato juice and chicken broth (or, if you wish, a mixture of chicken broth and white wine).

4.   Heat the oil and half the butter in a large skillet. When it is smoking hot, very quickly fry the slices of veal on both sides. Remove the pieces as soon as both sides are browned. Keep warm.

5.   Add scallions, mushrooms, green peppers, and tomato to the pan. Reduce the heat, cover, and let the vegetables heat through. It will take 3 to 4 minutes. Pour some of the tomato juice and some of the chicken broth over the vegetables. Cover again and simmer for 10 minutes. Remove vegetables with a slotted spoon and add to the veal. Keep warm.

6.   Pour the rest of the tomato juice and chicken broth into the pan and bring to a vigorous boil, scraping the bottom of the skillet. Keep boiling 3 to 4 minutes or until half the liquid evaporates. Strain the remaining liquid through a sieve over the veal and vegetables. Add black olives and the remaining half of the butter. Heat through and serve.

CHEF'S SECRET: The veal kept warm with the vegetables will cook thoroughly while you are preparing the sauce. It will not need additional cooking.

Calf's Feet with Mayonnaise

4 servings

1 pair calf's front feet, approximately 4 pounds (trotters)
2 tablespoons salt
1 teaspoon bruised black peppercorns
1 large onion stuck with a clove
2 or 3 sprigs parsley
2 or 3 celery ribs
1 tablespoon fresh or 1 teaspoon dried tarragon
1 cup vinegar

1 tablespoon sugar
1 bay leaf
1 portion crêpe batter, omit
  sugar (see index)
1 cup butter
1 cup lard or oil, for frying
1 lemon, cut in wedges
parsley or watercress, for decoration
1 cup mayonnaise

1.   Wash calf's feet and soak in water to cover overnight. Discard water and put the calf's feet with salt, peppercorns, onion, parsley, celery, tarragon, vinegar, sugar, and bay leaf in a large pot. Cover. Bring to a boil over medium heat. Adjust the heat and simmer for 2 hours and 30 minutes or 3 hours, depending on the size, or until you can penetrate the feet with a fork very easily. Remove from heat and let cool for a few minutes.

2.   Lift the feet from the liquid and let cool on a rack. When cooled, carefully remove meat and cartilage, discarding bones. You will have 8 to 12 pieces if you are careful, but probably 12 to 16 if you are trying it for the first time. Chill the meat.

3.   Dip each piece with a fork into crêpe batter and fry immediately in butter and other shortening over medium heat until golden brown. Remove to absorbent paper.

4.   Arrange in the middle of a serving platter. Surround with lemon wedges and parsley or watercress, and serve with regular or green mayonnaise (see index).

CHEF'S SECRET: Calf's feet are sometimes available in Mexican and Puerto Rican butcher shops. But you can order them in almost any supermarket if you give the meat manager enough time to get them.

Crown Roast of Lamb

8 servings

rack of lamb, 6 or 7 pounds	2 tablespoons Kitchen Bouquet
1½ to 2 pounds ground lamb (use trimmings from the rack of lamb and add more if needed)	½ cup oil
	½ cup butter
	1 clove garlic
3 tablespoons Chef's Salt (see index)	¼ teaspoon dry tarragon or 1 teaspoon fresh
2 cloves garlic mashed to a pulp with 1 teaspoon Chef's Salt	1 large egg
	⅓ cup water

1.   Preheat oven to 400° F.

2.   Ask the butcher to cut off all excess lamb from the rack right above the eye. Cut out the backbone on an angle so that the ends of the rib bones are cut off together with the backbone. Trim off chain bone, leaving no other bones but the ribs themselves. Have the butcher grind trimmings out of enough extra lamb to total 2 pounds.

3.   With a large kitchen needle and white yarn, sew together the two ends of the two sides of the rack, as shown in the illustration.

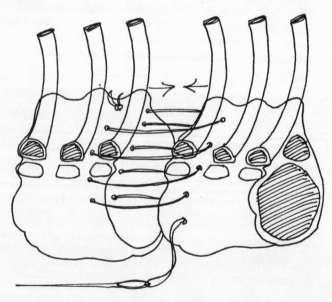

4.   Gently bend the two half-racks, bones facing outside, until

the other ends meet. Sew together. If you use U.S. Choice spring lamb, most likely each half-rack will be from 10 to 11½ inches long. Sewn together, the crown will comfortably fit a 9-inch cake pan.

5. Rub the surface (except the bones sticking out of the crown) with 2 tablespoons of the Chef's Salt; then rub the garlic mainly into the bone ends on the eye and around the bones on the top. Brush the crown with Kitchen Bouquet. In a small saucepan, heat the oil and butter to the smoking point. Pour about ¼ of it into a large (at least 9-inch) skillet that has been preheated over high heat. Place the crown of lamb into the smoking hot fat and let it stand in it for about 2 minutes. Meanwhile, spoon the remaining hot fat over the entire surface of the lamb. Be careful: use a large spoon or ladle with a wooden or plastic handle, or wear mittens while doing this. Remove the crown from the skillet and pour the shortening back into the small saucepan. Return the crown to the skillet over high heat. Heat the shortening to the smoking point again and ladle it on the crown a second time. Remove and let cool until you can handle it. Allow shortening to cool. When the surface of the lamb is cool enough for you to handle, place the crown into the cake pan, which has been brushed with some of the shortening. Fold enough aluminum foil into a rectangle so that when you press the middle of the foil inside crown, the sides of it will come up to the trimmed bones (approximately a 12 by 12-inch piece). Make it from heavy-duty foil. Brush the foil with some of the shortening.

6. In a bowl, mix by hand the ground lamb, 1 tablespoon Chef's Salt, 1 clove crushed garlic, tarragon, egg, and water. Place the mixture in the aluminum foil. Fold over the top of the foil and remove from the cavity. Place it on a cookie sheet or in a small cake pan, and place it in the oven.

7. After the ground lamb is in the oven for 30 minutes, put in the crown of lamb. Roast for 30 minutes. Then increase the heat to 450° F. and continue baking for approximately 15 minutes. Remove both and carefully unfold aluminum foil. Let it cool. Discard the fat oozing from the ground lamb. Remove the crown to a warm serving platter and place the roast ground lamb in the middle of the crown. Surround with vegetables of your choice. Place a white paper or aluminum foil chop-holder, or frill, on each bone and serve.

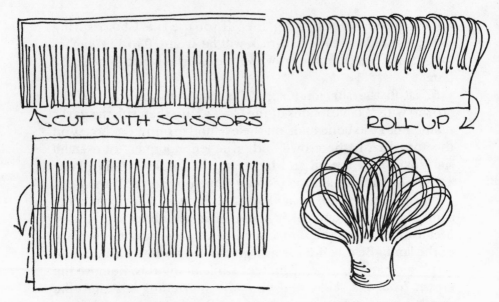

CUT WITH SCISSORS

ROLL UP

CHEF'S SECRET: A 9-inch cake pan or similar pan with low, straight sides will keep the crown in perfect shape. Basting the lamb with the hot shortening will also help, because it will firm up the outside of the crown.

The ground lamb must be baked alone for a longer time because, as good as lamb chops or lamb rack are when cooked medium rare or rare, ground lamb is not tasty unless it is cooked thoroughly. If you like lamb extra rare, cut down the cooking time for the lamb rack from 45 minutes to perhaps 40 or even 35 minutes. Don't forget that the cooking began when you basted the surface twice with the hot fat.

In many places it is difficult to purchase chop-holders, or paper frills. The accompanying diagram shows how to make them at home. Cut a piece of white paper or aluminum foil approximately 8 by 3 inches. Fold it in half so that it will be 8 by 1½ inches. Then fold the 8-inch length in half, and with sharp scissors cut from the fold toward the edge, making ⅛ inch strips about ¾ inch long. Unfold, turn inside out, gently refold, and roll around a round object about the thickness of the bone on which you plan to use the frill.

Glue the ends together with a nontoxic glue, such as library paste, or secure with a small strip of cellophane tape. If you are skilled enough, you can do as professional chefs do: fold the end of the paper to the inside so that the frill will keep its shape without glue.

Hungarian Lamb Stew

6 servings

3 pounds lamb shanks
1½ teaspoons Chef's Salt (see index)
1 teaspoon Kitchen Bouquet
6 cups water
4 to 5 black peppercorns, slightly bruised
1 clove garlic, crushed
1 green or red bell pepper

1 large onion
2 tablespoons shortening
1 teaspoon Hungarian paprika
2 teaspoons Hungarian paprika mixed with 2 tablespoons flour
2 large boiled potatoes, peeled and cubed

1.   Remove all the meat from the lamb shanks and cut it into 1-inch cubes. Reserve the bones. Sprinkle meat with Chef's Salt, add Kitchen Bouquet, and mix to coat all the pieces evenly. Let stand at room temperature.

2.   Gently cook lamb bones in the water with peppercorns, garlic, stem and core of the bell pepper, and a thick slice from the onion, for 2 hours or, if time permits, longer. Strain off liquid and discard spices, vegetables, and bones.

3.   Peel and chop the remaining onion. Place onion, shortening, and the 1 teaspoon of paprika in a cold sauté pan, cover, and slowly sauté over medium heat until onion starts to brown. Add lamb cubes, increase the heat to high, and brown the meat quickly on all sides, stirring constantly. Then add two cups of strained liquid, cover, adjust heat to medium, and simmer over low heat for 1 hour.

4.   After 1 hour, add remaining strained liquid and, if necessary, enough water to cover the lamb cubes. Remove from heat and cool the mixture quickly by placing the pot in a larger pot of ice water and stirring until cooled. Refrigerate overnight.

5.   Next day, remove all the fat that has accumulated on the top. In a separate pot, heat about 2 tablespoons of the fat together with the mixture of paprika and flour, until the mixture turns into a red substance. Slowly add the jelled juice and the lamb, stirring with a spoon until the mixture is smooth and without lumps. Add cubed potatoes and the remaining bell pepper, cut into thin slices. Reheat to the boiling point.

6.   Serve with crusty bread, and, if you wish, slice in some hot banana peppers before serving.

CHEF'S SECRET: Good lamb shanks are on the fat side, and the best way to get rid of this fat is as suggested in the recipe. Perhaps you have read in different cookbooks, and rightly so, that lamb stock should never be used under any circumstances. I agree with this rule in every dish except this Hungarian Lamb Stew, which should have the strong lamb taste that comes from the lamb broth.

If you wish, you can omit the potatoes or substitute a small Hungarian pasta called tarhonya, or the similar egg barley available in many stores.

Roast Leg of Lamb Turkish Style

8 servings

2 tablespoons salt
1 teaspoon whole black
  peppercorns
2 bay leaves, broken into pieces
1 teaspoon fennel leaves
1 teaspoon oregano
1 teaspoon marjoram
¼ teaspoon garlic salt (*not*
  garlic powder)

1 small boneless leg of lamb, 3
  to 4 pounds
1 cup chopped onion, including
  skin
1 cup chopped carrots
1 cup chopped celery

1.   Preheat oven to 425° F. In a mortar or in the bottom of a strong wooden salad bowl, crush together all spices until no large pieces are recognizable, except perhaps some bay leaf.

2.   Rub the whole surface of the boneless leg of lamb with the spice mixture; then roll and tie the leg.

3.   Distribute in a roasting pan the onion, carrots, and celery, and place the leg of lamb on the vegetables. Add enough water to have about an inch in the bottom of the pan. Roast, turning every 10 minutes, for approximately 1 hour, or until a good meat thermometer registers 100° F. in the thickest part of the leg. Remove lamb and set it on a serving platter.

4.   Press the vegetables through a fine sieve along with the liquid from the roasting pan. Skim off the fat. Serve the gravy as is or, if you prefer, thicken with 1 teaspoon cornstarch dissolved in ¼ cup cold water. Serve it with Rice Pilaf (see index).

CHEF'S SECRET: Don't start to slice the lamb for at least 30 minutes after removing it from the oven.

If your butcher sells already deboned, tied, ready-to-roast legs of lamb, prepare the spice mixture a day ahead. Bring it to the butcher and ask him to rub the inside before he ties it; or take a chance: untie the leg at home and tie it again after rubbing the meat with the spice mixture.

Around the Mediterranean this dish is often served with fresh chopped mint leaves sprinkled on the lamb after it is sliced.

Braised Lamb Chops

8 servings

8 shoulder lamb chops approximately 8 ounces each
1½ tablespoons Chef's Salt (see index)
2 tablespoons oil mixed with 1 tablespoon Kitchen Bouquet
4 to 6 tablespoons oil
1 cup chopped onions
1 cup chopped carrots
1 cup chopped celery and celery tops
2 cloves garlic
1½ cups beef consommé
½ cup tomato juice or 1 fresh tomato cut into pieces

4 tablespoons oil
4 tablespoons butter
16 to 24 small white boiling onions about the size of a walnut
16 to 24 carrot pieces, cut to same size as onions
16 to 24 pieces white turnip or yellow rutabaga, cut to same size as onions
2 tablespoons flour
1 tablespoon cornstarch
½ teaspoon Chef's Salt
½ cup water

1.   Preheat oven to 350° F. Sprinkle chops with Chef's Salt and brush with 2 tablespoons oil mixed with Kitchen Bouquet.

2.   In a heavy skillet, heat 4 to 6 tablespoons oil and sauté lamb chops 2 or 3 at a time until golden brown. Remove and place in a roasting pan with a cover. In the same skillet over medium heat, sauté onions until limp. Add chopped carrots and chopped celery. Stick a toothpick in each clove of garlic and add to skillet. Sauté vegetables, turning occasionally, for about 10 minutes.

3.   Spread vegetables over chops in roasting pan. Add consommé and tomato juice. Cover and bake 45 minutes, basting occasionally.

4.   Meanwhile, heat 4 tablespoons each butter and oil, mixed, to smoking point. Cook small whole onions until they start to get brown spots on the outside skin. Remove, increase heat, and add carrots and turnips. Cook until they brown at the edges. Keep warm.

5.   Remove garlic from roasting pan. Scrap off all vegetables from chops. Keep chops warm.

6.   Put pan vegetables with pan juices through a sieve or blender and blend smooth. Measure this liquid and add enough warm water for a total of 4 cups. Skim fat from the top. Bring to a boil over medium heat, and stir in mixture of flour, cornstarch, ½ teaspoon Chef's Salt, and ½ cup water. If too thick, add ½ cup more of stock, water, or wine.

7.   Place chops, onions, and pieces of carrots and turnips in the roasting pan. Pour the sauce over all. Cover and bake for 45 minutes. Serve with fluffy mashed potatoes or rice.

CHEF'S SECRET: This recipe is somewhat more complicated than the usual, but the results are much better. If you wish, you can prepare it a day ahead up to the point where you heat the pan juices and add the flour mixture. Do this on the day you plan to serve, but instead of baking 30 minutes, you will need 1 hour.

You can replace the tomato juice with beer and add more beer to your pan juices instead of water. Or you can replace the tomato juice with wine. If you like thin juice on the chops instead of gravy, cut down the flour to 1 tablespoon and the cornstarch to ½ tablespoon.

If you like the flavor of tarragon, chervil, or oregano, add some at the beginning and some again at the very end of the cooking process.

Lamb Navarin

8 servings

2 cups onions, chopped in ¾ to 1-inch pieces	10½-ounce can beef consommé, with enough water for a total of 3 cups
1 cup boiling water	

4 tablespoons butter
4 tablespoons other shortening
2 tablespoons Chef's Salt (see index)
½ cup flour
2½ to 3 pounds lamb, cut into pieces approximately 1½ to 2 inches

½ cup tomato purée
½ teaspoon crushed peppercorns
3 pounds potatoes
1 cup carrots, finely chopped

1.   Place onions in a metal bowl or small pot. Pour on the boiling water. Let stand for 2 to 3 minutes. Discard water and pat onions dry on absorbent paper, or shake them over heat until all water evaporates. Heat butter and shortening in a large, heavy pot or Dutch oven over medium heat, and add blanched onions.

2.   Sprinkle a mixture of Chef's Salt and flour over the cubed lamb, covering every piece. Add at once to the onions. Increase the heat and stir for about 10 minutes, scraping the bottom if the flour adheres.

3.   Add consommé, tomato purée, and peppercorns. Cover, adjust heat, and simmer over low heat for 1 hour, stirring every 10 minutes or so. Be sure to keep scraping the bottom of the pot so that the mixture will not burn.

4.   Peel the potatoes and cut them into pieces about the same size as the lamb. After the lamb mixture has cooked 1 hour, add the potatoes and carrots and stir well. Cover and simmer for an additional hour, stirring occasionally. Serve with a green salad in the summer, or with pickled beets or cabbage salad in the winter.

CHEF'S SECRET: Lamb Navarin is a dish with as many versions as there are cooks. This recipe is similar to the best I have ever tasted, at the world-famous Cafe Allard in Paris.

The flour will start to brown in the pot, and you will have a hard time keeping it from burning, but nothing else will give such a good taste to the dish. The carrots will turn the color to a deep orange. If you wish, you may add some garlic. Many recipes call for it. As much as I love it, I don't think it belongs here.

Haricot de Mouton Orleanaise
(Mutton and Turnip Stew)

8 servings

6 tablespoons shortening,
   preferably lard
2 pounds cubed boneless
   shoulder or neck of lamb (or
   3½ to 4 pounds with bones)
½ cup flour
3 cups boiling water
1 bay leaf
¼ teaspoon thyme

1 rib celery
1½ tablespoons salt
¼ teaspoon freshly ground
   black pepper
2 cups sliced onions
6 cloves garlic
4 cups diced turnips or
   rutabaga

1.   Preheat oven to 325° F. In a dutch oven or casserole, heat
4 tablespoons shortening. Add lamb in handfuls and keep
turning with a spatula, letting the fat heat up before each
addition. When the edges of the cubes start to turn golden,
sprinkle flour through a sieve over the meat. Stir and gradually
add boiling water. Add bay leaf, thyme, celery, salt, and pepper.

2.   Sauté sliced onions in 2 tablespoons shortening until limp.
Peel garlic cloves and gently press on each with the flat side of a
knife, hitting it with your hand to crush it. Drop crushed garlic
into the onion, sauté together for a minute or two, and add to the
casserole.

3.   As soon as the water begins to boil again over the meat,
cover the casserole and place in the oven for 1 hour. Add peeled,
diced, and rinsed turnips or rutabaga. Stir, cover, and bake for
another 1 to 1½ hours. Remove from oven, let stand for a few
minutes, and skim off excess fat. Ladle the stew into a serving
dish. Discard bay leaf and celery. Serve very hot.

CHEF'S SECRET: To many people, this dish has a strange name.
The most common meaning of the French word *haricot* is
"beans," but in gastronomy it refers to a dish made from lamb or
mutton—and not with beans, as you might think, but with
turnips. It is a kind of play on words. Long ago, when kitchen
help was abundant and cheap, the diced turnip was cut into the
shape of beans; so the dish looked like lamb and beans.

If you make this dish with tender young turnips, rather than with hard winter rutabaga or with large, hard winter turnips, it is sufficient to add the turnips for just the last hour, or even just for 45 minutes. If you are not fond of the turnip flavor, bake the lamb by itself and boil the diced turnips in lightly salted water. When they are done, discard the cooking water, fill the pot with cold water, let it stand for a couple of minutes, then pour it off and add the turnips to the lamb at the last minute.

Cabbage Stuffed with Hare or Rabbit

8 servings

1 head white cabbage, not too firm, approximately 6 to 7 inches in diameter
1 hare or rabbit
2 teaspoons salt mixed with ¼ teaspoon black pepper and ⅛ teaspoon white pepper
8 ounces slab bacon, cut parallel with the rind into thin slices approximately 5 by 2 inches

4 tablespoons butter
½ cup dry white wine
2 10½-ounce cans chicken broth
2 tablespoons unflavored gelatin
4 quails
1 teaspoon juniper berries, crushed with 1 teaspoon Chef's Salt (see index)
4 tablespoons butter

1.   Preheat oven to 350° F. Place cabbage in a pot with the core up. Pour on boiling water to cover. Over highest heat, cover and bring to a boil. When water starts to boil, remove from heat, pour off boiling water, and let stand uncovered for 10 minutes. Rinse with cold water until it cools throughout and drain.

2.   Debone the hare or rabbit (bone-in weight 3½ to 4 pounds, boneless weight approximately 2 pounds), and grind the meat through the medium blade of a grinder after cutting it into 1-inch cubes. Spice it with ⅓ of the salt and pepper mixture and form it into a firm ball.

3.   Lay cabbage in front of you on a towel covered with a piece of aluminum foil large enough so that you will be able to wrap the whole cabbage in it. Fold out the outside cabbage leaves carefully, without detaching them from the core. Remove from the middle of the cabbage exactly enough leaves to make room

for the ball of ground rabbit and replace the removed cabbage with the rabbit meat. Start gently to fold back the cabbage leaves, sprinkling them with the salt and pepper mixture, until all leaves are folded back to their original shape. Cover the outside surface of the cabbage with the slices of bacon. With the help of the towel, fold the aluminum foil over the cabbage until you have the entire cabbage enclosed in the foil.

4.   With half the butter, brush the inside of an ovenproof casserole with a tightly fitting lid. The casserole should be large enough to accommodate the cabbage and the chicken broth. Brush the other half of the butter on the outside of the aluminum foil. Place the cabbage in the casserole, add wine, cover, and bake 30 minutes. Remove, pour in chicken broth mixed with gelatin, and add enough water to cover cabbage more than halfway. Cover and return to oven. Reduce heat to 200° and bake 8 hours, basting every hour.

5.   After about 7½ hours, split the quails. Rub insides and outsides with the mixture of juniper berries and Chef's Salt. Heat butter in a heavy skillet over medium heat until it is very hot but not smoking. Add quail halves, skin side down, and quickly sauté to a golden brown. Now turn the quails, lower heat to medium, and finish cooking, skin side up, basting the quails occasionally. It will take about 20 to 25 minutes. Pour off the fat, keep the quails in a warm place on absorbent paper.

6.   Remove casserole from the oven. Carefully remove foil-wrapped cabbage. Open the foil and, after one or two minutes, lift the cabbage from the foil onto a large serving platter.

7.   Pour all the juices from the casserole into the pan you used to sauté the quail. Deglaze by scraping the bottom of the pan with a metal spatula until all bits loosen. Strain, skim fat, and transfer to a sauceboat. Surround the cabbage head with the quail and serve at once with boiled potatoes in their jackets or with baked potatoes.

CHEF'S SECRET: This dish sounds difficult, but it isn't. According to many nutrition experts, hare and rabbit are the most nutritious of all meats. If you have a hunter in the family, this is an excellent way to use what he bags. If you raise rabbits, it is a great change from the usual recipes. Most supermarkets sell frozen hare or rabbit, and in larger cities you can order fresh rabbit meat.

Boiling the cabbage will make the outside leaves elastic and soft so that they won't break easily. Still, be careful when you fold them back not to break the stems. The inside that you remove will make a great cole slaw the next day, or you can make finger-thick slices and put them around the cabbage head about two hours before serving. Since the aluminum foil will cool off very quickly after the cabbage is removed from the casserole, you won't have any difficulty removing it. The cabbage, on the other hand, will be extremely hot and will retain its heat for a long time, so be careful handling it.

If quail is not available, you can use small chickens (one-quarter to a person), drumsticks (one to a person), thick white wurst or other sausage spiced with juniper berries, or pork chops.

If you have a second rabbit, you can fry the rabbit meat and surround the cabbage with it.

Black Bear Sausage

10 pounds

1 cup finely minced onion
6 cloves garlic, finely minced
6 tablespoons salt
1 tablespoon saltpeter
1 tablespoon coarsely ground black pepper
1 teaspoon white pepper
1 tablespoon juniper berries, ground or crushed

4 tablespoons light brown sugar
1 quart lukewarm water
6 pounds lean bear meat
4 pounds pork shoulder
2 to 3 tablespoons sweet paprika
casing for sausage, approximately 3½ yards by 1¼-inch diameter

1.   In a saucepan, place onions, garlic, spices, brown sugar, and water. Let stand for about 5 hours at room temperature, stirring occasionally until salt, sugar, and saltpeter are dissolved.

2.   Warm the liquid over low heat just to the boiling point, stirring occasionally. Remove from heat and strain through a fine sieve. Cool to room temperature.

3.   Cut the bear meat and pork shoulder into 1-inch cubes and grind it twice through the largest setting of a meat grinder. Place it in a large container. Add the spicy liquid and 2 or 3 tablespoons sweet paprika. Work spices into the sausage with wet hands, making sure it is thoroughly kneaded. Add more salt or pepper to taste.

4.   With a sausage stuffer, fill the soaked, soft casing. Form 12-inch links and smoke over cold smoke 12 to 14 hours. Let it hang for one more day at room temperature; then refrigerate or freeze, packing it in aluminum foil. It will keep for 6 to 8 months in the freezer.

CHEF'S SECRET: The ideal bear for sausage is a 1 to 1½-year-old male, purchased in October or November. If you have no local source, contact Czimer Foods, R.R. 1, Box 285, Lockport, Illinois 60441, (815) 838-3503, and they will provide you with either bear or information.

Spices continue to act, even if frozen. That is why it is advisable not to leave any spices in the mixture. Let them dissolve in the water and then strain through a fine sieve to remove the spices.

Before starting to make the sausage, locate a smokehouse and ask if your sausage may be smoked there. The people at the smokehouse know what "cold smoke" means. It is the opposite of quick, or "hot," process.

Venison Sausage

10 pounds

1 cup finely minced onions
6 cloves garlic, finely minced
6 tablespoons salt
1 tablespoon saltpeter
1 tablespoon coarsely ground
   black pepper
1 teaspoon white pepper
2 tablespoons ground or
   crushed juniper berries
4 tablespoons light brown sugar

1 quart lukewarm water
6 pounds venison
4 pounds pork shoulder
1 lemon, approximately 1
   tablespoon of its juice and
   the zest from the entire peel
casing for sausage,
   approximately 3½ yards by
   1¼-inch diameter

Proceed exactly as with Black Bear Sausage, but before mixing by hand, add lemon zest and lemon juice instead of paprika. Smoke it exactly the same way as you would the Bear Sausage.

CHEF'S SECRET: Be careful when preparing the lemon zest. Scrape the white pulp as little as possible to avoid turning the mixture bitter. If the lemon rind is wrinkled and dehydrated, it won't have enough oil in the zest to flavor the sausage as it should. Buy a fresh, firm lemon with shiny, oily skin. Saltpeter is found in the prescription department of most drugstores.

Ragout of Venison

8 servings

4 pounds boneless venison, cut
    into 1-inch cubes
½ pound very lean slab bacon
2-3 cups water
½ cup lard
⅔ cup very finely minced
    shallots (or white parts of
    scallions)
2½ teaspoons Chef's Salt (see
    index)

4 tablespoons flour
1 small clove garlic, crushed
1 cup red wine
1 teaspoon brown sugar
½ cup tomato juice
1 cup stock (or water)
2 teaspoons Kitchen Bouquet
1 tablespoon cornstarch
1 cup sliced mushrooms
2 tablespoons butter

1.   Wash venison cubes and keep in water for about an hour. Remove, dry on a towel, and let stand at room temperature.

2.   Cut bacon into ½-inch cubes. In a small saucepan, boil bacon in 2 to 3 cups water for 15 minutes, then drain. Save the water for use in the ragout. Set boiled bacon aside.

3.   In a large pot, sauté shallots in shortening. Combine 2 teaspoons Chef's Salt, 2 tablespoons flour, and crushed garlic, and rub the mixture into the venison. Increase heat and add the meat to shallots in small amounts so that the heat in the pot won't decrease. Keep turning the few pieces of meat before you add more, and keep scraping the bottom with a metal spatula. When all the meat is in the pot, add ½ cup of the red wine, ½ teaspoon Chef's Salt, brown sugar, and tomato juice. Reduce heat to very low, cover, and cook, stirring occasionally, for about 30 minutes. Add stock or water and increase heat to medium. Add Kitchen Bouquet.

4.   Mix 2 tablespoons flour and the tablespoon of cornstarch into the second ½ cup of wine and stir into the pot until smooth. Simmer for 1 hour.

5.   Sauté mushrooms in butter. Add to meat 5 minutes before serving. Serve with noodles, rice, or potatoes.

CHEF'S SECRET: Soaking the meat will extract some of the wild taste, and having it at room temperature will help to make it more tender.

If you wish to add more vegetables than the mushrooms, mix 1 cup carrot slices and 1 cup frozen green peas (without defrosting) into the pot at the same time you add the liquid-cornstarch mixture.

Roast Venison, French Style

8 servings

4 to 6 pounds rack or loin of venison
1 tablespoon salt
½ teaspoon crushed black pepper
½ teaspoon juniper berries

4 tablespoons red currant jelly
4 tablespoons butter
8-ounce piece of bacon
2 cups consommé mixed with 2 cups red wine

1.   Wash and dry the venison, rub it all over with salt, pepper, and juniper berries, and let it stand at room temperature for 2 to 3 hours.

2.   In a small bowl, mix currant jelly and butter with a wire whip until it turns into a pink substance. Don't let it get too thin. If the kitchen is too warm, refrigerate the mixture.

3.   Cut the bacon into even-sized pieces about 2½ inches long and ¼ by ¼ inch thick. Lay the pieces on a cookie sheet or aluminum foil and freeze.

4.   Preheat oven to 450° F. With a small, sharp paring knife, pierce as many holes in the venison as the number of pieces of bacon you cut. Enlarge the holes in the meat with the sharpened end of a wooden spoon. Remove only 2 or 3 pieces of bacon at a time and insert one piece into each hole in the meat. Repeat until all bacon is used.

5.   Place the venison in a roasting pan, uncovered, in the oven. In 10 minutes, brush with about ¼ of the butter-jelly mixture. Let it roast for 30 minutes, brush again, and pour half the consommé-red wine mixture into the roasting pan. Roast for 30 minutes, brush again with the butter mixture, and baste with pan juices. Repeat after 20 minutes and add the rest of the consommé-red wine mixture. After a total cooking time of 1½ hours, remove and let stand at room temperature.

6.   Scrape out all residue together with the liquid from the roasting pan. Pour through a fine sieve. Skim off fat and boil the liquid in a small saucepan until it reduces to half its volume and has a syrupy consistency.

7.   Slice the meat along the backbone into very thin slices. Spoon over it 1 or 2 teaspoons of the sauce and serve with green noodles or other pasta. If you wish, you may add 2 tablespoons

of good cognac and 2 tablespoons red currant jelly to the sauce, or you can stir in 4 or 5 tablespoons cream.

CHEF'S SECRET: As a rule, the French won't touch venison until it has hung three or four weeks outdoors, or until it has been refrigerated for two or three weeks if the weather will not permit hanging outdoors.

The meat will be medium rare. A meat thermometer inserted into the thickest part would measure 120° to 130°, and the color would be pink.

If you don't want to lard the meat, omit the bacon and insert small slivers of frozen butter into the small holes you cut in the meat.

4

Poultry

People who don't travel much, or who don't pay attention to food when they do travel, don't realize that one of America's greatest contributions to the gastronomic world is our achievement in poultry science. I travel a lot—in the last few years in South America, Africa, Japan, Hong Kong, and most of Europe —so I feel I have sound basis for comparison. I love poultry and I eat it wherever I go, so I can say from firsthand experience that American poultry has no equal in quality, quantity, uniformity, or yield per bird.

Some doom advocates, who consider themselves "experts" on everything, claim that American poultry isn't tasty or nutritious, is full of chemicals, loaded with poison, etc., etc. The truth is that three generations of Americans have grown up on great quantities of American poultry—and have grown taller and healthier than their counterparts in many countries, with a longer life expectancy. Of course, their good health is not attributable merely to poultry, but I like to think it has helped.

Being a chef, I am concerned with ease of preparation, perfect taste, eye appeal, and economy. I believe the dishes in this chapter reflect those concerns. The versatility of chicken perhaps surpasses all other domestic birds, and its size lends itself to perfect portion control. Birds of one and a half to two pounds give two ample portions, but the best buy is the bird that weighs two and a half to three pounds. This size yields four ample servings.

Because of its taste and texture, chicken is easy to combine with accompaniments; it is good with starches, vegetables, fruits, and even other meats. It goes equally well with potatoes, rice, or pasta, and with a little skill and imagination it can be turned into so many varieties of dishes that its uses are almost unlimited. It is equally good hot and cold, and hardly anyone exists who really objects to its taste.

Capons, ducks, and turkeys are almost as versatile and, comparatively speaking, always worth the price. Thanks to modern research, capons are larger and fleshier than they used to be, ducks are leaner and more tender, and turkeys now come in any size and shape you wish. In addition to the recipes in this chapter, you will find poultry as an ingredient in many recipes in other chapters. Some recipes are old and some new, but all are easy to prepare, delightful to taste, and very economical.

Stuffed Whole Spring Chicken

8 servings

2 spring chickens, 2 to 2¼
  pounds each
½ pound ground beef
½ pound ground pork
⅛ pound ham, chopped (op-
  tional)
½ cup chopped onion
1 tablespoon shortening
1 egg
3 to 4 tablespoons chopped
  parsley
¼ teaspoon dry marjoram
4 slices day-old white bread
salt and freshly ground black
  pepper to taste

½ teaspoon dry tarragon
⅛ teaspoon garlic salt (*not*
  garlic powder)
1 package fresh soup vegetables
  (carrots, celery, parsnips,
  etc.)
4 cups water, or 2 cups chicken
  broth and 2 cups water, or 2
  cups chicken broth, 1 cup
  white wine, and 1 cup water
4 tablespoons shortening
1 tablespoon flour
1 tablespoon cornstarch

1. Remove from the chickens the bags with necks, giblets, hearts, and livers. Chop the livers fine with a knife; set other pieces aside.

2. In a mixing bowl, combine ground beef, ground pork, and ham. Sauté onion in 1 tablespoon shortening until translucent and work it into meat.

3. Add liver, egg, parsley, marjoram, and bread, broken into ¼-inch pieces. Work the mixture together with your hands, adding ¼ cup or so of water if necessary. Add salt and freshly ground black pepper to taste.

4. With your fingers, loosen the skin over the chicken breasts. Start at the neck and move your fingers toward the wings; then work from the breast bone to the inside of the thigh. Divide the stuffing into four portions and gently push it in between the skin and the flesh of the chickens. Rub tarragon and garlic salt into the skin over the breasts. Preheat oven to 375° F.

5. Wash, clean, and cut up the soup vegetables and distribute them in the bottom of a large roasting pan with a tightly fitting lid. Add the necks, giblets, and hearts, and sprinkle with a little salt and pepper. Pour two cups of the water (or other liquid) into the pan; then place the chickens over the vegetables.

6. Heat 4 tablespoons of shortening in a small pan until it starts to smoke. Spoon it carefully over the chicken. (This will

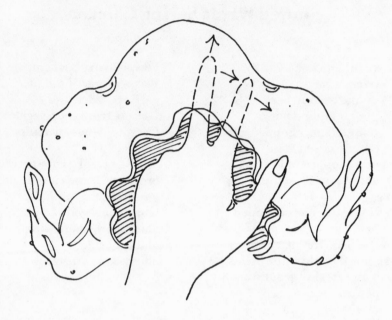

give the skin a beautiful crispness and color.) Cover the pan and roast 1 hour.

7.   Remove chickens from pan. Strain pan juices and discard vegetables and giblets. Skim off fat. Put chickens back in the roasting pan, heat fat to the smoking point, pour the fat over the chickens, and roast uncovered about 30 minutes.

8.   Meanwhile, in a saucepan, mix flour and cornstarch with pan juices and remaining water (or other liquid). Whisk while bringing to a boil. Remove chickens from the oven and let stand in a warm place for 10 minutes. Split each chicken in half and place skin side up on a warm serving platter. Spoon on some of the sauce and serve the rest in a sauceboat.

CHEF'S SECRET: If you wish, tie the two legs together with white butcher string or soft, not too thin yarn, after the stuffing is done. It will hold the chickens in a nicer shape. You can also fold the wings under the back by gently lifting both wings at once away from the body, holding them with three fingers, and then pressing the second and third joints downward with your thumbs until they go under the back. Then push the first joints back to the body. The wings will stay folded and the breasts will look plumper.

Chicken Breasts Baked with Prunes in Acorn Squash

8 servings

4 acorn squashes
1 cup dark brown sugar
½ cup butter
8 chicken breasts, boneless or
  with only the wing bone in
  (so-called "airline breasts")

40 pitted prunes
1 tablespoon salt
¼ teaspoon ground white
  pepper
1 cup water
juice of 1 lemon
1 lemon sliced paper-thin

1.   Preheat oven to 400° F. Split the acorn squashes in half. Remove and discard seeds. Sprinkle each with 2 tablespoons of dark brown sugar to cover the flesh and the cavity. Place 1 tablespoon butter in each cavity. Bake the squash on cookie sheets for 1 hour and 30 minutes.

2.   Debone the chicken breasts, if necessary. Scrape back the flesh from the wing joint. Place a pitted prune in each breast on the flesh side, fold over, and sprinkle with salt and white pepper.

3.   Remove squash from the oven and pour out the butter from each into a small saucepan. Place a breast in each half squash with the wing bone up. Pour the butter over the breasts.

4.   Pour 2 cups water into a baking dish large enough to accommodate all the squash halves. Place the squash in the dish and distribute the remaining prunes around it. Cover and bake for 20 minutes. Remove prunes from the water and put four around each chicken breast inside each squash. Squeeze the juice of a lemon on the breasts and cover each with 2 to 3 paper-thin slices of lemon.

5.   Increase heat to 425°. Uncover the dish and bake for an additional 10 minutes.

CHEF'S SECRET: Many butchers and chain stores offer "airline breasts," or you can ask the butcher to prepare the breasts for you so that the first wing joint remains on the breast. You can also use boneless chicken breasts, skin on. They will not be as pretty, but there will be no other difference.

From the 2 cups (or more) of water that you put into the baking dish when you prepare the acorn squash (depending on the size of the dish you use), there will be very little left when you finish.

If you wish, you can stuff the pitted prunes with a piece of precooked carrot, a whole almond, or a piece of pecan or walnut.

After baking the squash for 1 hour and 30 minutes, and before putting the chicken in, pierce holes with a round toothpick or with a thin bamboo skewer into the flesh of the squash, being careful not to pierce through the skin. This will allow the taste of butter, brown sugar, prunes, and chicken to ooze into the flesh of the squash.

Be careful when you split the squash in half. The skin is quite hard. The best way to attack it is to scrape a thin line from the stem end toward the flower end with a strong nail or an ice pick. Or ask somebody to saw it for you with a small hand saw. But don't try to attack it with a knife before it is marked with a pick.

Chicken Breasts with Bananas

8 servings

4 whole chicken breasts, each approximately 1 pound
salt and pepper to taste
2 tablespoons shortening
2 tablespoons butter
8 medium-sized bananas, not too ripe

8-ounce can crushed pineapple
1 tablespoon cornstarch
2 tablespoons brown sugar
1 cup shredded coconut
8 portions rice, prepared according to package directions

1.   Remove bones from chicken breasts. Cut breasts, with skin on, lengthwise into finger-thick slices. Sprinkle with salt and pepper. Melt shortening and butter in a sauté pan, and when it is smoking hot, add the chicken strips and cook very fast, stirring constantly, for 4 to 5 minutes. Remove the pieces from the pan to a warmed platter.

2.   Peel the bananas. Cut each lengthwise in half, then crosswise into four pieces. Mix the banana pieces with the cooked chicken strips on the hot platter.

3.   Strain the juice from the canned pineapple, and add enough water to it to make 1 cup. Dissolve the cornstarch in this liquid, then slowly pour it into the sauté pan in which the chicken

was cooked. Stir constantly over medium heat until the mixture turns into a thick, pudding-like substance. Add crushed pine-apple, keep stirring until it heats through, then pour the mixture over the chicken breast and banana strips.

4.   Sprinkle with brown sugar and coconut, and place under a preheated broiler, as close to the source of heat as possible, for 45 seconds to 1 minute, or until the sugar melts and starts to bubble and the coconut browns.

5.   Serve with fluffy rice.

CHEF'S SECRET: It is important to leave the chicken skin on the breasts for this recipe because the skin is needed for consistency, besides being the tastiest part of the whole bird. (The experiments of the noted food scientist Dr. Charles Rogers proved that almost all the taste components of poultry are in the skin, not in the flesh or muscle.) Nevertheless, if someone among your guests just hates chicken skin, take it off after cooking, not before.

This dish can be made from beginning to end, even for an unskilled homemaker, in 15 to 20 minutes for 8, and in even less time for 4 people.

Serve chilled tomato or vegetable juice with fresh celery stalks as a first course, and a good cheese with crusty bread as dessert, and you have a complete meal in no time.

Chicken Breasts Kiev

8 servings

4 fresh boneless whole chicken
  breasts, 8 to 12 ounces each,
  with or without the wing bone
  attached
12 tablespoons chilled unsalted
  butter
1 teaspoon lemon juice

1 teaspoon finely chopped
  chives
1 tablespoon finely chopped
  parsley
salt and pepper to taste
flour for dusting
2 eggs, slightly beaten
2 cups fine, dry Italian bread
  crumbs
oil for deep-frying

1.   Remove and discard the skin from each breast. Cut off the wing tip and its adjacent bone and leave only the short leglike

bone attached to each breast. Cut each breast in half down the center.

2.   Place breast pieces smooth side down on a cutting board and pound them as flat as possible with the flat side of a mallet. Be careful not to tear the flesh; if you do, you can correct the tear by overlapping the edges and pounding them until sealed. Double-folded aluminum foil can be placed over each breast to prevent the flesh from flying loose.

3.   Cream the butter with the lemon juice, chives, parsley, and salt and pepper to taste.

4.   Shape the butter into 8 equal cone-shaped pieces, about 3 inches long. Freeze in waxed paper until firm.

5.   Lay a piece of butter in the center of the flattened breast and cover with any loose pieces of flesh. Fold one wide side of the breast over it. Twist the wing bone of the breast around to seal it. This prevents the butter from seeping through when the meat is deep-fried. Fold in the other ends. It can be patted into its final shape after flouring.

6.   Roll each piece in flour; dip in egg, then in the bread crumbs. Pat until breading has adhered well. Refrigerate at least 1 hour before frying. Freeze if they are to be used another day. They can be fried when frozen.

7.   Preheat oven to 200° F. Have at least 4 inches of oil in the bottom of a deep-fryer. Heat the oil until a deep-fat thermometer registers 360° F.

8.   Fry two pieces at a time until golden brown, about 5 minutes (longer if frozen). Place them on a baking sheet lined with absorbent paper and hold in the oven for no longer than 10 minutes. Serve as soon as possible.

CHEF'S SECRET: I have found the following technique best for shaping the butter into cone shapes. Have on hand a small bowl with cold water and a larger bowl with ice water. Divide the butter mixture into 8 portions and drop each from a wet spoon into the cold water. Dip your hands into the ice water and with cold hands form a cone between your two palms. Hold the bottom of your palms and the little fingers closely together. Then, with the help of your index fingers, move your palms loosely back and forth. Drop the formed cone into the ice water and leave until firm.

If you are a beginner, it is advisable to brush all edges of the chicken flesh with egg white before placing the butter in the middle and rolling it up. Egg white will help to hold the chicken breast in shape.

Chicken in Parsley Sauce

8 servings

2 large chickens, approximately 3 pounds each
12 to 16 peppercorns, slightly bruised
2 tablespoons salt
1 cup sliced carrots
½ cup chopped parsley root or parsnip

1 cup chopped celery
½ cup chopped onion
1 clove garlic
¾ cup butter
½ cup flour
1 cup green parsley, finely chopped

1.   Cut chicken into serving pieces—drumsticks, thighs, wings, breast halves. Place the chicken on the chicken bones, giblets, and necks in a large soup pot. Sprinkle peppercorns and

salt over the chicken. Add carrots, parsley root, celery, and onion. Add 3 quarts water to cover chicken and vegetables. Add garlic and cover the pot. Bring to a boil over medium heat; then adjust heat to low and gently simmer for 45 minutes to 1 hour or until chicken is tender. Remove chicken to a serving platter and keep warm. Discard garlic. Strain the liquid through a sieve.

2.   Measure out 2 cups of the cooking liquid into a saucepan. Bring to a vigorous boil.

3.   In another saucepan, melt ½ cup butter and the flour, stirring constantly with a wire whip over high heat until the flour and butter start to bubble. Lower heat as soon as the flour starts to turn light yellow, because you don't want this mixture to turn brown.

4.   Remove from heat and slowly stir in the 2 cups of boiling stock. Keep stirring with a wire whip until it thickens. If it gets too thick, add more stock mixed with water or milk until the sauce has the consistency you want.

5.   Add remaining ¼ cup butter and the parsley. Correct seasoning by adding more salt or freshly ground pepper.

6.   Coat the chicken pieces on the serving platter with part of the sauce.

7.   Surround the chicken with boiled small potatoes or fluffy rice, and serve the rest of the sauce in a gravy boat.

CHEF'S SECRET: By cooking the chicken in just enough liquid to cover, you will have a very strong broth that will give an excellent flavor to the sauce. If you wish, you can add milk to the sauce, or mix an additional cup of the stock with water. The sauce will be good both ways.

Incidentally, the same sauce is also excellent on boiled beef, boiled turkey, or on other boiled meats. It used to be a great American favorite about 100 years ago, but somehow it fell out of favor. It would be worthwhile to reintroduce it. If you like a piquant sauce, add the juice of ½ lemon.

To make it easy to remove the garlic, stick a toothpick into it before adding it to the broth. It will not be lost among the other vegetables and will be easy to remove.

Hungarian Csirke Pörkölt

8 servings

2 fryers, 2½ to 3 pounds each
8 ounces slab bacon or smoked
    pork jaw, cut into ¼-inch
    cubes
3 cups finely sliced onions
2 to 3 tablespoons water
3 tablespoons Hungarian
    paprika

1 tablespoon Chef's Salt (see
    index)
2 cups bell peppers sliced into
    julienne strips 1½ to 2 inches
    long and ¼ inch wide
4 cups tomatoes, peeled and cut
    into pieces approximately ½
    inch by ½ inch

1.   Cut the chicken into small pieces. Cut the wing into three joints. Split the drumstick along the bone into two pieces. Split the thigh along the bone into two pieces. Cut the breast into three segments crosswise after splitting it in half down the middle. Retain the small bones, neck, heart, and gizzard. Keep the liver for another use.

2.   In a large, heavy pot with a tightly fitting lid, render the bacon or smoked jaw. Add onions and water. Cover the pot and cook over medium-high heat 15 to 20 minutes.

3.   When onions are limp and yellow and all the water has evaporated, add 2 tablespoons paprika. Increase heat to high and add the pieces of chicken 4 to 5 at a time, stirring constantly. Add Chef's Salt and about ⅓ of the green peppers. Cover the pot and lower the heat to medium. Cook about 30 minutes; then stir. Add remaining green peppers and tomatoes and stir again. Then cover and cook over low heat for another 30 minutes.

4.   Remove cover, increase heat to high, and stir through the whole mixture once or twice. Taste, and, if necessary, add a sprinkling of sugar to counteract the acidity of the tomato. Sprinkle the top with the remaining paprika, and stir.

5.   Transfer to a deep serving dish and serve with Hungarian galuska or spaetzle, with noodles or rice, or with Egg Barley (see index).

CHEF'S SECRET: This is a classic Hungarian way to prepare chicken. Be careful not to add too much liquid to the onions; the idea is that after the onions cook in a mixture of fat and water, the water evaporates and the onions start to brown. As you increase the heat and add the chicken pieces, 4 to 5 at a time, the chicken pieces and the onion will start to brown a bit, and this taste will add a very characteristic quality to the chicken which you cannot obtain any other way.

The tomatoes will of course add a considerable amount of liquid as they start to cook, but in half an hour they will cook down sufficiently to arrive at the proper consistency for the sauce. There won't be as much sauce as with Chicken Paprikash, but it will be rich and pungent.

Boned Chicken with Pâté

8 servings

4 ounces chopped fresh
mushrooms
1 tablespoon freshly chopped
green parsley
4 tablespoons butter
2-ounce can imported French
goose pâté with truffles
1 egg
1 cup milk or cream

2 cups toasted bread cubes (or
commercial croutons)
1 teaspoon dry chervil (or
tarragon or rosemary, as you
prefer)
salt and pepper to taste
1 frying chicken, 2 to 2½
pounds
10¾-ounce can chicken broth

1. Sauté mushrooms with parsley in 2 tablespoons butter for 2 to 3 minutes over medium heat. Remove and cool.

2. Mix pâté by hand or with a rotary beater in a bowl, combining it with egg and milk or cream; then add mushroom mixture and fold in croutons, chervil, salt, and pepper. Let stand at room temperature.

3. Lay the chicken breast down, with the neck away from you. With a sharp knife, gently cut along the back from the neck to the tail. With a very sharp paring knife, holding the tip of the knife always on the bone structure, first cut off the left side until you get to the place where the wing joins the carcass. Cut around the round bone; then proceed down to the tail end, until you get to the end of the rib cage. Starting again close to the neck, gently remove the breast meat where it joins the wishbone and collar

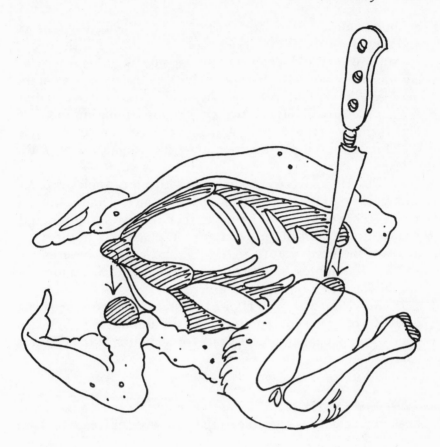

bone. With your index finger, loosen the breast from the rib cage and keel bone. Loosen the thigh bone from the hip. Repeat this procedure with the other side of the chicken; then lift out the carcass. Now you have only four bones in the whole chicken: the left and right wing bones, consisting of three joints, and the two leg bones, each consisting of two joints.

4.   Leave the two wings as they are. Loosen the flesh around the knob of the thigh and ease the flesh off the thigh bone until you reach the joint at the drumstick bone. Carefully cut around the drumstick bone and thigh joint, and pull out the bone from the drumstick. Repeat with the right side.

5.   Preheat oven to 350° F. Place a sheet of aluminum foil 12 inches wide and 24 inches long on the table. Spread the remaining 2 tablespoons butter on the middle of the foil. Lay the

deboned chicken on it, skin down. Stuff each empty drumstick and thigh with about 1 tablespoon of the stuffing. Pile the rest of the stuffing on the chicken and pull the sides together where the cut was made down the backbone. With a thread, starting at the neck, sew the skin carefully together until you get to the tail; then sew up the cavity. Lift the two ends of the aluminum foil, fold over the back of the chicken, and close the front and back so that the aluminum foil package resembles the original shape of the chicken.

6.   Place in a covered roasting pan with one can chicken broth and moist roast under cover for approximately 1 hour. Remove and let cool enough to be handled; then remove aluminum foil. Baste chicken with the juice around it, place back in the oven, increase the temperature to 450° F. and roast uncovered for another 10 minutes, basting once or twice. Or place it under the broiler for 2 to 3 minutes to brown.

7.   Serve hot with your choice of starch and vegetable. If you prefer it cold, let it cool completely in the aluminum foil. Press it gently with a plate and refrigerate for 24 hours. Slice and serve cold.

CHEF'S SECRET: Use the carcass bones and the liver, giblets, and heart for a chicken vegetable soup if you wish, or freeze for later use.

The instructions for deboning the chicken sound lengthy and complicated. I suggest that first you read the text from beginning to end without doing anything; then read it aloud a second time while you have the chicken right in front of you. Go through the motions without using a knife; just use your fingers as you are reading. Then start to do it, and remember to hold the knife as you would hold a pencil or pen while you write.

Concentrate on the tip of the knife just as you concentrate on the tip of your pencil or pen while you write. This will be the greatest secret you can learn from this book—to handle the knife properly. If you consider it a part of your hand, just as you consider your writing instrument, you will never cut yourself and the knife will never go in the wrong direction.

The knife must be sharp. When you debone, whatever it may be, hold the knife so that the point and the cutting edge are always toward the bone.

Chicken and Kohlrabi

8 servings

2 fryers, 2 to 2½ pounds each
1 clove garlic mashed to a pulp
    with 1 tablespoon salt
8 ounces smoked bacon or salt
    pork, or ½ cup butter and ½
    cup oil
2 cups finely chopped onion
2 tablespoons sweet Hungarian
    paprika
freshly ground black pepper to
    taste
½ cup tomato paste mixed with
    ½ cup water, or 1 cup tomato
    purée

1 cup coarsely chopped green
    pepper
4 to 5 bunches kohlrabi, enough
    to yield 7 cups julienne
pinch of sugar
½ cup chopped green parsley
4 tablespoons flour and 2
    teaspoons salt mixed with
    1 cup light cream or half-and-
    half
2 cups sour cream
2 tablespoons chopped green
    parsley for decoration

1.   Cut the chicken into small pieces as follows: drumstick; thigh; third and second wing joint; first wing joint and third of breast; halve the rest of the breast. From each chicken half you will have six pieces. Save neck, giblets, heart, and liver from each chicken. Sprinkle pieces with mashed garlic.

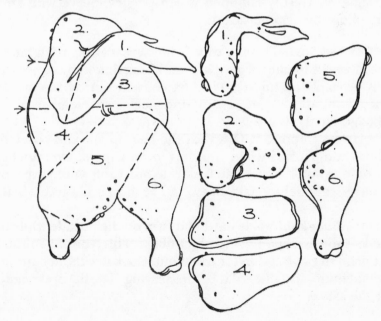

2. Chop the bacon and render it. Or heat butter and oil in a heavy kettle. Add onions and half the paprika. Lower heat, cover, and cook for about 10 minutes or until onions are a yellow-red pulp. This is extremely important. Raise heat as high as possible. Add chicken and black pepper, stirring constantly with a wooden spoon as you add the chicken pieces. Brown chicken.

3. After all pieces including neck, giblets, heart, and liver are added, add tomato paste or tomato purée, and chopped green pepper. Cover, set the heat to low, and gently cook the chicken for approximately 30 minutes.

4. Add kohlrabi cut in julienne strips 1½ inches long and ½ by ½ inch thick. Add sugar and ½ cup chopped parsley, and cook over low heat for another 20 minutes.

5. Add remaining paprika, stir, and gently pour in the flour-salt-cream mixture. Be careful that it does not lump.

6. Now you have a choice of how to continue. Either set the heat low and cook the chicken without lifting the cover, over the lowest possible heat, for another 30 minutes; or preheat the oven to 275° F., and place the covered pot in the oven for 30 minutes.

7. Whichever way you choose, after a half-hour transfer the mixture to a serving dish, ladle the sour cream over it, and sprinkle on freshly chopped green parsley. Serve with small dumplings or firm macaroni.

CHEF'S SECRET: This is a dish from a great Hungarian family, one of whose members gave it to me a long time ago as a present. It is perhaps the finest way to fix chicken during the months when kohlrabi, an interesting and neglected member of the cabbage family, is available.

It is very important to adjust the heat to low and cover the onions and paprika when you start to cook them. On high heat the onions would immediately start to burn and would turn into crunchy, caramelized bits that would be most undesirable in this dish.

Sometimes kohlrabi is hard and firm on the outside while the inside is soft and spongy with thick fibers. This type of kohlrabi is not good to eat, but don't throw it out. Cook it without cutting it into julienne, and discard it before serving. The flavor is needed for the sauce.

Perhaps you wonder why so little water is called for in this dish. If you cook the chicken under cover over very low heat, all the juices oozing out of the chicken and all the moisture from the kohlrabi and green peppers will produce a divine, thick sauce.

Roast Capon

8 servings

1 cup sliced carrots
1 cup sliced celery
1 large onion, peeled and
   quartered
1 clove garlic
1 bay leaf
1 quart water

2 tablespoons Chef's Salt (see
   index)
1 large capon, 7½ to 8 pounds
4 tablespoons cold butter
pinch salt
pinch sugar

1.   Preheat oven to 350° F. Place carrots, celery, onion, garlic, and bay leaf in a roasting pan with a tightly fitting lid. Pour in about a quart of water, or enough to have approximately 1 inch of water in the pan. Sprinkle 1 tablespoon Chef's Salt into the water.

2.   Rub the inside and outside of a large capon with the remaining Chef's Salt. Place the capon, breast down, in the roasting pan. Cover and roast for 1½ hours. Remove the pan, carefully lift the lid away from you, and turn the capon breast up. Baste with the juice in the roasting pan.

3.   Increase the heat to 450° F. Rub the breast of the capon with the cold butter. Return to the oven. In 10 minutes rub with cold butter again. In 5 minutes rub it again and distribute over the breast the rest of the butter broken into small pieces. Sprinkle a pinch or so of salt and a pinch of sugar over the breast. Return to the oven for another 5 minutes. Remove and serve with the pan juices skimmed and defatted in a sauce boat.

4.   Discard the vegetables or, if you wish, discard only the garlic and bay leaf and run the rest of the vegetables through a blender and add them to the gravy.

CHEF'S SECRET: Capons are the finest-tasting members of the chicken family. Their special taste is entirely different from fryers, broilers, or roasters. That's why capons are not usually heavily spiced.

Rubbing the cold butter into the breast will make it beautifully brown and crisp.

If you wish to serve the capon cold, proceed exactly as for hot roast capon; but after 1½ hours covered roasting, remove from the oven and let it stand in the roasting pan, breast side up, under cover, for an hour. Then remove it, put it on a platter, let it cool to room temperature, and refrigerate.

Cold Capon with Blueberry Relish

8 servings

1 large onion, peeled and sliced	1 orange
1 stalk celery, chopped	½ lemon
2 to 3 sprigs parsley	½ cup brown sugar
1 bay leaf	1 cup water
1 large capon	4 cups blueberries
2 tablespoons salt	½ cup sweet gherkins, finely
¼ teaspoon white pepper	chopped
2 pounds potatoes	lemon slices (optional)
2 teaspoons salt	fresh parsley sprigs
1½ cups mayonnaise	

1.   In a large soup pot with a tightly fitting lid, place onion, celery, parsley, and bay leaf.

2.   Rub inside and outside of a large capon with 2 tablespoons salt mixed with white pepper. Place it on top of the vegetables and add water to cover. Bring to a boil uncovered, then cover, adjust heat, and simmer gently for 2 hours. Remove capon and set it aside to cool. You can use the stock for soup or keep it frozen or refrigerated for later use.

3. Meanwhile, wash, peel, and cut potatoes into ½-inch cubes. Place in a saucepan, add 2 teaspoons salt, cover with water, and cook over medium heat for approximately 15 minutes from the time the water starts to boil, or until tender but firm. Pour off boiling liquid from potatoes. Fill the pot with cold water, pour off immediately, and place potatoes on an absorbent towel in a thin layer so that they will dry well. After potatoes cool to room temperature, mix with mayonnaise and refrigerate in a bowl.

4. Cut the orange in half, cut the half-lemon in two, and grind them both through the medium or large holes of a meat grinder. Place in a small pan with the brown sugar dissolved in 1 cup water. Bring mixture to a boil and add washed and dried blueberries. Stir, cover the pot, and cook for approximately 5 minutes or until some of the blueberries start to pop. Stir the finely chopped sweet gherkins into the mixture and place the relish in a glass serving dish. Chill.

5. When the capon is cool enough to handle, carefully remove the two half-breasts in one piece each. Remove the thighs; cut in half. Remove the drumstick; cut in half. Cut the wings so that the first and second joints stay together and the third joint closest to the breast is cut off, resembling a small drumstick.

6. Make a mold of the potato-mayonnaise mixture in the middle of a large serving platter. Arrange the cold capon pieces over the potato-mayonnaise mixture and surround the capon with a border of the blueberry relish. If you wish, decorate the meat with a few slices of lemon, a few sprigs of parsley, or small dots of the blueberry relish (the size of a walnut) placed on each slice of lemon, and serve.

CHEF'S SECRET: The blueberry relish will gain an excellent taste and a crunchy texture from the gherkins. It is very good with any kind of cold meat, especially with other poultry and with ham, but it is also a great accompaniment to fried, boiled, poached, or broiled fish.

You may have noticed that this recipe has no carrot. The capon should remain as snow-white as possible, and carrot always gives a yellowish tint.

Capon in Aspic

8 servings

2 cups sliced carrots plus 1
   whole carrot, scraped
2 cups sliced celery
1 onion, skin on, studded with 2
   cloves
10 to 12 black peppercorns,
   crushed
2 tablespoons Chef's Salt (see
   index)
1 tablespoon salt

1 bay leaf
1 large capon (7½ to 8 pounds)
6 quarts warm water
½ cup finely grated carrot
1 teaspoon sugar
3 envelopes unflavored gelatin
   dissolved in 1 cup water
watercress, lemon wedges,
   black olives, and
   mayonnaise, for garnish

1.   In a large heavy soup pot with a tightly fitting lid, place carrots, celery, onion, peppercorns, Chef's Salt, salt, and bay leaf.

2.   Wash and wipe the inside and outside of the capon. Put the capon in the pot with the vegetables and add 6 quarts warm water. Bring to a boil over medium heat; then adjust heat to low and simmer for 2 hours.

3.   After 2 hours skim the fat from the top. Place it in a narrow, tall container, and put it in the freezer to chill quickly.

4.   Simmer capon for another 30 to 45 minutes or until a fork goes easily into the thigh.

5.   In a small sauté pan, heat 2 tablespoons of the fat you removed from the cooking liquid and add grated carrot and sugar. Over high heat, stir until sugar melts and carrots start to brown slightly. Pour 1 cup of the cooking liquid into the carrot mixture, stir, and pour the mixture into the soup pot. Let it simmer for another minute or two; then gently stir in dissolved gelatin. Cover and simmer for 15 minutes.

6.   Remove pot from heat and carefully lift out capon. Fish out whole carrot and plunge it immediately into ice water. Strain cooking liquid through a strainer; then wet a kitchen towel, wring it out, put it into the strainer, and carefully ladle the cooking liquid through the wet towel, discarding the last cup or so.

7.   Cool the capon; then carefully skin it and set all skin aside along with the cut vegetables.

8.   After an hour, skim fat from the top of the cooking liquid.

Put 2 tablespoons of the liquid into a cold saucer. Put the saucer into the refrigerator and check in about 10 minutes to see if it jells or not. If it jells and has the consistency of a gelatin dessert, then the "aspic" is good. If it doesn't jell in 10 minutes in the refrigerator, place all the liquid back in a pan over medium heat and bring to a *gentle* boil. Boil until about ⅓ of it evaporates. If any white froth comes to the top, skim it off.

9.   Make another test by putting 2 tablespoons of the liquid into a saucer and placing it in the refrigerator for 10 minutes. If it still does not jell, stir into the liquid one more envelope of unflavored gelatin dissolved in ⅓ cup cold water.

10.   Meanwhile, carefully remove the capon pieces from the carcass, discarding the bones and keeping the largest pieces (breasts and thighs) on a tray. After 15 minutes, put all capon meat into the refrigerator.

11.   Cut even, round disks from the whole carrot and, with a small star cutter, cut stars from the slices. In a large oval or rectangular Pyrex dish, arrange the stars on the bottom, dipping each piece first in the gelatinous liquid. Spoon some of the liquid over the stars, and chill the dish in the refrigerator for 10 minutes. Dip the large pieces of capon into the gelatinous liquid and place them with their meatiest surface toward the carrot stars.

12.   Cover the large pieces with the small pieces of capon picked off the bones, and ladle on enough of the liquid to completely cover the meat.

13.   Refrigerate overnight. The next day, dip the glass dish for a minute into warm water, and unmold on a serving platter.

14.   Serve the capon in aspic garnished with bunches of watercress and wedges of lemon alternated with black olives, and with a good mayonnaise.

CHEF'S SECRET: The grated carrots will give a beautiful amber color to the aspic, and the carrot stars will give a nice decorative touch to the dish. Capon, especially the skin and the bones, has a certain amount of natural gelatin; the additional gelatin will make the dish firm enough to mold.

It is not difficult to make this dish, but you must be very careful to skim all the fat so that the gelatinous substance will be clear, and to test the aspic so that it is not too thin.

If you have extra aspic left over, put it into a flat-surfaced, fairly large container, perhaps a glass pie plate. Let it jell, cut it into triangles, and use it to decorate the unmolded aspic. Or chop it into very small cubes and place the cubes in a pastry bag without a tube. Press it from the pastry bag onto a border around the unmolded dish.

Capon is excellent for this dish because it is tender and easy to cut. If you like a piquant taste, add to the gelatinous liquid the strained juice of a lemon, or add a little white vinegar and a tablespoon or so of white wine.

Roast Duck with Fresh Green Peppercorns

4 servings

2 ducks, approximately
  5 pounds each
1 cup sliced carrots
½ cup sliced celery
½ cup chopped onion
1 bay leaf
2 cloves garlic mashed to a
  paste with 2 tablespoons
  Chef's Salt (see index)
12 to 16 crushed black
  peppercorns

2 to 3 cups water
4 tablespoons butter
4 tablespoons oil
1 tablespoon butter mixed with
  1 tablespoon flour
2 tablespoons canned green
  peppercorns in brine, well
  rinsed
½ cup dry white wine
green parsley for garnish

1. Preheat oven to 350° F. Wipe the ducks very carefully inside and out until they are absolutely dry. Place carrots, celery, onions, and bay leaf in the bottom of a roasting pan with a fitted cover. Rub the inside and outside of the ducks with the garlic mashed with Chef's Salt. Be sure that both ducks are rubbed evenly. Rub the inside of the ducks with the crushed peppercorns. Place the ducks, breast down, on the vegetables and pour in the water. In a skillet, heat butter and oil to the smoking point. Spoon the hot shortening over the ducks.

2. Roast the ducks, covered, for 1½ hours. Then remove the lid, turn the ducks breast side up, increase the heat to 450° F., and continue to roast, basting occasionally with the pan juices, for another 30 minutes. Remove and keep the ducks in a warm place.

3. Strain the pan juices into a tall container. Let stand for a few minutes. Remove almost all the fat from the top of the liquid. Skim the last part of the fat by putting 3 or 4 ice cubes into a wet kitchen towel and moving it slowly over the top of the sauce with the ice cubes half immersed.

4. Pour this defatted juice into a small pan, bring to a boil, and add the flour-butter mixture bit by bit and the green peppercorns. Stir in the white wine. Continue stirring until it starts to boil again; then simmer for 15 to 20 minutes over very low heat.

5. Before serving, split the ducks in half. Place on a cookie sheet or baking sheet with a very low rim, skin side up, and place in a preheated 450° F. oven for about 10 minutes. Remove to a serving platter.

6. Surround the ducks with fresh green parsley and ladle a little of the sauce with the fresh green peppercorns in it over the ducks. Serve the rest of the sauce in a sauce boat. Accompany with rice, wild rice, or mashed potatoes.

CHEF'S SECRET: Until now it has been difficult to get green peppercorns, but now several companies sell them. They are very pungent. Be sure to rinse them well to remove the brine in which they are preserved.

Duck with Rice

8 servings

1 duckling, 4½ to 5 pounds	1 cup water
1 tablespoon Chef's Salt (see index)	3 cups washed rice
	6 cups boiling water
4 tablespoons lard or duck fat	2 teaspoons Chef's Salt (see index)
2 cups chopped onion	
1 cup sliced carrot	1 teaspoon marjoram
½ cup sliced celery	½ cup fresh parsley, chopped
½ cup sliced parsnip or parsley root	1 cup sliced mushrooms
	2 tablespoons butter

1. Cut up the duckling into small pieces. Use neck, giblets, and heart. Set the liver aside and sprinkle Chef's Salt on all other pieces. Preheat oven to 350°F.

2. In a skillet heat half the lard or duck fat. Add the onions

over high heat, and stir until they start to brown. Add carrots, celery, and parsnip and stir until they start to brown. Transfer the browned vegetables into a large ovenproof casserole. Add salted duck pieces, stir, and pour in about 1 cup of water. Cover and place in oven for 45 minutes. After 30 minutes, skim off as much fat as possible, stir, and add more water if necessary.

3.   Meanwhile, add remaining shortening to the skillet. When the shortening is smoking hot, add the washed rice. Stir the rice with a wooden spoon until it starts to brown and crackle.

4.   Remove casserole from oven. Carefully lift the lid, add the fried rice and 6 cups boiling water. Stir. Add Chef's Salt, marjoram, and half the parsley. Cover and return to the oven. Bake for another 30 to 45 minutes, or until the rice is cooked and the meat is tender.

5.   Meanwhile, gently sauté mushrooms in butter. Just before serving, sauté the duck liver, cut in slices, in the same butter.

6.   Remove the duck and rice to a serving platter, cover with the sautéed mushrooms and duck liver, and sprinkle with remaining parsley. Serve immediately.

CHEF'S SECRET: This delightful dish can stretch one duck as a main course for eight hungry people because the accompanying rice will be rich from the duck juices and fat. Yet the dish will not be greasy, because the rice will absorb the fat.

If the duck has lumps of fat around the cavity, by all means remove them when you cut the duck. You may render the fat and keep it for later use. Before adding the rice to the mixture of vegetables and duck, if you see that it has too much fat swimming on top, spoon off some of the fat into a small metal container and chill it for later use.

Potted Duck

approximately 24 slices

1 duckling, 4½ to 5 pounds	2 large cloves garlic
1 tablespoon plus 2 teaspoons Chef's Salt (see index)	8 to 10 whole black peppercorns, bruised
8 ounces lean veal	1 bay leaf
8 ounces pork shoulder	½ teaspoon dried tarragon

1 small carrot

1 small onion (the size of an egg)

4 envelopes gelatin

1 ounce cognac or brandy

1.   Preheat oven to 400° F.

2.   If you use a frozen duck, remove it from the freezer, submerge it in a large container of tap water for 2 hours, wipe it dry, and refrigerate it for at least 12 but not more than 24 hours. To defrost it to refrigerated temperature without first submerging it in tap water, allow at least 24 to 36 hours in refrigerator.

3.   Remove the bag containing neck, liver, heart, and gizzard from the cavity. (Be careful, sometimes the liver alone is in an extra small bag inside the neck cavity.) Wipe the duck dry with a towel and rub the surface inside and outside with the one tablespoon Chef's Salt. Let it stand.

4.   Rub the surface of the veal with one teaspoon Chef's Salt and rub the pork with the other teaspoon of Chef's Salt.

5.   Slice the carrots and onions and quarter the cloves of garlic. Distribute on the bottom of a roasting pan with a tight-fitting lid. Add the peppercorns, bay leaf, and tarragon. Pour into the pan one quart water. Place the duck, breast side down, and the pork and veal in the roasting pan. Sprinkle 2 envelopes of gelatin on the back of the duck and one envelope each on the top of the veal and pork. Cover and place in the oven. Be sure that the lid fits tightly; if not, cover the roasting pan with aluminum foil and then put the lid on.

6.   Roast for 1 hour. (When you remove the roasting pan from the oven, lift the lid carefully so that the hot steam will escape toward the rear of the pan without burning your arm or face.) Turn the duck breast side up, and turn the pork and veal. Tilt the roasting pan and baste all the meats. Replace cover and roast for another 30 minutes.

7.   Remove the duck, pork, and veal and place on a wire rack or a baking sheet. Strain the pan juices through a sieve into a tall, narrow container. Let it stand an hour at room temperature; then put it into the freezer so that the duck fat which comes to the top will be easy to remove. Discard the carrots and peppercorns; retain the bay leaf, onion, and garlic.

8.   When the duck is cool enough to handle, gently remove

the skin from the whole duck. Then remove the two breast halves by hand.

9. Press the breasts flat between the bottom of two plates and refrigerate. Debone the duck and discard bones. Cut up the gizzard and liver and debone the neck. Check the veal and pork and discard any bones. Grind duck skin, meat, veal, and pork with the onions and garlic twice through the disc with the largest holes. Do not grind the bay leaf; you will use it later.

10. Prepare an oval-shaped tureen (approximately 2 quarts) or a round glass casserole by gently brushing the inside with some of the duck fat you removed from the top of the cooking liquid.

11. Press half the ground meat firmly and evenly into the bottom of the dish. Cut the breasts lengthwise into finger-thick strips, and lay the strips parallel so that they are evenly distributed over the ground meat.

12. Press the second half of the ground meat over the strips of breast.

13. Warm the cooking liquid to lukewarm; add cognac or brandy and slowly, spoon by spoon, ladle it over the ground meat, waiting until the liquid seeps down.

14. Place the casserole on the bottom shelf of the freezer. Leave the duck fat at room temperature, and after one hour remove the duck from the freezer and spoon enough duck fat on top to cover. Place the bay leaf in the middle and chill for at least 24 hours before serving.

CHEF'S SECRET: Perhaps this recipe sounds very different from other recipes for similar dishes. Please trust me.

Sprinkling the gelatin onto the meat before baking is not customary, but through hundreds and hundreds of experiments I have convinced myself that even if the method is unconventional, the results are classic.

If you dissolve the gelatin in cold water and then mix it with the hot roasting liquid before pouring it over the duck, you will always have a gelatin taste whatever you do. Sprinkling the gelatin will give you the same taste cooks obtained a hundred years ago by extracting the gelatin from calves' feet and pork rinds. The pork and veal will absorb most of the juices oozing out of the duck, and the only flavor will be that of the duck.

When you cut the potted duck, always cut with a warm, very

sharp knife, and wipe the knife with a wet cloth after each slice. If your guests are not embarrassed to admit that they don't know how to eat and enjoy it, don't hesitate to explain that the best way to eat potted duck is to spread a little of the top layer of duck fat on a bit of warm toast and then cut a small piece from the potted duck and put it into your mouth with the toast. Chew it slowly, and swallow it only after it is well warmed by chewing. Many people hurry through a meal, swallowing everything before the taste, aroma, and fragrance of the food have a chance to develop from the warmth of the tongue and palate.

Serve very tart, crisp gherkins or pickled onions with the potted duck. A well-chilled white wine goes well with it, too.

Deviled Turkey Breast Steaks

8 servings

1 boneless turkey breast, 4 to
  4½ pounds
1 tablespoon Chef's Salt (see
  index)
2 tablespoons melted butter

Sauce:

½ cup cranberry sauce
2 tablespoons lemon juice
2 tablespoons brown sugar
¼ teaspoon freshly ground
  black pepper
5 to 6 drops Tabasco

1. Split the breast into two pieces. Remove the skin and cut each half into 4 equal steaks. Pound each gently with a mallet or with the edge of a heavy plate to approximately ½ inch thick.

2. Sprinkle with Chef's Salt and brush both sides with some of the melted butter.

3. Broil under a preheated broiler, approximately 6 inches from the heat, for 2 minutes on each side.

4. In a small bowl, combine cranberry sauce, lemon juice, brown sugar, pepper, and Tabasco. Brush this mixture liberally on one side of the turkey steaks. Broil with the brushed side up for 2 to 3 minutes; then turn, brush the second side, and broil for another 2 to 3 minutes. Repeat this one more time so that each side is brushed twice and broiled twice. Serve immediately with plenty of cranberry sauce and baked potatoes or French fries, and a big salad.

CHEF'S SECRET: Turkey breast—broiled, pan-fried, or grilled quickly—is not very well known, but it should be. It is surprisingly tender and tasty. Be careful not to overcook it or it will dry out. This method will definitely keep it from drying, and the cranberry sauce will add a perfect crust to the steak.

If you prepare it on an outdoor charcoal grill that has a cover, by all means cover it for the last turn. The smoky flavor will be pleasant.

Turkey in Avocado with Cranberries

8 servings

4 medium-sized ripe but firm
  avocados
2 cups cooked turkey cut into
  ½-inch cubes or julienne
½ teaspoon Chef's Salt (see
  index)
1 cup cranberry-orange relish

½ cup mayonnaise
1 can cranberry sauce
8 lettuce leaves
8 sprigs parsley
additional mayonnaise for
  garnish (optional)

1. Split avocados in half. Remove pits. Cut pits in half with a strong knife and return a half-pit to each avocado half. Chill.

2. In a bowl, mix turkey, Chef's Salt, cranberry-orange relish, and mayonnaise. Chill.

3. From a can of cranberry sauce cut 4 slices approximately ⅓ inch thick, and cut each slice in half. Chill.

4. Remove pits from avocado halves. Divide turkey-cranberry mixture among avocado halves. Place each half on a lettuce leaf. Cover half the filling with a half-slice of cranberry sauce. Decorate with a sprig of parsley and serve with additional mayonnaise if you wish.

CHEF'S SECRET: Splitting the avocado pits and placing them back in the avocado prevents the avocado from turning brown. The easiest way to split an avocado seed without cutting yourself is first to score the brown outer skin with a sharp nail, and then to cut along the scoring. Another method is to hold the pit with a kitchen prong and insert into it the tip of a strong knife, moving the knife back and forth until it goes in deeply enough to split the pit easily.

Turkey Croquettes

8 servings

½ cup finely minced onion
2 tablespoons butter
4 cups ground cold turkey
1½ teaspoons Chef's Salt (see index)
¼ teaspoon poultry seasoning or sage
2 eggs plus 2 tablespoons water

4 slices white bread
1 cup milk
1 cup flour
2 eggs plus 2 tablespoons water, for coating
2 cups bread crumbs
4 cups (approximately) liquid shortening

1.   Sauté onions in butter until limp and translucent. In a large bowl mix ground turkey, Chef's Salt, and onions.

2.   Add poultry seasoning, the two eggs beaten with water until smooth and light yellow, and 4 slices of white bread trimmed and soaked in the milk until all the milk is absorbed. Mix to a medium-soft consistency. If necessary, add a sprinkling of bread crumbs to make it firmer, or 1 or 2 tablespoons of milk or water to make it somewhat looser. The mixture should be easy to handle and to shape. Divide the mixture into 16 equal parts. With wet palms, shape into small cone-shaped croquettes. Roll each first in flour, then in egg beaten with cold water, and finally in the dry bread crumbs. Place on absorbent paper and chill.

3.   Approximately a half-hour before serving, heat half the shortening in a large heavy skillet and fry the turkey croquettes over medium heat 2 to 3 at a time, adding shortening as necessary, until golden brown. Place on absorbent paper and keep in a 200° F. oven until serving time.

CHEF'S SECRET: Be careful to let the shortening regain its high temperature after you remove the first fried croquettes, so that the next ones are not placed in merely warm shortening. Warm shortening will be absorbed by the bread crumbs and will make the croquettes heavy and greasy. Hot shortening fries the crumbs without penetrating the croquette.

If you like especially light croquettes, separate the eggs and beat the whites with a small pinch of salt until they are very stiff. Then gently mix a part of the croquette mixture into the egg white and slowly add the egg white to the whole mixture. The croquettes will be light as a cloud.

Turkey Stew

8 servings

8 pounds turkey wings cut into
  1-inch pieces
2 tablespoons Chef's Salt (see
  index)
1 teaspoon celery salt
½ teaspoon curry powder
½ cup shortening
3 cups finely minced onions
1 cup grated carrots

3 cups water
1 cup white wine
4 tablespoons flour
2 tablespoons cornstarch
1 cup water or white wine
2 cups fresh green peas, or 10-
  ounce package frozen green
  peas

1.   Ask the butcher to cut up the turkey wings into 1-inch pieces with his saw. Sprinkle the pieces with Chef's Salt, celery salt, and curry powder. Let stand at room temperature for an hour or so.

2.   Meanwhile, in a large, heavy pot with a tight-fitting lid, melt the shortening. Over high heat, add onions and grated carrots and stir until they start to brown. Immediately add the turkey pieces, keep stirring, and pour in the 3 cups water and 1 cup white wine. Bring to a boil, then reduce the heat to low. Cover and gently simmer for approximately 1½ to 2 hours, or until the turkey pieces are fork tender. Skim fat, if any.

3.   Mix flour and cornstarch with cold water or white wine. Add to it 1 cup of the hot stock from the pot. Stir until smooth; then pour the whole mixture back into the pot, stirring with a wooden spoon. Add peas. Bring to a boil, lower heat, and simmer for 10 minutes. Serve.

CHEF'S SECRET: If the liquid you add at first is not enough to completely cover the turkey, add more, just to cover. But be careful—do not make it too soupy.

If, after the addition of the flour and cornstarch, the stew is too thick, dilute with a little more water or wine, according to your taste.

The carrots for this dish are grated so that they will cook down more easily. Only their coloring and flavor will remain, not the carrots themselves.

If you don't like the taste of curry powder, omit it or replace it with another spice or herb of your taste.

Instead of the green peas you can add cubed carrots, cauliflower, or corn.

5

Fish & Shellfish

There was a time when most fish and shellfish were unknown to land-locked people. The only fish consumed was local fish, because of great difficulties in transportation and storage. Modern refrigeration and freezing has changed all this. If we can say that freezing—proper freezing, that is—will actually improve food, then fish is certainly the strongest point in the argument. Modern fishing vessels all over the world process their catches within a few hours after the fish are netted, and frozen wind tunnels in the processing ships freeze the catch so quickly and thoroughly that no spoilage can occur.

In the past, almost all "fresh" fish were served covered with sauces, vegetables, and condiments, mainly to disguise the fact that it spoiled quickly. Now, thanks also to modern transportation and distribution, the availability of all kinds of seafood and fresh-water fish is no more than a question of demand and supply—if you really want it, you can get it.

The main rule in preparing fish is not to overcook it. Unfortunately, this rule is commonly violated. Almost every fish should be cooked only until it is firm. If you are not sure, test gently with two round toothpicks or with a skewer. You can even

159

remove some of the inside flesh from a whole baked or poached fish without disturbing its appearance, then continue cooking for a few minutes if necessary. If you have poached a fish and lifted it out with great care and difficulty from the poaching liquid, and it turns out to be undercooked, it doesn't have to go back into the liquid for finishing. You can put it in the oven, on a cookie sheet, for a few minutes at 350° F.

You will notice in this chapter that the recipes are very sparingly "embellished" with strong-tasting ingredients that would take away the most important attribute of fish, its subtle taste and texture.

Among the shellfish dishes is a recipe for one of the finest ways to prepare a good lobster, one that is often misspelled. I am referring to *Lobster à l'armoricaine,* a dish that takes its name from its place of origin in Brittany, in the small coastal region Cotes-du-Nord. Editors and proofreaders are forever trying to turn this dish into *Lobster à l'américaine,* but if you check with such world-renowned experts as the Countess de Toulouse-Lautrec or Jean Conil, one of the most renowned cookbook authors of the twentieth century, you will see that the dish is indeed *à l'armoricaine.*

One more word of warning about how to recognize a fresh fish. Many cookbooks used to tell the homemaker to look into the eyes of the fish to see if they are bright and clear. But how can you look into the eyes of a skinned, boned whitefish fillet, neatly wrapped in plastic? My advice is to look for the busiest fish market in your community, and there you will find the best fish without looking into the accusing eyes of a lake trout.

If you want to check something, don't use your eyes but your nostrils. Yes, the nose knows. Fresh fish, even when frozen, has no "fishy" smell.

Boiled Lobster

4 servings

4 live lobsters, 1½ to 2 pounds each
sea water, or water with 1 tablespoon salt per quart

handful seaweed if available, or (European style) 1 teaspoon caraway seed per 2 quarts water

METHOD I: 1.   Place the 4 lobsters in a large empty pot. Add water to cover plus one inch. Remove the lobsters, add salt, and cover. Bring to rapid boil.

2.   Plunge lobsters headfirst into boiling water. Add seaweed or caraway seed. Cover pot. When the water starts to boil again, set timer for 10 minutes for 1½-pound lobsters, 15 minutes for 2-pound lobsters.

3.   When time is up, remove lobsters immediately and plunge into cold water or keep the pot under running cold water for 1 to 2 minutes to stop the cooking. Serve on a silver platter covered with a white napkin. Surround lobster with the green seaweed that was boiled with it.

METHOD II: 1.   Place lobsters in an empty pot. Cover with warm tap water. Add salt and seaweed or caraway seed. Cover pot and bring to a rapid boil.

2.   As soon as boiling starts, remove the pot from the stove. Proceed as in Method I, using the same cooling times.

CHEF'S SECRET: I lived for seven years in New England and watched experienced chefs and outstanding housewives using both methods with excellent results.

Timid persons who are afraid of the lobster will probably find the second method easier. Experienced ones tend to like the first. The main point in both cases: Don't overcook.

Many experts suggest laying the boiled lobster on its back, armor down, and splitting it lengthwise down the belly. I see no advantage in this method. As a matter of fact, it can lead to disaster. The easiest, best method is to place the boiled lobster belly down on a carving board (never on a tabletop!) and insert a knife (with the cutting edge toward the tail) in the middle of the body armor about an inch behind the tip of the head. Plunge the knife with a firm downward thrust until the tip hits the carving board, then bring the handle of the knife with one swift movement down toward the tail, like a lever, so that the entire cutting edge is used.

If the lobsters are 2-pounders, precrack the 2 big claws in the kitchen with a good lobster cracker; but if they are smaller, let the guests have the joy of cracking and picking.

Live lobster is almost always shipped in seaweed. This kind of seaweed looks like canned spinach with little air bubbles inside the leaves, and it is dark blackish green. But when you boil it, it goes through a miraculous chemical change and turns into an emerald green that makes a beautiful contrast with the red hue of the lobster.

Lobster Armoricaine

8 servings

4 live lobsters, 1½ to 2 pounds each
½ cup oil
4 tablespoons butter
1 tablespoon finely chopped shallots
1 small clove of garlic mashed to a pulp with 1 teaspoon salt
2 ounces cognac or brandy
1 pint dry white wine

2 cups peeled, cored, and seeded fresh tomato, chopped
½ bouillon cube diluted in 2 tablespoons boiling water
1 tablespoon freshly chopped parsley, or 1 tablespoon parsley flakes
pinch cayenne pepper
2 tablespoons cold butter

1. Cut lobsters into pieces as follows: first cut the lobster lengthwise down the middle; then cut the tail halves crosswise so that each tail makes six pieces. Break off the claws, cut off the legs, and cut open the two large legs. Crack the claws. Split the armor in two. Remove and discard the sac.

2. Collect all the soft parts, green liver, and coral in a plastic container. Save for later use.

3. In a heavy Dutch oven or skillet with a good tight lid, melt the oil and butter together until they are smoking hot. Add the lobster pieces all at once. Toss briskly over high heat until the shell gets red. Pour off the fat and discard it.

4. Sprinkle the shallots and crushed garlic over the lobster. Toss with a spatula.

5. In a small pan, warm the cognac. Light and pour it flaming over the lobster and kill the flames immediately with the white wine. Add the tomatoes, bouillon, parsley, and cayenne pepper. Cover the pan and cook gently over medium heat for about 20 minutes.

6. Remove all the lobster pieces. Cool so that you can handle them; then quickly remove the meat from the shell. Put it in a casserole and keep it warm. Save the half shells of the body and decorate the lobster meat with them.

7. Put the cooking liquid back on the stove over high heat. Add the chopped coral, green liver, and intestines to the sauce and add 1 tablespoon of the cold butter. Cook for 2 to 3 minutes.

8. Remove from the heat and stir in the remaining cold butter bit by bit. Pour the sauce over the lobster. Sprinkle with additional fresh green parsley if you wish, and serve immediately.

CHEF'S SECRET: This recipe may be more difficult to read than it is to prepare. I would advise you to read it two or three times and have all ingredients on hand before you begin. Before you even touch the lobster, prepare the tomato, garlic, shallots, wine, brandy, and butter. Taste the chopped tomatoes and if they are too acidic and leave a sour taste in your mouth, sprinkle them with a teaspoon of sugar.

It is hard to remove the lobster pieces from the shell if you don't have the right tools. A lobster pick, a shrimp fork, or a small sharp knife does the job best.

Don't throw out the pieces of shell. Cut them fine with lobster scissors and put them in a sauté pan with 4 to 6 tablespoons of butter. Sprinkle with ½ teaspoon Spanish paprika. When the shells start to sizzle, pour on 1 can of chicken broth and 1 cup of light cream. Bring to a boil, strain, and cool. Then freeze and use as a base for lobster bisque. When you are ready to use it, remove the butter from the top and melt it in a soup pot. When it starts to sizzle, stir in 2 tablespoons flour and 2 tablespoons cornstarch diluted in 2 cups of cold milk. Then add the reheated chicken stock-cream mixture. Bring to a very gentle boil. Add a few tablespoons of sherry or a touch of brandy and serve.

King Crab Salad

4 servings

2 packages frozen Alaska King Crab (6 ounces each), or 2 cans Alaska King Crab (7¾ ounces)
1 cup mayonnaise
2 tablespoons prepared mustard
2 tablespoons lemon juice
½ teaspoon sugar
pinch cayenne pepper
pinch dry mustard

½ cup finely chopped celery (if possible, tender stalks from the middle)
1 firm, not too tart apple, peeled, cored, and finely chopped
pressed yolks and chopped whites of 2 hard-boiled eggs
lettuce leaves
parsley for decoration

1. If frozen, defrost crab meat according to package directions.

2. In a bowl, mix mayonnaise, mustard, lemon juice, sugar, cayenne pepper, and dry mustard. Set aside some large pieces of crab meat for decoration.

3. Shred and fold crab meat, celery, apple, and egg whites into the mayonnaise mixture. Heap the salad over the lettuce leaves. Sprinkle it all over with sieved egg yolk and decorate the salad with the large pieces of crab meat. Chill.

CHEF'S SECRET: The egg whites and the apple are very good fillers for the expensive crab meat: They are bland, and together with the celery and the shredded crab meat they give four distinctive textures to the salad without overpowering the delicate taste of the crab.

Press the egg yolks carefully. If possible use a stainless steel sieve with fairly large holes, and don't scratch off the particles that stick to the bottom of the sieve, but gently tap the edge of the sieve on the dish in which you press the yolk, so that the particles remain loose and don't stick together. To sprinkle the yolk over the salad, use a fork, gently scraping out the particles from the container onto the salad.

Spicy Shrimp and Pork Salad

8 servings

½ teaspoon ground coriander
3 cloves garlic, minced
1 teaspoon freshly ground
  black pepper
3 tablespoons vinegar
2 tablespoons lime or lemon
  juice
1 teaspoon salt
1 teaspoon sugar

¼ teaspoon chili powder
2 cups cooked pork, cubed
  small
1 pound cooked shrimp, diced
  small
1 cucumber, peeled and sliced
lettuce leaves or greens of your
  choice
1 teaspoon mint

1. In a bowl combine the first 8 ingredients.

2. Add pork, shrimp, and cucumber. Mix.

3. Let stand at room temperature for about one hour, tossing occasionally. Then chill in refrigerator for an hour.

4. In a large salad bowl, arrange the lettuce leaves or other greens. Pile in the salad and sprinkle the top with chopped fresh mint or with dry mint steeped for ½ hour in hot water.

CHEF'S SECRET: Any leftover pork may be used for this dish as long as it is not too fatty. For the shrimp, you may use broken pieces or the inexpensive but tasty tiny shrimp.

If you wish to make individual servings, mix the mint into the salad before dividing it into portions. Or, instead of the chopped mint, add 1 fresh mint leaf on top of each serving.

This dish, eaten with freshly cooked oriental-style rice, can be a main course for a luncheon or a delightful small fish course for an oriental dinner. Instead of serving hot rice, you may serve it with cold rice prepared as follows:

Place in a bowl 4 cups boiled oriental-type (sticky) rice. Add 2 tablespoons white vinegar, 2 teaspoons sugar, and a very light sprinkling of monosodium glutamate. Press it into a large square on a wooden surface. Moisten with some water. Cut the rice into 8 portions. Between your palms form 2 rice sticks from each portion. Sprinkle with black sesame seed and serve with salad.

Black sesame seed is available in every oriental store. It is sold in a small plastic grinder that grinds the seeds properly for use.

Scallops Prepared as Snails

4 servings

2 tablespoons corn oil
1 teaspoon minced onions
4 tablespoons butter
½ cup bread crumbs
2 cloves garlic mashed to a pulp
   with 1 teaspoon Chef's Salt
   (see index)

1 pound scallops
4 tablespoons sherry
2 teaspoons freshly chopped
   green parsley
1 lemon

1.   Preheat oven to 450° F. In a saucepan, heat corn oil, add onions, and sauté over medium heat.

2.   In another small saucepan, heat 2 tablespoons butter and toast bread crumbs until golden brown. Set aside and keep warm.

3.   Add garlic and remaining 2 tablespoons butter to onions. Heat through; add scallops. Increase heat to high and sauté scallops very quickly, shaking pan back and forth all the time. It will take about 2 minutes. Discard liquid from saucepan.

4.   Add sherry; lower heat to medium. Cook for 1 more minute.

5.   Divide into 4 portions, spoon into 4 shells or other ovenproof containers, sprinkle each with bread crumbs, and bake 6 to 8 minutes.

6.   Sprinkle with parsley and serve with ¼ lemon per person.

CHEF'S SECRET: Many people eat canned snails (which taste like rubber bands) because they like garlic butter. But tender baby scallops are a much tastier excuse for garlic butter.

If the scallops are large, cut each into 2 to 4 pieces before sautéing them. Instead of sherry, you can use another white or even a red wine, if you wish.

Fillet of Sole Maison Gyarmathy

4 servings

4 Dover sole fillets (or lemon
   sole, gray sole, or flounder)

6 ounces small, firm, snow-
   white mushrooms

½ cup butter
1 quart water
1 tablespoon salt
½ cup vinegar
6 to 10 whole peppercorns, crushed
½ bay leaf
1 lemon, sliced

½ cup half-and-half or light cream
2 egg yolks
salt and pepper to taste
4 slices dry toast, each lightly toasted and cut into 4 triangles

1.   Coat the bottom and sides of an ovenproof dish with a little of the butter. Add the sole.

2.   In a saucepan, bring water, salt, vinegar, peppercorns, bay leaf, and sliced lemon to a vigorous boil. Ladle over fillets and let stand 10 to 15 minutes.

3.   Meanwhile, slice mushrooms to the thickness of a matchstick. Sauté in half the butter for 1 minute over medium heat.

4.   Drain liquid from the sole and discard spices and lemon. Distribute mushrooms over fish.

5.   Preheat oven to 350° F. Add the remaining butter to the sauté pan. Melt slowly and stir in the half-and-half with a whisk.

6.   In a metal or heat-resistant bowl, beat egg yolks until lemon-colored. Add 1 tablespoon of the cream and butter mixture. Beat vigorously and continue to add cream and butter in small amounts, beating after each addition. Do this off the heat but close enough to it so that the cream and butter mixture does not cool.

7.   When all cream and butter has been added, ladle the sauce over the fish. Add salt and freshly ground pepper to taste and bake 12 to 15 minutes.

8.   Place 4 toast triangles on each plate and serve the fish, mushrooms, and sauce over the triangles.

CHEF'S SECRET: I had the pleasure of enjoying this heavenly dish at the palatial home of Monsieur Gyarmathy, art director and stage designer of the world-famous "Follies." His "gentleman's gentleman" prepares this incomparable dish with such ease and elegance that it is a joy just to watch him. The preparation is done on the table top next to the stove. The fish is not exposed to direct heat until it goes into the oven for the final 15 minutes.

Don't be afraid to undercook fish. If it happens, you can always put it back in the oven for another 2 to 3 minutes. The easiest way to see if the fish is cooked is to open it carefully with two forks at its thickest place. If it is cooked, it will have lost all its shininess and will be a dull white. Another test is to press the surface gently with your finger. If the touch is springy, the fish is not done yet. To perfect this technique, cook one piece of fish until it is overdone, let it cool a bit, and place it next to a piece of raw fish. Try to press both with your finger, not looking while you do, until you can tell the difference.

Fillet of Sole Suchet

8 servings

8 sole fillets, 4 ounces each
2 teaspoons Chef's Salt (see index)
2 eggs
1 tablespoon lemon juice
6 tablespoons milk
2½ to 3 cups sifted dry bread crumbs
½ cup melted butter

2 large carrots, approximately 6 to 7 inches long and 1¼ to 1½ inches thick, or 3 smaller carrots
1 teaspoon salt
4 tablespoons chopped parsley, or 1 small can black truffles, cut julienne (optional)

For the sauce:

2 tablespoons finely chopped shallots or scallions (white parts only)
3 tablespoons butter
¼ teaspoon celery salt
¼ teaspoon Chef's Salt
pinch white pepper

3 tablespoons flour
½ cup dry white wine
1½ cups fish stock, clam juice, or water
dash of sugar
2 to 4 tablespoons light cream or half-and-half

For the border (Duchess Potatoes):

4 cups mashed potatoes
4 egg yolks
2 egg whites
½ cup light cream or half-and-half

4 tablespoons butter
1½ teaspoons Chef's Salt
1 tablespoon Hungarian paprika

1. Preheat oven to 375° F.

2. Sprinkle fillets with Chef's Salt. In a bowl, beat together eggs, lemon juice, and milk. Place bread crumbs in a pie pan. Melt butter and brush a cookie sheet with very little of it. Cover with aluminum foil and brush the foil well with more butter.

3. Dip the fillets one by one, first in the egg wash, then in bread crumbs. Press bread crumbs into the fish. Shake off excess, dip fish in the egg again, and then into the bread crumbs again. Place breaded fish on the foil and butter the top of each fillet with the remaining butter. Bake uncovered for 30 minutes.

4. While fish bakes, peel and cut carrots into matchstick-sized pieces 1½ inches long by ⅛ inch thick (julienne). Place in a small pot, add the teaspoon salt, and fill with cold water to cover plus ½ inch. Bring to a boil and remove after 2 minutes of boiling. Strain, discard water, and cool carrots by running cold water on them.

5. *Sauce:* In a skillet, sauté shallots in butter over medium heat for about 5 minutes. Combine celery salt, Chef's Salt, white pepper, and flour; then mix with dry white wine. Stir mixture into shallots, add fish stock, and bring to a boil over medium heat. Correct seasoning with a dash of sugar if wine is too acidic.

6. Stirring constantly with a wire whip, add light cream or half-and-half, reduce heat and simmer the sauce over very low heat for about 15 minutes.

7. **Duchess Potatoes:** Mash enough boiled potatoes in the bowl of an electric mixer to have 4 cups. Using the paddle or dough hook, add egg yolks one by one, egg whites, cream, butter, and Chef's Salt. Beat until slightly yellow and fluffy. Transfer to a pastry bag with a ½-inch star tube and pipe it around the edge of an ovenproof serving platter. Sprinkle with paprika and heat through in the oven. (Do this during the last 10 minutes of cooking time for the fish.)

8. Arrange fish on the platter, pour about half the sauce over fillets, and sprinkle with half the carrot slices. Ladle on the second half of the sauce and distribute on top the remaining carrots. If you have black truffles, cut them julienne and spread over the carrots. If you do not have truffles, sprinkle on freshly chopped green parsley and serve at once.

CHEF'S SECRET: The breading for the fillets is a little different from regular breading, because they are baked instead of deep fried. This breading will not be golden, crispy, and crunchy, but the white wine sauce would make the other type of breading soggy.

Some types of paprika get dark brown very fast in the oven and turn bitter. It is best to try the paprika on just a dab of Duchess potato. Put it on a piece of aluminum foil and stick it in the oven. If the paprika you have turns an ugly dark brown in a few minutes and acquires a bitter smell and taste, you should sprinkle it on the potatoes *after* baking.

Please note that before you lower the heat under the white wine sauce, you must stir constantly to prevent scorching or lumping. White wine sauces are very delicate and must be watched carefully.

Serbian Fish Fillets

8 servings

2 tablespoons oil
2 pounds potatoes, approximately 8 to 10 medium, very thinly sliced
2 cups very thinly sliced onions
1 tablespoon Chef's Salt (see index)
1 tablespoon paprika

½ teaspoon black pepper
1 tablespoon flour
2 whitefish fillets, heads removed, about 2 pounds each; or 4 1-pound fillets
8 slices bacon, each cut in half
2 cups sour cream mixed with 1 cup milk

1.   Preheat oven to 375° F.
2.   Line bottom and sides of a baking pan with foil and brush with oil. Lay sliced potatoes loosely in the pan and distribute onion rings on top.
3.   Combine Chef's Salt, paprika, and black pepper. Add half to the flour. Sprinkle the other half over the potatoes and onions.
4.   Rub both sides of each fish fillet with the mixture of Chef's Salt, spices, and flour. Lay the fillets in front of you and in each fillet cut 4 gashes about ½ inch deep, through the skin. Insert ½ slice bacon in each gash so that some of it is in the gash and the rest lays on top of the fish. Lay the fillets skin side up on the

onions and bake 10 minutes. Cover the fillets with half the sour cream mixture and bake for another 20 to 25 minutes, depending on the thickness of the fillets.

5.   Carefully remove the fillets with a spatula and set aside, keeping them warm. Return potatoes and onions to the oven and increase the heat to 450° F. Bake about 15 minutes, then transfer to a serving platter. Carefully place the fillets on top of the potatoes. Cover with remaining sour cream mixture and serve with a green salad or with a cucumber salad.

CHEF'S SECRET: To make the gashes in the fish, insert the tip of the knife under the skin with the cutting edge up and cut away from you. This will prevent the knife from losing its edge. Or, cut into the skin with a kitchen scissors and then make the gash in the fish.

The potato slices must be sliced very thin. If you are not good at this, use the two straight blades of a four-sided grater, or cut them on a vegetable slicer.

If you can't get 2-pound fillets and have to use smaller ones, boil the sliced potatoes for 2 to 3 minutes and fry the onion rings in 2 tablespoons shortening for 2 to 3 minutes before adding so as not to overcook the fish.

This same dish can be made with many other kinds of fish, such as lake trout or pike.

Baked Grouper

8 servings

4 tablespoons oil
3½ to 4 pounds grouper fillets
1 tablespoon Chef's Salt (see index)
2 tablespoons fresh parsley, chopped
1 teaspoon dry tarragon
1 teaspoon dry rosemary

½ teaspoon chervil
2 tablespoons butter
1 large bunch fresh green parsley
2 large lemons
1 recipe Hot Herb Butter for Fish (see index)

1.   Preheat oven to 375° F. Cover the rack of a broiler pan with aluminum foil. Brush 2 tablespoons oil on the foil. Rub both

sides of fish with Chef's Salt. Mix chopped parsley, tarragon, rosemary, and chervil in a cup with butter and 2 tablespoons oil. Spread mixture on the flesh side and place the fish, skin side down, on the foil. With a small, sharp knife, gently make 2 or 3 lengthwise cuts into the fish, being careful not to go deeper than half the thickness of the fish. Then cut it 6 to 8 times crosswise. Bake the fish for 20 minutes.

2.   Check doneness by inserting 2 forks in the thickest part of the fish and trying to pull it apart. If it flakes and is not translucent, the fish is ready. Remove it to a large serving platter. Surround with fresh parsley and lemon wedges. Serve with Hot Herb Butter, flambé it, and serve Sauce Louis (see index) on the side. Offer with it plain boiled potatoes or Duchess Potatoes (see index) and a fresh green vegetable.

CHEF'S SECRET: Grouper is not a well-known fish, but it is gaining in popularity because of modern freezing facilities around the Mexican Gulf, where most of it is caught. It is a delicately flavored, delightful fish. Don't overcook.

Red Snapper Creole

8 servings

⅓ cup oil
½ cup diced onion
½ cup thinly sliced celery
½ cup diced green bell pepper
¼ cup flour
1½ cups hot water
8-ounce can tomato sauce
¼ cup tomato catsup
1½ teaspoons salt

2 tablespoons sugar
¼ teaspoon garlic salt
2 bay leaves
1 pinch thyme
1 dash Tabasco sauce
2 pounds Red Snapper fillets, cut into 1-inch slices
2 teaspoons lemon juice

1.   In a heavy (if possible, cast iron) skillet, heat the oil to the smoking point. Add the onion, celery, and green pepper, and sauté until tender. Stir in the flour; then add hot water, stirring constantly for a smooth mixture. Add all the remaining ingredients except the red snapper fillets and the lemon juice. Cover and cook over low heat for 15 to 20 minutes.

2. Add red snapper and cook for an additional 5 minutes.
3. Remove from heat; discard bay leaves. Add lemon juice and serve with cooked rice.

CHEF'S SECRET: Red snapper, which is abundant in the Gulf of Mexico, is the ideal fish for this recipe because it is always available throughout the United States. Never try to cut it with the skin up. As with all other fish, lay it with the skin on the cutting board, flesh side up, for cutting. The knife won't become dull and the strips will be much more even.

This is an ideal dish for fishing picnics. You can prepare it at home up to the point of adding the fish fillets and the lemon juice, and you can finish it with the fresh fish right next to the river or lake over an open fire. If you wish to make it for outdoor finishing, I suggest you replace the canned tomato sauce with 1 pound of fresh tomatoes, peeled, and cook the sauce for half an hour instead of the suggested 15 to 20 minutes. Because of the high acidity in the tomatoes, you won't have to worry about the sauce turning sour during the day. Of course, if you prepare it ahead, freeze the sauce overnight and leave home with the frozen sauce in a plastic container.

Whitefish with South African Lobster Tail Soufflé

8 servings

4 tablespoons butter
½ cup white wine mixed with ½ cup water
8 boneless whitefish fillets, 4 ounces each, or other fish fillets, same size
1½ to 2 teaspoons Chef's Salt (see index)
4 cups boiling water with 1 tablespoon salt
2 South African lobster tails, 6 to 7 ounces each

1 large bowl ice water
2 slices white bread, crusts removed, soaked in ½ cup milk with a pinch of white pepper and a dash of salt
5 large or 6 medium eggs, separated
4 tablespoons sifted white bread crumbs

1. Preheat oven to 350° F. Preheat broiler.
2. Have butter at room temperature and spread it into the

bottom of a shallow ovenproof dish large enough for the 8 whitefish fillets. Pour the wine-water mixture into buttered dish.

3.   Sprinkle Chef's Salt on both sides of each fillet and lay them skin side down in the dish.

4.   In a saucepan, bring to a boil the salted water. When it boils, add the lobster tails. If the tails were frozen, boil for 8 minutes from the time the water starts to boil again; if thawed, for 5 to 6 minutes.

5.   Remove lobster tails; plunge immediately into ice water.

6.   Break bread into milk sprinkled with the salt and pepper.

7.   Separate eggs carefully. Stir yolks into milk-bread mixture.

8.   Carefully remove meat from lobster tails by cutting along the inner edge under the armor, from the middle under the tail, up toward the front. After cutting on both sides of the membrane, lift out the tails and cut each crosswise into three sections. By hand, shred each section lengthwise into "threads" or "flakes" by holding it firmly in one hand and pinching off pieces the thickness of a matchstick until all is shredded. If you do it correctly, you will get about 2 cups of loosely packed lobster meat.

9.   Thirty minutes before serving, bake fish for 10 minutes and remove from oven.

10.   Beat egg whites with a dash of salt until they form soft peaks. Remove ⅓. Beat the ⅔ until they form dry hard peaks; put back the other ⅓ and beat for an additional 30 seconds. Sprinkle half the bread crumbs over the egg whites and gently fold in with a rubber spatula. Sprinkle the remaining bread crumbs on the shredded lobster. Fold half the egg whites into the egg yolk-bread mixture. Sprinkle the shredded lobster tail on top and gently fold in. Then fold the whole mixture into the remaining egg whites. Lay the soufflé on top of the fillets and bake for an additional 10 minutes without opening the oven door.

11.   Remove from oven. Place under preheated broiler about 6 inches from the source of the heat. Close broiler door and shut heat off immediately. As soon as the top starts to brown, remove and serve immediately with fluffy rice or boiled potatoes.

CHEF'S SECRET: A small amount of South African lobster tail can raise a few plain fish fillets from the ordinary to the festive.

The technology of the shredding is Oriental. I watched my mother-in-law shred small pieces of lobster tail into gorgeous mounds of tasty shreds. The secret is that the taste buds receive several hundred times as many "taste messages" by this method as they would if you were to chew a cube or chunk of the same food. This is the principle on which the shredding of cheese, the "French cutting" of vegetables, and many other culinary procedures are based.

Cucumber Crowns with Salmon

8 servings

4 large cucumbers
1 7-ounce can salmon
1 cup homemade or good
   commercial mayonnaise
½ teaspoon dry tarragon
¼ teaspoon dry chervil

1 tablespoon rinsed capers
   (leave 8 whole; chop the rest)
2 lemons
parsley sprigs
4 pimiento-stuffed olives

1. Peel cucumbers, leaving on some of the green skin. Cut each cucumber into two pieces as shown in the illustration. Cut two crowns from each piece by moving a sharp paring knife in and out of the cucumbers, cutting equal-sized V cuts.

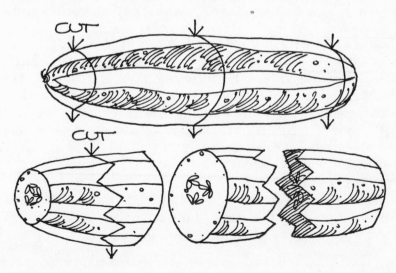

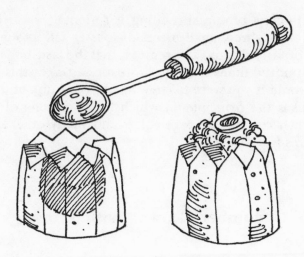

2.   With a melon-ball cutter, scoop out the seeds and moist pulp from the cucumber crowns, being careful not to scoop completely through to the bottom. Sprinkle the cucumbers very lightly with salt, let them stand for 5 to 6 minutes, and then rinse in ice water. Pat dry with a towel and refrigerate.

3.   In a large bowl, mix salmon with mayonnaise, tarragon, chervil, and chopped capers. Squeeze in the juice of ½ lemon. Spoon the filling into the 16 cucumber crowns, arrange them on a serving platter—in a bed of lettuce, on a paper doily, or surrounded with sprigs of parsley—and decorate every second one with a whole caper and the others with a spanish olive half, cut side up. Cut the remaining ½ lemon in 2 pieces and the whole lemon in 6, so that you have 8 wedges, one for each serving.

CHEF'S SECRET: For this dish select very firm, vivid dark-green cucumbers, at least 5 to 5½ inches but not longer than 7 inches. They should be at least 1½ inches or more in diameter. After peeling, you can cut up the two ends, chop them fine, and mix with the salmon. They will add a crunchy texture.

If you let the cucumbers stand for a few minutes after salting them, the salt will draw out a certain amount of the liquid. But you must wash the salt out immediately; otherwise the cucumbers will go limp.

Beginners sometimes cut through the bottom of the crown while scooping out the inside of the cucumber. If this happens, don't worry; simply place the crown on a slice of cucumber.

A commercial mayonnaise will always be greatly improved if

you add a pinch of sugar, a pinch of salt, and a few drops of lemon juice, and gently stir. Or you can improve it by adding a teaspoon of prepared mustard.

If you wish, you can fill the cucumber crowns with tuna fish or any other seafood, or with leftover finely chopped cold meat or shredded poultry.

Most people think of a cucumber as a cold vegetable or salad ingredient to be eaten raw. Try filling the crowns with ground beef, highly spiced, and bake them at 350° F. in a lightly buttered ovenproof serving dish. After 15 minutes, spoon on top ½ cup sour cream mixed with 2 or 3 tablespoons mayonnaise. After 30 minutes, sprinkle the top with some paprika. Bake for another 5 minutes and serve as a hot first course.

Smoked Salmon or Trout Mousse on Toast

8 servings

8 slices bread
4 tablespoons melted butter
2 egg yolks
½ cup flaked or chopped smoked salmon or lox, or 1 cup smoked trout, smoked chub, or other smoked fish

4 tablespoons sifted white bread crumbs
4 egg whites at room temperature
1 to 2 tablespoons lemon juice
4 large or 8 small black olives
8 sprigs parsley, for decoration

1. Preheat oven to 400° F. Preheat broiler.
2. Trim crusts and lay the slices of bread on a cookie sheet. Brush both sides with some of the melted butter. Refrigerate.
3. Put egg yolks and some of the smoked fish in an electric mixer. Set the blender first for "chop" and then for "mince" (about medium speed), and slowly add remaining fish alternately with bread crumbs until the mixture turns into a paste. Scrape the paste into a bowl.
4. Beat egg whites until they form shiny peaks. Gently fold about a quarter of the egg whites into the fish-egg mixture. Fold in lemon juice and another quarter of the egg whites. Now fold the mixture into the remaining egg whites.
5. Remove bread from refrigerator and place it immediately under the broiler. Toast one side quickly. Remove and

refrigerate again for 4 to 5 minutes. Meanwhile, transfer the smoked fish mixture into a pastry bag with a star tube approximately ½ inch wide. Toast the second side of the bread, then turn it over and pipe the soufflé on the 8 slices of toast, dividing equally.

6.   Bake 5 minutes. Turn off the heat and let stand in the oven for another 8 to 12 minutes without opening the door. Remove. Decorate each slice with black olives and parsley sprigs and serve at once.

CHEF'S SECRET: If you make this dish with smoked chub or smoked whitefish, you won't need to use a blender. These fish are soft enough to be mashed into pulp with a fork; but the sliced smoked salmon will have to be processed in the blender.

When I beat egg whites, I always follow the rule of a fabulous old pastry chef with whom I worked for a while in Austria. He taught me first to beat about ⅔ of the egg whites to very dry peaks, almost to the point of overbeating, and then to add the last third and keep beating. You would think that after this addition the first ⅔ would collapse. Not so. It will pick up moisture and form beautiful, shiny and soft but strong peaks. The method is worth trying. Be careful not to have any trace of yolk in the whites, and be sure that the bowl and the whip are free of fat. It is best to wipe the bowl and whip with a vinegar-dipped kitchen towel and then rinse with cold water before beating.

Some smoked fish is too mild to be enjoyed without adding salt, so add some if it is needed.

Nova Scotia Salmon Service

Perhaps one of the finest gourmet delicacies ever invented is smoked salmon. In Europe the Scotch and in the New World the Nova Scotia salmon are unsurpassed. But this delicacy can turn into a disaster if it is not served properly and if it is not accompanied properly. Just as chamber music is designed for a few selected instruments, smoked salmon is designed to be enjoyed with a few selected side dishes.

First of all, it should be sliced so thin that you can read through the slices. A Parisian restaurant once had a fabulous captain who could slice salmon tissue-thin. The owner, to prove the point, ordered some plates designed with newspaper reproductions on the surface—and the captain sliced the salmon so that one really could read the text through the slices. After a couple of years he left and opened his own small country restaurant. The owner could never find another man who could master the slicing, so the plates have been in storage ever since. How do I know? I have one of the plates hanging in my office.

If you purchase smoked salmon that is machine cut and packed in oil, wipe off the oil with paper towels, place the slices between two sheets of strong plastic wrap, and very gently pound the slices until they are two or three times their original size and turn a very pale pink. Be careful not to destroy their texture. Remove the slices from the plastic with a wide metal spatula or with a slicer (a wide- bladed long knife with a rounded end, often used for slicing roast beef).

Always serve the salmon at room temperature, never cold. Accompany with freshly chopped onion that has been soaked for 5 minutes or so in cold water with 1 or 2 teaspoons lemon, then gently pressed out in a towel. Serve also with rinsed capers, juicy ripe lemons cut in half and covered with a double cheesecloth to prevent the seeds from falling out during squeezing, and an excellent quality fresh rye or wheat bread with fresh sweet butter.

If you can't get sweet butter, take a stick of salted butter and break it in half. Put it in a bowl with 2 or 3 cups of room-temperature water and squeeze the butter with both hands, pressing and kneading until the salt and other chemicals go into a solution with water. Then lift out the washed butter and put it in a strong, wet cloth. Gather the cloth until the butter forms a ball, then squeeze out all the water.

Be sure to have plenty of good chilled beer or a pleasant but dry, well-chilled white wine on hand.

Eating salmon like this is a heavenly experience, especially if you follow the rules for eating as well as those for service. To eat Nova Scotia salmon you must train your palate just as you must train your ears for chamber music. The first bite you take should be nothing but salmon, about the size of two postage stamps. Place it on the middle of your tongue if possible, without touching either your lips or tongue with the fork. Close your mouth and let your tongue and upper palate engulf the salmon and warm it to your body temperature. The volatile oils that preserve the frail scent of the smoked fish will start to evaporate, filling your mouth with a very pleasant, warm, sweet sensation. The mild saltiness will awaken all your taste buds.

Now start to chew the salmon very slowly, turning it with your tongue from molar to molar in the back of your mouth. Without opening your mouth, swallow. Now take a deep breath and have four or five short but powerful sips of the beer, or two sips of the wine, to rinse the fish taste from your mouth and to enjoy the fragrance and cooling effect of the beer or wine.

Next, take a small piece of bread with a touch of butter. Chew and swallow it. Take a second piece of bread, placing on it a piece of salmon. On top of the salmon put two or three small bits of the sweet onion, one or two capers, and a few drops of lemon juice. Don't use a fork. Lift the little canapé by hand to your mouth. Bite into it right in the middle. Place both bites in your mouth. Close your mouth and chew slowly, playing sensuously with the food, turning it back and forth with your tongue, and enjoying the crunch sensation of the onion, the mellow fragrance of the caper, the unique texture of the salmon, the bland coarseness of the bread, and the sweetness of the butter.

Close your eyes if you wish, as if you were listening to music. Keep repeating this procedure and you will decide, I'm sure, that the salmon was well worth the price you paid for it.

Old-Fashioned Stuffed Gefilte Fish

6 to 8 servings

1 to 1½ pounds whitefish, cleaned and boned, but left whole
salt and plenty of freshly ground black pepper
juice of 1 lemon

2 tablespoons freshly chopped parsley
1 large egg beaten with ½ cup milk
1 envelope (1 tablespoon) un-flavored gelatin

1 bay leaf
1 small clove garlic, sliced (optional)
½ cup oil
2 cups skinless, boneless, flaked smoked chub
2 slices white bread without crusts

1 large carrot, scraped and sliced, preboiled until done
2 to 3 cups water
lemon and parsley for decoration

1.   Wash and dry whitefish. Sprinkle inside with salt and black pepper, half the lemon juice, bay leaf broken in small pieces, and sliced garlic if you use it.

2.   Fold fish back to its original shape, brush with oil, and place in refrigerator for about 30 minutes. Turn it over and let stand for another 30 minutes.

3.   Preheat oven to 350° F. Flake the smoked chub and break the bread into small pieces. Loosely mix chub, bread, and parsley with salt and black pepper to taste. Pour beaten egg over chub mixture and toss lightly.

4.   Remove bay leaf and garlic from whitefish and discard. Fill the fish with the stuffing. Sprinkle half the gelatin on the cut belly edge of the fish and press the top half down on it. Lay it on well-oiled aluminum foil in a baking pan. Put carrots around the fish and brush with oil. Pour water and remaining lemon juice mixed with the other half of the gelatin around the fish and bake for 20 to 25 minutes.

5.   Remove from oven and let stand for 2 to 3 minutes. Then pour off the liquid into a tall, narrow container. Carefully remove the fish to the serving dish. Let it cool. Skim the oil from the cooking liquid and spoon it on the fish while still lukewarm.

6.   Chill before serving. Cut into 6 to 8 pieces, decorate each piece with a slice of lemon and parsley, and serve.

CHEF'S SECRET: This recipe lends itself to easy multiplying. You can prepare 3 to 4 of the stuffed fish with just a little more work than it takes for one.

We tried to use other types of fish but were not very successful. Perhaps the closest to whitefish was lake trout.

Pompano en Papillote

4 servings

2 tablespoons oil
1 teaspoon Chef's Salt (see
 index)
4 pompano, cleaned, head and
 tail removed
½ cup sliced scallions, white
 and green parts mixed

4 teaspoons butter
juice of ½ lemon
4 slices lemon
4 tablespoons mayonnaise
4 teaspoons finely chopped
 green parsley

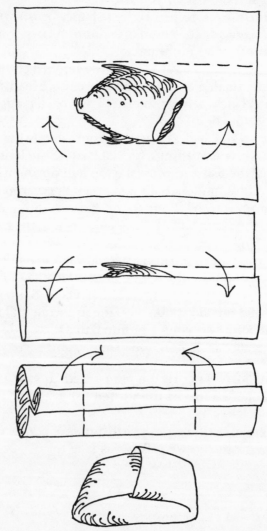

1.   Preheat oven to 375° F. Dip two fingers in a little oil and gently rub the middle of 4 squares of parchment, approximately 10 by 10 inches. Sprinkle the Chef's Salt inside and outside of the pompano and rub it into the flesh.

2.   Place a wet kitchen towel in front of you and put on it one sheet of the oiled parchment, oily side up. Place a pompano in the middle and heap on the pompano ¼ of the sliced scallions. Place 1 teaspoon cold butter on the scallions and sprinkle with some of the lemon juice. Fold the parchment over the fish as shown in the illustration. Place it on a wet cookie sheet. Repeat with each fish and sprinkle some water on the parchment. Bake on the cookie sheet for approximately 20 minutes. If the pompano is more than 6 ounces, bake 25 to 30 minutes. Be careful not to overcook.

3.   Remove each parchment to a plate. Open the papillote. Cover half of the scallions on the top of each fish with a slice of lemon, the other half with a generous teaspoon of mayonnaise. Sprinkle with fresh parsley and serve in the papillote.

CHEF'S SECRET: If you can't get real parchment, use aluminum foil. Don't try imitation parchments because they usually contain chemicals. They will either burn or impart a very bad taste to the fish. Of course, you can prepare any small fish this way. We tried it with perch fillets and it was delicious.

6

Vegetables

One of the greatest culture shocks after my arrival in America as an immigrant in 1951 was to see the relationship between meat and vegetable on a lunch or dinner plate. Not only in my native Hungary but all over Middle Europe and large parts of Eastern Europe, the main part of the meal is the vegetable. The meat is just a side dish. So when I saw the tremendous hunks of meat—the thick double pork chops, the half-chickens with a few green peas, a couple of carrots, or three or four spears of asparagus modestly hiding next to it under a bunch of parsley— I was quite surprised.

But it didn't take me long to get my fill of meat and yearn for the type of meals I had known in the Old World—a big plate of squash, thickened with starch and laced with sour cream, with a thin slice of veal roast or meat loaf on top of it, or a big bowl of thick beans, lentils, or peas with a two-inch piece of sausage or a slice of roast pork, or the many vegetable dishes that use meat only as an ingredient in their preparation.

Now there seems to be a strong vegetarian movement in the United States, with more and more people trying to cut down on their intake of meat. This is not a book on nutrition—doesn't intend to be and doesn't pretend to be. Nutrition is a responsible science, and nutritional requirements should be the concern of an individual and his physician. But because vegetables can be good eating and because more and more people are interested in them, I have included some vegetable recipes—without making any claim to nutritional advice.

The most important element in vegetable cooking is *timing*. Certain vegetables must cook, simmer, braise, or bake for a long time. On the other hand, many vegetables are overcooked by most people.

First I must defend frozen vegetables. They are so often unfairly criticized and belittled by so-called purists who find no use for them at all. Fresh vegetables were unquestionably best when people could walk out to their garden and see which was the freshest vegetable to pick; or when homemakers could walk to the market where local farmers' wives sold vegetables picked the night before at a local farm. But look what happens today. Fresh green peas are harvested on Monday in California; Tuesday they are carried on to the wholesale buyer who buys up all the green peas in a farming area and takes them to the warehouse; on Wednesday the orders go out to the wholesalers so they can be at the wholesale market on Thursday morning—from where they are delivered to the chain-store produce department on Friday to be sold Saturday morning.

At the same time, green peas are harvested at 8 A.M. Monday in Minnesota, are in the freezer plant by 9, and are shelled, sorted, blanched, deep frozen, packaged, and safely in the warehouse by 2 P.M., retaining a tremendous amount of their freshness until the minute they land in your saucepan.

Which green peas will be fresher—the ones that spent a week on the road or the ones that were preserved naturally by freezing within a few hours of being harvested?

Yes, I prefer fresh vegetables, and I always try to use them in season, in abundance, and consider the frozen ones as substitutes. I would never suggest that you cook frozen carrots instead of fresh, or frozen white cabbage, or frozen onions, but I would certainly recommend that if you want corn on the cob in February, you should buy it frozen.

Canned vegetables, too, have a legitimate and useful place in the household. I don't care for restaurants in Paris that serve canned green peas in canned artichoke bottoms, topped with canned mushrooms, no matter how many stars they have in the guide books. But I certainly would not suggest to a homemaker today that she pick, shell, hull, soak, and cook kidney beans for a bean salad, or cook up a storm for a few slices of beets. Canning does a perfect job for many, many vegetables, and even canned green peas and canned green beans can be excellent if handled properly.

The difference between a true vegetarian and a convert is the same as between a virgin and a divorcée. The true vegetarian, just like the virgin, doesn't know what he or she is missing. On the other hand, divorcées, just like the people who are converted to the million-year-old-"new" fad of vegetarianism, know what they are missing. Because they know what they are missing, I included a few dishes in this chapter that, although they are pure vegetables, resemble the "forbidden fruit" meat.

Dilled Baby Carrots with Brown Sugar

8 servings

5 to 6 baby carrots per person
1 quart boiling water plus 1
    tablespoon salt
1 tablespoon butter

1 tablespoon oil
2 tablespoons chopped dill
4 tablespoons brown sugar

1.   Wash and scrape carrots. Ideally, they should be 2½ to 3 inches long and about ½ inch in diameter.

2.   Plunge carrots into boiling water, boil 5 to 6 minutes, discard water, cover the pot, and keep the carrots warm.

3.   Melt butter and oil in a heavy skillet; add the carrots and half the dill. After turning the carrots so they are coated with butter, sprinkle on brown sugar. When the sugar starts to melt, gently shake the pan back and forth or turn carrots with a spatula until they are evenly coated.

4.   Just before serving, sprinkle the rest of the dill over the carrots.

CHEF'S SECRET: The best way to scrape carrots is with a non-metallic scrubbing pad which takes off all the dirt but leaves on some of the skin. Dill weed is very delicate and it loses much of its fragrance if it is cut with a knife. Always snip it with a good pair of scissors. Try adding some lemon zest and a few drops of lemon juice to the carrots. This will give them a new "life" and a new taste.

Potato Croquettes

8 servings

1 pound potatoes, cooked and
    peeled 1 day ahead
3 eggs
1 tablespoon soft butter
1 cup flour

salt and pepper to taste
flour for dusting
24 toothpicks
shortening for frying
24 parsley sprigs

1.   Grate the potatoes or mash them until they are coarse but even. Do not overmash or grate them too fine.

2.   Separate the eggs. In a bowl, mix 2 egg yolks and 1 egg white with the soft butter. Add 1 to 2 tablespoons flour and salt and pepper to taste.

3.   Place the potatoes on a dusted pastry board. Make a well in the middle and pour in the egg-butter mixture.

4.   Sprinkle some of the remaining flour over the potatoes, the remainder into the well. With your finger tips, mix the potatoes and the flour from the rim of the well toward the middle quickly, until all the moisture is absorbed and the mixture is an even consistency. If it is too soft, add a little more flour, but not too much.

5.   Spread the mixture out into a rectangle. Cover with a wet cloth and let stand for about 15 minutes. Then divide the mixture into 24 even portions.

6.   Beat the remaining egg yolk with the 2 egg whites until the mixture is frothy. Run the mixture through a fine sieve into a shallow bowl. Place some dusting flour in another shallow bowl.

7.   Moisten your palms with a wet towel, but be careful they are not too wet. From each portion of dough, form carrot shapes between your palms. Insert a round toothpick in the thick end of each croquette.

8.   Holding the toothpick, dip each croquette into the egg mixture; then roll in the flour. Place on absorbent paper on a tray. When all the croquettes are made, place in the freezer for at least 1 hour.

9.   Half an hour before serving, heat enougn shortening in a large frying pan to cover about one-third of the croquettes at a time. Once the shortening reaches the smoking point, start to add the croquettes. Hold them by the toothpicks and add, one by one. Keep turning gently with a metal spatula until they are golden brown. Remove to an absorbent paper towel.

10.   Just before arranging on a serving platter, remove the toothpick from each "carrot" and replace it with a parsley sprig.

CHEF'S SECRET: This is probably one of the most elegant ways to serve potatoes, especially with dishes that have a good deal of sauce or gravy. It is a traditional accompaniment of venison in fine Continental restaurants.

Egg yolk and butter will make the croquettes tender, and egg white will help to firm them up.

Never "drop" anything into a frying pan. Always submerge gently to avoid grease burns and fires. The toothpicks are a great help in submerging the croquettes one by one.

If you wish, instead of making "carrots" you can make 16 "pears" from the same amount of potatoes. For each pear, use two cloves. Insert one in the thick, floured end with the blossom end of the clove out, and stick the other in the opposite end with the flower in the croquette and the stem standing out. You do not need enough shortening to completely submerge the pears. A pear is nice if one side is darker than the other, but keep turning the pears gently in the hot shortening.

Sometimes, depending on what the croquettes are to be served with, you may wish to add spices to the dough, such as cinnamon, nutmeg, mace, or cloves.

Creamed Turnips with Carrots

8 servings

4 cups sliced turnips	1 tablespoon cornstarch
4 quarts water	¼ teaspoon pepper
2 teaspoons salt	2 tablespoons parsley
3 cups sliced carrots	1 tablespoon sugar
4 tablespoons butter or oil	juice of ½ lemon
2 cups milk	¼ teaspoon sage (optional)
2 tablespoons flour	

1.   Slice turnips approximately ⅛-inch thick. If the turnip is large, first split it in half, then slice. Combine 2 quarts water and 1 teaspoon salt in a pot, add turnips, cover, and bring slowly to a boil. As soon as it starts to boil, remove from heat and keep under cover for 10 minutes. Discard water. Keep warm.

2.   Repeat the same procedure with the sliced carrots.

3.   In a saucepan, heat the butter or oil. Combine milk, flour, cornstarch, ½ teaspoon salt, and pepper. When butter is melted, stir milk mixture into the hot butter with a wire whip, adding it in small amounts and stirring constantly. As soon as the mixture in the saucepan stops boiling, stop adding and keep stirring until it boils again. Then add more milk mixture and stir. When all the milk mixture is in the pan, adjust heat to low, stir for another

minute, then add the turnips, carrots, parsley, sugar, lemon juice, and sage. Gently mix and keep under cover over very low heat for about 30 minutes. Adjust seasoning if necessary by adding a little salt, and serve.

CHEF'S SECRET: With today's butter and starches, and with good heavy aluminum kitchenware or similar utensils available, this is the fastest and best way to make a white sauce. In most cookbooks you will find the old method—combining the shortening with the flour, heating it through, and then adding the milk. This used to be as important as the basic black dress, but today, when most homemakers prefer basic blue jeans, I feel that my revolutionary method is more appropriate.

Cooking the turnips and carrots in separate pots makes more work for the dishwasher, but both vegetables will retain their own identity, and the dish will taste much better.

Savoy Cabbage

8 servings

3 pounds savoy cabbage
(approximately 2 heads)
1 pound potatoes
1 tablespoon salt
1 teaspoon bruised caraway
seeds
4 tablespoons shortening
1 tablespoon grated or finely
minced onion

2 tablespoons flour
1 tablespoon cornstarch
1 cup milk
4 tablespoons lard
4 tablespoons flour
1 teaspoon dry marjoram
½ teaspoon sugar
¼ teaspoon black pepper

1. Break off and discard wilted outside leaves from the cabbage. Wash thoroughly; take off about ⅓ of the leaves. Rinse each leaf and cut into ½-inch strips. Cut out the core and split the head into 8 wedges. Place wedges and strips of leaves in a large pot. Cover with water and set to boil over medium heat, covered.

2. Peel potatoes, wash, and cut into cubes 1 to 1½ inches.

3. When the water with the cabbage comes to a boil, immediately discard and replace with fresh cold water. Add potatoes, salt, and caraway seed, and set to boil again. After it comes to a boil, simmer 45 minutes, then pour off and discard half the liquid.

4.   In a small saucepan, heat the shortening with onions over medium heat, stirring. Mix flour, cornstarch, and milk. When the onions start to turn yellowish brown, stir in the milk mixture with a wire whip and, as soon as it comes to a boil, add to it one cup of the cooking liquid. Stir until smooth and pour it into the cabbage pot. In the same saucepan you used to cook the onions, heat 4 tablespoons lard and stir into it 4 tablespoons flour. Stir until the mixture foams and then turns brown. Ladle into it some liquid from the cabbage, and after stirring it smooth, pour into the pot. Add remaining ingredients, bring to a boil and simmer for 15 minutes over low heat. Serve with sour cream or just as it is, sprinkled with paprika for color or with freshly chopped parsley.

CHEF'S SECRET: Savoy cabbage is a neglected member of the cabbage family, though it is versatile and very tasty. Good savoy cabbage is pale gray-green on the outside and lemon yellow on the inside. The head is firm and the core is not too large.

Pouring off the first water helps to remove the characteristic odor present in almost every member of the cabbage family.

If you like this dish thicker, ladle out some of the cooking liquid before adding the sauce.

Sugar-Loaf Cabbage

8 servings

1 head firm white cabbage, approximately 2 to 2½ pounds
2 teaspoons salt
¼ teaspoon pepper
2 tablespoons cornstarch
6-ounce can tomato paste
2 cups tomato juice

¼ cup sugar (or more, depending on sweetness of tomato paste)
2 tablespoons wine vinegar
1 tablespoon chopped fresh dill or dried dill weed (or more, depending on taste)

1.   Cut the cabbage into strips about ¼ by 1 inch. Place it in a large pot, add salt and pepper and water to cover. Cover and cook over medium heat until tender, approximately 30 minutes. Drain in a colander, reserving one cup of cooking liquid and discarding the rest.

2.   Cool the one cup cooking liquid, dissolve the cornstarch in it, and then add tomato paste, tomato juice, sugar, vinegar, and dill. Bring this mixture to a boil in the pot in which the cabbage was cooked, stirring constantly, then add the cabbage. Cover and remove from heat. Let stand in a warm place for 25 to 30 minutes before serving.

CHEF'S SECRET: Don't forget to mix cornstarch thoroughly with the cold liquid *before* adding the tomato paste.

Sugar-loaf cabbage is firmer, tastier, and sweeter than the regular white cabbage—but if you cannot get it, use the regular instead. The same dish is very good when made from large (8 to 10 inch) firm zucchini, peeled, seeded, and cut into (or grated into) matchstick-sized pieces.

If you have a small apartment with not much ventilation in the kitchen, first pour boiling water on the raw cabbage, cover, let stand for 10 minutes, then drain, rinse, and cook in fresh water to cover with the salt and pepper.

Creamed Sorrel

8 servings

2 pounds sorrel (sour grass)	1 tablespoon sugar
4 tablespoons butter	½ teaspoon salt
1 cup sour cream	¼ teaspoon ground white
1 egg	pepper

1.   Pick over sorrel and discard stems. Wash and drain.
2.   Cook with butter but with no liquid added in a covered saucepan on low heat, about 20 minutes.
3.   Cool and chop fine with a French knife. Return to saucepan. Mix sour cream and egg, add sugar, salt, and white pepper. Gently fold into the chopped sorrel. Heat and serve.

CHEF'S SECRET: This dish is what the French use to cover their poached turbot. Its pungent taste really covers everything. It is also an excellent dish with fried or poached eggs, a great accompaniment to boiled meats or fried ham, or a wonderful filling for pancakes or crêpes sprinkled with grated cheese and baked.

Sometimes, instead of sour cream, the dish is prepared with sweet cream and lemon juice. Or, instead of using any cream, you can make a light roux from 2 tablespoons shortening and 2 tablespoons flour heated through until it is a pale yellow. Dilute with 1 cup chicken stock or water, off the heat, stirring constantly. Fold it into the sorrel and simmer for a few minutes.

Beanburgers

8 burgers

¼ cup oil
1 cup finely minced onions
1 teaspoon salt
¼ teaspoon freshly ground
   black pepper
4 slices white bread, crust
   removed

½ cup water
2 16-ounce cans red kidney
   beans
2 tablespoons catsup (optional)
2 cups bread crumbs
2 eggs

1.   Heat ¼ cup oil in a skillet until very hot. Add onions and sprinkle with salt and pepper. Sauté until the onions turn limp and start to brown. Let them cool off the fire for a few minutes.

2.   Tear bread and put in a bowl. Pour water on the bread and add the red kidney beans, well rinsed, dried, and coarsely chopped on a cutting board with a French knife.

3.   Add catsup, about 1 cup of the bread crumbs, and the onions. Add eggs and work into a loose mixture with wet hands. It should be mixed through but not pressed together. Let it stand for at least 30 minutes or longer.

4.   Spread ½ cup bread crumbs on a cutting board, making a surface approximately 10 by 16 inches. Spread the mixture evenly over the bread crumbs. Divide the 10-inch side in half so that you have two 5-inch strips each 16 inches long. Divide the mixture into 4 sections along the 16-inch length. You now have eight portions, 4 by 5 inches each.

5.   Sprinkle the last ½ cup bread crumbs on top, and form the portions into patties resembling hamburgers. Place the patties on a foil-covered cookie sheet and broil 6 to 8 inches from the source of heat for 3 to 4 minutes a side. Serve on toasted, buttered buns with catsup, onion rings, and pickles.

CHEF'S SECRET: No tools will be as good for mixing bean-burgers as your hands. Wash thoroughly, dry and dip them into ice water. Spread your fingers on both hands and gently go along the inside surface of the bowl under the mixture, until your fingers meet at the bottom. Loosely lift the bottom part, gently shaking your hands as you would toss a salad, turning the bowl as you do. This will assure a good texture. If you wish, you can substitute soybean or protein meat substitutes for part of the beans.

Corned Bean Hash

8 servings

16-ounce can white beans
16-ounce can red kidney beans
2 cups potatoes, cut into ¼-inch
 cubes
2 cups water
4 tablespoons Bac★Os,
 crumbled
6 tablespoons shortening
1 cup finely minced onion

4 tablespoons catsup
1 vegetable-flavored soup cube
 dissolved in ½ cup water
¼ teaspoon black pepper
1 cup bread crumbs mixed with
 2 tablespoons Bac★Os
 crushed to resemble corn
 meal
8 poached eggs

1. Rinse beans, leave them in the cans, fill cans with cold water, and let stand at room temperature.
2. Peel and cut potatoes into cubes. Bring to a boil 2 cups water. Add potatoes, stir, return to a boil, and remove immediately from heat. Pour off water, place the pot back over the heat, and shake it until the potatoes dry. Sprinkle the crumbled Bac★Os on the potatoes and let them cool.
3. Meanwhile, heat 4 tablespoons of the shortening and sauté onions until golden brown. Add onions to potato mixture and blend.
4. Drain beans and shake dry. Cut them coarsely with a French knife; then mix with potato mixture. Add catsup, dissolved soup cube, and pepper. Sprinkle bread crumbs on the mixture and gently mix by hand to form 8 patties.
5. Heat remaining shortening in a skillet. Ease in 4 patties, one at a time, and fry over high heat for 3 to 4 minutes; turn,

lower the heat, and fry for another 6 to 8 minutes. Keep patties warm and repeat with remaining patties. Remove to a serving platter. Place a poached egg on each patty and serve at once.

CHEF'S SECRET: The only thing that can go wrong with this recipe is the handling—chop the beans so that you don't have large pieces on the one hand or mush on the other. And form the patties with as little handling as possible.

White Bean Croquettes

8 servings

4 slices bread, with the crust
2 eggs
½ cup water
1 16-ounce can white beans
1 teaspoon salt
¼ teaspoon white pepper
¼ teaspoon celery salt
1 vegetable soup cube (optional)

2 tablespoons grated onions
2 tablespoons grated carrots
¼ cup oil
2 cups fine bread crumbs
2 cups oil and 1 cup other shortening, for frying

1.　Tear bread into pieces. Beat eggs with water and pour over bread. Rinse and add drained white beans, salt, white pepper, celery salt, and, if you wish, 1 vegetable-flavored soup cube, either diluted with the eggs or crushed and sprinkled.

2.　Heat onions and carrots in ¼ cup oil until they turn into a yellow liquid with small speckles of the vegetables in it. Pour this over the bread mixture and add about ½ cup of the bread crumbs.

3.　With wet hands, mix the ingredients, but do not press, into a smooth paste. Divide into 16 equal portions, roll each one in bread crumbs, and shape into cones.

4.　Heat the 2 cups oil and 1 cup other shortening in a pan 5 to 6 inches in diameter and at least 3 inches deep, to 340° F. or until a small piece of bread pressed between your fingers and dropped into the shortening sinks almost to the bottom and then shoots to the top with a small ring of bubbles around it.

5.　Ease 5 to 6 croquettes into the shortening at 10-second intervals and fry them to a golden color. If the croquettes do not submerge, baste them with a long-handled spoon. Or after a couple minutes of frying place the croquettes gently on their side in the shortening.

6.   Remove croquettes to absorbent paper, let the shortening heat again, and repeat the process until all croquettes are done. Serve with mushroom sauce, sorrel sauce, or any other sauce of your choice, or with creamed vegetables instead of meat.

CHEF'S SECRET: For meat eaters, this is a great side dish with ragout of venison or another stew.

If you wish, you can form the croquettes into pear shapes. Press a whole clove into the middle of the bottom and a piece of twig into the top for a stem. Or form small balls and serve them with roast pork or roast duck.

If you want 16 pieces all the same size, pour the mixture from the bowl into a round pie pan and cut into 16 slices as you would cut a pie. Chill after cutting, and then form a cone from each slice.

Hungarian Green Beans

8 servings

6 cups fresh green beans cut or
  broken into 1-inch pieces
⅓ cup vinegar
2 teaspoons salt
4 slices bacon cut into ½-inch
  squares
2 tablespoons butter
1 small clove garlic
1 teaspoon salt

2 tablespoons sugar
3 tablespoons flour
1 tablespoon cornstarch
2½ cups buttermilk
½ cup water
2 tablespoons fresh parsley,
  chopped
1 cup sour cream

1.   Wash beans and drain. Pour into a saucepan ⅓ cup of vinegar, salt, and water to cover the bottom of the pan 1 inch high. Add beans. Cover, bring to a quick boil over high heat, then adjust to low. Cook 20 to 25 minutes, or until beans are tender. Shake the pot occasionally, holding the lid tight.

2.   Fry the bacon with the butter until the bacon squares turn golden brown and shrivel up. Remove, press out excess fat, and place on absorbent paper for later use. Reserve the bacon fat.

3.   In a saucepan, mash the garlic to a pulp with the salt, add sugar and the fat rendered from the bacon, and heat through.

4.   With a wire whip, mix flour and cornstarch with 1½ cups buttermilk and the water. Increase the heat under the saucepan and, in a slow stream, pour the buttermilk mixture into the hot fat, stirring constantly. When it comes to a boil, remove from heat, add to the green beans, and mix. Add half the parsley, remove from heat, and leave the beans covered in the pot.

5.   Mix remaining parsley, sour cream, and remaining buttermilk, place it in a serving dish, and slowly add the beans, stirring constantly. Sprinkle top with parsley and bacon chips Serve with pork or veal.

CHEF'S SECRET: Cooking the beans this way will keep them very crisp and will reduce the cooking time.

If you want to make this dish in the winter from canned beans, start it by frying the bacon together with the butter and mix the salt, garlic pulp, and sugar into it. Then proceed. Add the rinsed canned beans at the end and heat through for only 2 to 3 minutes. It is surprising how fresh the canned beans will taste.

Green Beans with Tomatoes

8 servings

4 tablespoons butter	2 cups tomato juice
2 tablespoons shortening	1 tablespoon sugar
1 cup sliced onions	1 teaspoon salt
1 cup tomatoes cut into chunks	6 cups green beans
1 cup chopped bell peppers	1 tablespoon salt

1.   In a large saucepan, heat butter and shortening, add onions, and stir until edges begin to brown. Add tomatoes, bell peppers, tomato juice, sugar, and 1 teaspoon salt. Lower heat to simmer, and cover.

2.   While the tomato-vegetable mixture simmers, place green beans and 1 tablespoon salt in another saucepan, cover with hot water, and bring to a rapid boil over high heat. Remove cover; boil for 20 minutes. Discard cooking water and add the steaming hot beans to the simmering tomato mixture. Let simmer for another 15 to 20 minutes, then serve.

CHEF'S SECRET: In Europe this is a favorite way to cook green beans, zucchini, summer squash, eggplant, or kohlrabi. It can be made a day or even two days ahead, then chilled and heated at the last minute. The large amount of tomato makes the dish safe for summer.

If you wish, you can add an herb of your choice, and if you like spicy hotness, add a few slices of hot green pepper.

This dish is often served with hot dogs, frankfurters, or other sausages steamed right in the beans.

Yellow Wax Beans with Dill

8 servings

2 tablespoons chopped onion
4 tablespoons shortening
6 tablespoons fresh parsley, chopped
6 cups young wax beans broken into pieces
2 tablespoons flour
2 tablespoons cornstarch

1 teaspoon Chef's Salt (see index)
2 cups chicken stock
1 cup light cream or half-and-half
2 to 3 tablespoons wine vinegar or tarragon vinegar
¼ cup fresh dill weed

1. In a saucepan over high heat, sauté the onions with the shortening. Add 2 tablespoons parsley and washed, wet wax beans. Cover, adjust heat to medium, and cook, stirring occasionally, for 15 minutes. If the water evaporates, add a few tablespoons, but not more.

2. In a bowl, mix flour, cornstarch, Chef's Salt, chicken stock, and light cream. Blend smooth with a wire whip and slowly pour over the beans, stirring with a wooden spoon. Bring to a boil and adjust heat immediately to simmer. Add 4 tablespoons parsley, vinegar, and fresh dill. Mix, cover, let simmer for 5 more minutes, and serve.

CHEF'S SECRET: Wax beans have a distinctive flavor. The blandness of the other ingredients in this dish lets the true flavor of the wax beans come through wonderfully.

If you wish, you can add a dab of sour cream to the dish before serving. Or if you want the dish to taste very festive, stir an egg yolk together with 3 to 4 tablespoons sour cream, put it into the serving dish, then slowly add the beans, mixing lightly.

Mock Chops

8 servings

2 large eggplants, approximately 6 to 7 inches long and 3 to
3½ inches in diameter
4 tablespoons salt
1 cup flour
2 eggs beaten with 2
tablespoons water
2 cups sifted bread crumbs
2 cups oil, for frying

Mushroom sauce:

2 tablespoons butter
1 tablespoon finely minced onion
1 tablespoon chopped parsley
1 cup sliced mushrooms
2 tablespoons flour
1 tablespoon cornstarch
1 teaspoon salt
¼ teaspoon mushroom powder
1 cup milk
½ cup sour cream
½ cup buttermilk

1.   Cut each eggplant, with skin on, into 8 diagonal slices. Cut
each slice into a shape resembling a lamb chop (see illustration).
Salt both sides and let the chops stand for an hour, turning after

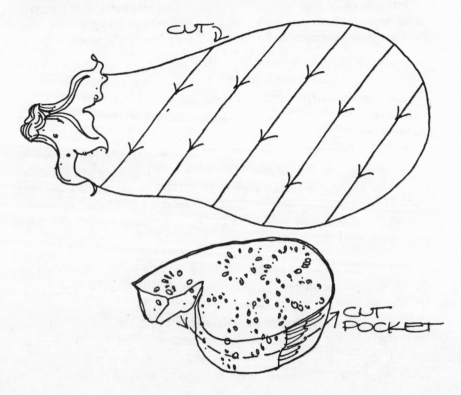

30 minutes so that the salt penetrates the slices. After an hour, rinse in cold running water, then lay the slices in ice water for about 30 minutes. Remove and wipe dry with a kitchen towel. Dip into flour, shake off excess; dip into egg wash, then into bread crumbs.

2.   Heat the oil to about 320° F. and fry the mock chops, 3 or 4 at a time, depending on the size of the skillet or pot you use. Remove to absorbent paper and keep warm.

3.   In a saucepan, heat butter, onions, and parsley over medium heat. When onions turn limp and translucent, add mushrooms and increase the heat. With a spatula, turn mushrooms for a minute or so in order to coat them with the onion-parsley mixture.

4.   Mix the 2 tablespoons flour, the cornstarch, salt, and mushroom powder together. Stir into milk and pour over mushrooms, stirring constantly. When sauce comes to a boil, lower the heat and simmer for about 10 minutes. Let stand, covered, for at least another 10 minutes. Ladle some of the hot sauce into a mixture of the sour cream and buttermilk, then pour the mixture into the hot sauce. Arrange mock chops on a serving platter. Cover with some of the sauce and serve the rest in a sauceboat.

CHEF'S SECRET: You can also serve the mock chops without the mushroom sauce and with a creamed vegetable or salad instead.

Eggplant Provençale

8 servings

4 tablespoons oil
8 small eggplants or baby eggplants, approximately 4
   inches long and 1 to 2 inches
   in diameter
2 small firm tomatoes
2 bell peppers

2 medium onions,
   approximately the size of a
   large egg
1 teaspoon salt
½ teaspoon black pepper
1 teaspoon rosemary
1 teaspoon thyme
½ cup soft butter

1.   Preheat oven to 375° F. Brush a large roasting pan with oil. On each eggplant make 6 slashes about ⅔ of the way into the

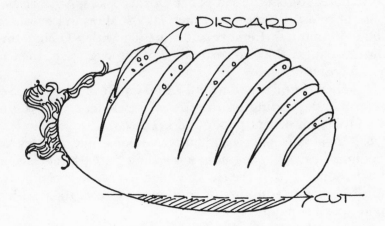

eggplant. Cut from each a sliver as shown in the illustration. Discard slivers. Cut the bottom, opposite the slashes, flat. Place eggplants in the roasting pan. Cut the tomatoes into 16 thin wedges. Cut from the bell peppers 16 small, wedge-shaped pieces. Cut the onions into 16 wedges.

2. Insert in each eggplant 1 slice of tomato, then a slice of green pepper, then onion. Repeat until you have 6 pieces of vegetable in each small eggplant.

3. Mix salt, pepper, rosemary, and thyme. Add to butter and, with a teaspoon, cream the butter and spices together. Divide half the mixture among the 8 eggplants, putting a little bit on top of each in a narrow strip, so that as they cook the butter will melt down on the vegetables.

4. Bake for 30 minutes. Baste eggplants with 1½ to 2 cups warm water. Bake another 30 minutes. Increase the heat to 400° F. Let the top of the vegetables brown. Remove. Put on a serving platter and distribute the second half of the butter-spice mixture on the tops of the eggplants. Serve immediately with fish.

CHEF'S SECRET: In most supermarkets almost year round you can purchase these small baby eggplants. Some are a little larger, some a little smaller, but this is their average size.

If you have an herb garden, or if you can get a few branches or twigs of any of the herbs used in this recipe, place on each serving one little branch of the herb dried, dipped in a little cognac, and ignited.

For a variation you can, after placing the vegetables in the eggplant, cover each one with a slice of country bacon or ranch-style bacon. In this case sprinkle the herb mixture over the vegetables and omit the butter.

Curried Cucumbers

8 servings

4 large cucumbers, approximately 6 to 7 inches long and 2 to 2½ inches in diameter
2 tablespoons salt
2 quarts water
2 tablespoons butter
2 tablespoons oil
1 cup peeled and cubed apple

½ cup finely chopped onion
2 teaspoons curry powder, or more to taste
½ cup water
1 ripe banana
½ teaspoon salt
¼ teaspoon freshly ground black pepper
½ teaspoon sugar
½ cup cream (optional)

1.   Split unpeeled cucumbers in two lengthwise. Scoop out and discard the soft inside and seeds. Peel halves and cut lengthwise into finger-thick slices. Crosscut slices into 1½ to 2-inch diagonal pieces. Sprinkle with salt, let stand for an hour; then rinse with cold water, pat dry, and set aside.

2.   Bring water to a boil, add cucumbers, and return to a boil over high heat. Immediately remove from heat, discard the water, and let the cucumbers stand, covered.

3.   In a saucepan, heat the butter with the oil. Add apples and onions, and sauté under cover, without any liquid, over low heat for 15 minutes. Add curry powder and ½ cup water, and cook covered for another 10 minutes.

4.   In a large bowl, mash the banana with a fork and add with salt, pepper, and sugar to the simmering curry sauce. Remove from heat, add cucumbers to the sauce, and let stand for about 15 minutes. If you wish, add cream and stir in before serving.

CHEF'S SECRET: If you first scoop out the soft part of the cucumber and then peel it, you will find it much easier.

If you have the time, the dish looks very nice if instead of the diagonal cuts you "olive" the cucumbers. To olive a vegetable (potato, carrot, turnip, etc.) you cut pieces approximately 2 by ¾ by ¾ inches, then with a sharp paring knife round the edges so that the piece looks like a large olive.

Squash in Dill Sauce

8 servings

4 pounds (approximately)
    summer squash or large,
    mature zucchini, or 2 pounds
    of each
4 teaspoons salt
½ cup vinegar
2 cups water
2 tablespoons butter

2 tablespoons lard
1 teaspoon sugar
1 cup finely chopped fresh dill
1 teaspoon Hungarian paprika
4 tablespoons flour
½ cup chicken stock or water
1 cup sour cream mixed with 1
    cup buttermilk or plain milk

1.   Peel and core summer squash, discarding soft inside and seeds. Cut crosswise into approximately 3-inch segments. Cut the segments lengthwise into ¼-inch julienne, or use a grater, grating the squash through the large hole, slowly, and being sure to press the squash at a right angle.

2.   Mix the salt, vinegar, and 2 cups water, pour over the grated or cut squash, and let stand for 1 hour.

3.   Fold a wet kitchen towel double. Take as much of the grated squash as you can hold in two hands, place it in the middle of the wet towel, gather the corners, hold them in one hand, and keep turning the towel with your other hand to squeeze out as much of the liquid as possible from the squash. Repeat until all squash is squeezed. Quickly wash squash in cold water; press out the water the same way until the squash is dry.

4.   In a pot, heat butter and lard with sugar, ½ cup of the dill, and the paprika. As soon as they heat through (about 2 to 3 minutes), add the squash and keep stirring with a wooden spoon over high heat until all squash is in the pot. Cover and adjust heat to lowest possible. Simmer squash until tender, about 20 to 25 minutes. Increase heat to medium, remove lid and through a sieve shake the flour into the squash, stirring constantly until all the squash is coated. Pour chicken stock or water slowly into the squash and continue stirring.

5. Just before serving, mix some of the cooked squash into the sour cream-buttermilk mixture, adding it spoon by spoon to prevent the sour cream from curdling. Then add the whole mixture to the squash, remove from heat, cover, and let stand about 10 minutes. Transfer to a serving dish and sprinkle the top with the remaining ½ cup of chopped fresh dill.

CHEF'S SECRET: In specialty stores you can purchase a wooden grater designed for cutting squash into julienne. Besides gourmet shops, German, Austrian, Hungarian, and Swiss grocers carry this gadget. So do Japanese and other Far Eastern stores. Of course, this tool can be used for many other things besides squash. If you cannot get it in any stores near you, you can order it from Mail Order Dept., Hungarian Enterprises, 11802 Buckeye Road, Cleveland, Ohio 44120.

If you have a jar of dill pickles, Kosher pickles, or Polish pickles in the refrigerator, add ½ cup of the pickling liquid together with the chicken stock or water. It will give an excellent flavor.

If no fresh dill is available, replace each ½ cup dill with one tablespoon dry dill weed steeped in water mixed with vinegar in equal parts, or in dill pickle juice and water mixed in equal parts, using approximately 2 tablespoons each—a total of 4 tablespoons to steep one tablespoon of the dried dill weed.

Zucchini Polonaise

4 servings

1 pound zucchini	2 cups sour cream
2 quarts boiling water	1 hard-boiled egg, riced
2 teaspoons salt	through a sieve
1 cup bread crumbs	1 tablespoon finely chopped
2 tablespoons butter	fresh green parsley
2 tablespoons oil	

1. Wash zucchini; split each into six spears after cutting off stem end. Boil the spears for 5 minutes in 2 quarts vigorously boiling water with salt added. Cool immediately under running cold water, and drain. Preheat oven to 350° F.

2.   Sauté bread crumbs in butter and oil until golden brown. Distribute 2 tablespoons sour cream in the bottom of a 2-quart ovenproof glass dish. Arrange half the zucchini neatly over the sour cream; then cover with more sour cream. Repeat and cover with sour cream again, using a total of 1 cup. Distribute bread crumbs evenly over the top of the casserole and bake for 15 minutes. Add the rest of the sour cream, spreading it around the edges 1½ to 2 inches, so that the middle of the bread-crumb crust is not covered. Bake another 10 minutes. Remove. Sprinkle the riced egg, mixed with the chopped parsley, over the sour cream border. Serve at once.

CHEF'S SECRET: This dish was originally made with asparagus, but the season for asparagus is short and the price is usually much higher than zucchini. Try it with zucchini and you will be surprised how close you can get to the asparagus taste. If you wish to make it with asparagus, pre-boil the asparagus 2 to 3 minutes longer than the zucchini. For a main-course dish, add 8 to 12 ounces ground beef between the two layers of zucchini.

7

Eggs, Cheese, Rice & Pasta

The closest relatives in this chapter are the first and the last—eggs and pasta. We can hardly imagine good pasta without some form of eggs in it, just as many egg dishes have as an ingredient some flour. Napkin Dumplings are a good example. Because, as a rule, they are served with heavy meat dishes, in most people's minds they too are heavy and rich. Not so. They are actually very light, and not as fattening as you might think. They serve as a great vehicle to carry sauces, gravies, and juices from plate to mouth.

Certain kinds of cheeses make wonderful ingredients in many dishes, but I really prefer cheeses on their own. The United States has always produced tremendous quantities, but until the last twenty or thirty years, the quality was average, without exciting taste sensations, textures, or aromas. This state of affairs has changed dramatically, and today many small American cheese manufacturing companies can hold their own with the greatest of France, Switzerland, and Holland. I have tasted several U.S.-manufactured Brie and Camembert cheeses and some American Blue and Swiss, which not only equal cheeses from other countries but in many cases surpass them.

Some American cheeses are beginning to acquire reputations in other parts of the world, and cheese experts and connoisseurs are urging traders to supply foreign markets. Beer Cheese, Wisconsin Brick, California Monterey Jack, Palatel from Wisconsin, and some of the fine cheeses from DeKalb, Illinois, are representing the American cheese industry in European capitals. Still, my personal preference among the thousand (if not more) kinds I have devoured throughout my cheese-loving life, is Stilton. But whatever *your* favorite is, I'm sure you'll find some delectable cheese recipes in this chapter.

Hungarian-Style Scrambled Eggs

4 servings

8-ounce slab bacon, with rind
  on
¼ cup thinly sliced onions
¼ cup sliced green peppers
8 eggs
8 tablespoons milk or half-and-
  half

½ teaspoon salt
¼ teaspoon freshly ground
  black pepper
1 tablespoon sweet Hungarian
  paprika

1. With a very sharp knife, cut the bacon slab into 4 equal pieces and prepare slices as shown in the illustration.

2. Place bacon in a cold skillet, put over medium heat, and cook bacon pieces on both sides, turning occasionally, until they turn into "crowns," as shown in the illustration. Set the crowns aside and keep warm.

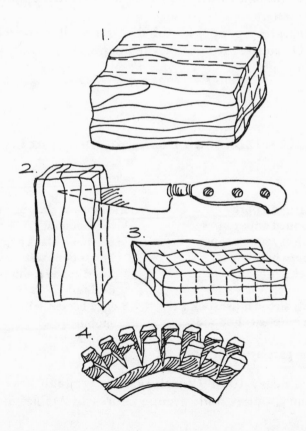

3. Add sliced onions and green peppers to rendered bacon fat in same skillet. Sauté for 5 minutes, increase heat to very high, and immediately pour in eggs, beaten with milk, salt, and pepper. The edges will start to cook at once. Move the cooked egg from the edges with the circular motion of a large cooking spoon toward the middle of the pan and scrape the bottom, letting the soft egg from the middle move toward the outside. As soon as all the egg starts to firm up, scrape to the middle and immediately remove skillet from heat. Keep stirring for another minute and remove soft, but not runny, eggs to a serving platter.

4. Sprinkle top with paprika, arrange bacon crowns, and serve at once with rye toast, generously buttered.

CHEF'S SECRET: If the bacon is too streaky with lean meat and does not render ¼ to ⅓ cup of fat, add some butter or oil. This dish is good only if it is prepared in plenty of hot shortening.

If you wish, you can add half a pound of smoked Hungarian sausage to the bacon drippings together with the onions and green peppers.

The ideal green pepper for this dish is the yellow sweet banana pepper. Of course, if you like hot peppers, you can use hot banana peppers.

Oriental Omelet with Pork, Shrimp, and Oysters

8 servings

½ pound ground pork
¾ cup chopped onion
¼ teaspoon cayenne pepper
2 tablespoons oil
½ cup stock (chicken, veal, or beef)
1 cup thinly sliced mushrooms
½ cup ready-to-eat chopped shrimp
¼ teaspoon parsley

2 teaspoons chopped mint
¼ teaspoon sage
¼ teaspoon black pepper
1½ teaspoons salt
2 dozen oysters, shucked and drained
8 eggs beaten with 4 table- spoons water
1 cup oil

1. In a heavy 10 or 12-inch skillet, over high heat, brown ground pork, onion, and cayenne pepper in 2 tablespoons oil.

Keep breaking up the pork into small lumps while cooking. When brown on all sides, reduce heat to medium, add stock, stir, cover, and simmer for 20 minutes.

2.   Add mushrooms, shrimp, and seasonings. Cook, stirring, for 5 minutes. Add oysters. Cook for 3 minutes, stirring occasionally. Remove from heat and cool.

3.   When lukewarm, add the mixture to the eggs and water, which have been beaten to a frothy light yellow.

4.   In the same skillet, heat 3 to 4 tablespoons from the cup of oil, and pour one ladle of the egg mixture into it. As it starts to cook, quickly fold all edges toward the top so that you will have a round omelet approximately 4 inches in diameter. Quickly turn over, fry for another minute, and remove to a serving platter. Repeat seven more times, adding more oil if necessary. Serve with soy sauce and plenty of hot cooked rice.

CHEF'S SECRET: When you have mastered the speed needed for good results, this dish will be excellent and will turn into a family favorite. It is important that as soon as the eggs start to set you fold them toward the top. Also be sure you keep the round shape.

Baked Fish and Eggs

8 servings

8 fish fillets (flounder, gray sole, lemon sole, etc.)
1 tablespoon Chef's Salt (see index)
8 slices precooked thin bacon

8 large eggs
2 tablespoons soft butter
8 toasted English muffins
8 sprigs parsley

1.   Preheat oven to 350° F. Sprinkle the fish fillets with Chef's Salt, roll them up, and wrap each roll with a slice of bacon. Secure with a round toothpick and place in an 8-cup muffin tin. Bake 15 minutes.

2.   Meanwhile, brush a second 8-cup muffin tin with butter and gently break a whole egg into each muffin cup (break the eggs first, one by one, into a saucer). Sprinkle with a little salt, if you wish, place in the oven 5 minutes after you start to bake the fish, and bake for about 10 minutes.

3.   Meanwhile, toast and butter the muffin halves. Place one fish fillet rolled in bacon on one half, and a baked egg on the second half. Serve at once.

CHEF'S SECRET: The muffin tins for baking the fish don't have to be buttered because the precooked bacon will give you e-nough shortening to prevent the fish from sticking. Instead of butter to brush the muffin tins in which you bake the eggs, you can use some of the fat rendered from the bacon when it was prefried. If you wish, 2 or 3 minutes before removing the eggs from the oven you can sprinkle some good red paprika on each egg yolk.

Pipérade

8 servings

4 tablespoons oil
4 cups peeled, seeded, and
   chopped tomatoes (1½ to 2
   pounds)
2 cups seeded and chopped red
   bell peppers, or 1 cup
   chopped pimiento
4 cloves garlic
1 teaspoon Chef's Salt (see
   index)

1 tablespoon sugar
8 slices ham, approximately 3
   ounces each (total 1½
   pounds)
8 slices toast
8 eggs
½ cup milk
2 tablespoons oil
3 to 4 tablespoons chopped
   chives or chopped parsley

1.   Heat the oil in a heavy skillet over medium heat.
2.   When oil is smoking hot, add tomatoes and stir with a wooden spoon. Add peppers. Increase the heat a bit and keep stirring as liquid from tomatoes evaporates. After 5 minutes, add 2 cloves garlic mashed to a pulp with Chef's Salt. Sprinkle mixture with sugar. Lower heat and continue to stir until consistency of tomato paste. Set aside in warm place.
3.   Under broiler, about 4 inches from the source of heat, quickly broil ham slices on both sides just enough to heat them through and until they start to get a brown edge.
4.   Rub toast on both sides with cut surface of remaining 2 cloves garlic. Place on each slice of toast a slice of ham and arrange on a large serving platter.

5.   Set tomato mixture over high heat. Beat eggs together with milk and oil and pour into tomato mixture, stirring constantly with a metal spatula for about 1 minute or just until tomatoes and eggs mix and eggs set. Spoon on top of ham and toast. Sprinkle generously with chives or green parsley, and serve at once.

CHEF'S SECRET: If you use pimiento instead of red bell peppers, cook the tomatoes alone in the hot oil and then with the garlic, Chef's Salt, and sugar. Only then add the pimiento, because it is already cooked.

If you wish, you can pan-fry the ham and keep it warm, but it won't be as attractive as with the little scorched edge from the broiler.

Serve extra buttered toast with this dish, especially if you don't use the heavy-crusted country bread they serve in the Pyrenees.

Feta Cheese Mix

2 to 2½ pounds

1 pound feta cheese
8 ounces cream cheese
1 cup butter
1 tablespoon prepared mustard
2 tablespoons Hungarian or
   Spanish paprika

2 teaspoons whole caraway
   seeds
⅓ cup very finely minced
   onions or scallions
⅓ cup beer

1.   In the bowl of an electric mixer, blend ⅓ of the feta cheese, grated or pressed into small crumbs with a fork, ⅓ of the cream cheese, and ⅓ of the butter. Use a paddle or dough hook if you have either.

2.   When this mixture is smooth and blended, add mustard, paprika, caraway seeds, and onions. Beat the mixture for 2 or 3 minutes, then stop, scrape the walls of the bowl, and add the second third of the feta cheese, cream cheese, and butter. Beat again for 5 minutes. Scrape the bowl and add the remaining cheese and butter. Set the speed to low and while mixing, slowly pour in the beer. When all the beer is incorporated, set the speed to high and beat for another 2 or 3 minutes.

3.   Remove and pour into a high mound in the middle of a serving platter. Chill. Sprinkle the top with some additional paprika, if you wish, or with finely chopped parsley, or both. Surround with radish roses and serve with heavy rye bread or toast.

CHEF'S SECRET: This is a pleasant and surprisingly good cheese spread for cocktail parties or as a first course. In Europe it is made either with feta or with a similar cheese such as Brinza or Liptoi—all soft goat or sheep cheeses resembling baker's cheese or smooth cottage cheese. For variation, you can add a 2-inch piece of anchovy paste, or a tablespoon of rinsed, chopped capers, or 2 tablespoons of finely minced Hungarian salami.

Rice Pilaf

8 servings

2 cups long-grain rice
2 tablespoons oil
3 tablespoons butter
1 tablespoon finely minced
   onion

½ teaspoon salt
⅛ teaspoon black pepper
3 tablespoons freshly chopped
   parsley
4 cups boiling water

1.   Preheat oven to 375° F.

2.   Wash rice in a colander. Cover colander with a lid or a plate and shake to dry rice as much as possible. Let it stand for a few minutes and shake again.

3.   Heat oil and 1 tablespoon butter with onion, salt, pepper, and 1 tablespoon parsley in a heavy metal casserole over medium heat. When onions start to turn yellow, add about ⅓ of the rice and stir with a wooden spoon to coat it with the shortening. Repeat twice more until all rice is in the pot. Stir until rice heats through, turns opaque, and starts to crack and pop.

4.   When rice starts to turn yellow, add 4 cups boiling water in small amounts, being careful not to burn your hand with the steam. Keep stirring with the wooden spoon as you add the boiling water. Cover and bake for 45 minutes to 1 hour. Stir once after 30 minutes and again after 45 minutes.

5.   Before serving, fluff the Pilaf with two forks. Add remaining 2 tablespoons butter and let it melt into the rice, then add remaining parsley.

CHEF'S SECRET: As a child, I watched an old Turkish woman make this rice in the home of a classmate in grade school. She used more butter and more oil than this recipe does, and the end result was greasier than this version. Nevertheless, I have always found that this type of rice goes very well with Western-style dishes. It is very different from the Oriental method of cooking rice, though its taste resembles fried rice. The basic recipe given here can be prepared with many variations:

(a) Add to the above ingredients 4 tablespoons red zane corinth (a Mediterranean raisin, tiny and dark, resembling the English red currant).

(b) Add 4 tablespoons chopped, sliced, or slivered almonds, plain or roasted.

(c) Add 4 tablespoons pine nuts or pistachios.

If you don't have a metal casserole or serving dish, fry the rice in a frying pan, add water, and then transfer to a glass or china ovenproof dish.

Dirty Rice

8 servings

1 pound chicken necks and backs
½ pound gizzards
½ pound chicken livers
1½ teaspoons Chef's Salt (see index)
4 teaspoons black pepper
4 tablespoons oil

½ cup finely minced onions
2 to 3 tablespoons tomato paste or ½ cup tomato juice
1 tablespoon Kitchen Bouquet
3 cups rice cooked according to package directions
2 tablespoons fresh green parsley, coarsely chopped

1.   Preheat oven to 350° F. Wash chicken backs and necks in a colander and cut into 1-inch pieces. Wash gizzards and trim inside surface if necessary. Remove the yellowish-gray loose skin. Cut gizzards into quarters. Cut livers into small pieces. Sprinkle Chef's Salt and pepper on all the chicken pieces and let stand in a bowl at room temperature, first mixing by hand so that the spices penetrate every piece.

2.   In a heavy pot with a tightly fitting lid, heat the oil until very hot. Add onions in small amounts, stirring until they brown. Add chicken parts and stir so that they start to brown immediate-

ly. Keep stirring and browning over high heat for at least 10 minutes, stirring every 2 minutes so that they won't stick to the bottom and burn. Add tomato paste or juice, Kitchen Bouquet, and just enough water to cover. Bring to a boil. Add precooked rice. Stir it through until the rice looks dirty. Cover and bake for 45 minutes. The rice should be mushy and moist. Pile it in the middle of a serving dish and sprinkle with parsley. Serve with fried chicken, pork, or fried fish.

CHEF'S SECRET: This dish is a favorite of poor people in Louisiana, but wealthy gourmets like it, too. For a variation, omit the chicken backs and necks, increase the amount of gizzards and liver, and add some raw, peeled, chopped shrimp. Or omit the chicken entirely and replace it with very finely minced pork, increasing the Kitchen Bouquet to 2½ or 3 tablespoons.

Alsatian Noodles

8 servings

4 quarts water
4 tablespoons salt
8 tablespoons corn oil
1½ pounds noodles

6 tablespoons butter or lard
½ teaspoon salt
¼ teaspoon white pepper

1. Set water with salt to boil. When it starts to boil, add 2 tablespoons oil. Let oil coat the top and adjust heat so that water boils gently. Add 1¼ pounds noodles slowly, by handfuls, waiting 10 seconds after each addition. When all noodles are in, stir with a wooden spoon that reaches to bottom of pot. Cover but leave about a ½-inch opening between pot and lid. Stay and watch; within a minute or so the water will start to foam and run over. Remove lid and stir noodles again with wooden spoon. Adjust heat somewhat lower and keep boiling as long as the package instruction indicate. Rinse if it is suggested.

2. In a skillet large enough to accommodate noodles, heat 6 tablespoons butter or lard with 6 tablespoons oil. Crush with a rolling pin remaining ¼ pound noodles (wrapped in a clean kitchen towel) until they resemble crushed cornflakes. Sauté in

hot shortening mixture, stirring constantly until they turn golden brown.

3.   Slowly add boiled noodles and mix gently with 2 forks so as not to break them. Sprinkle salt and white pepper on top. Heat through and serve.

CHEF'S SECRET: We always serve Alsatian noodles with Beef Stroganoff. Guests often ask me what is sprinkled on top of the noodles, and when I tell them "noodles," they are surprised—until I explain how the dish is made. The interesting thing is that the taste of the toasted raw noodles will be so surprising and pleasantly different from the boiled noodles that your guests will think they are some kind of strange nuts or specially treated almonds.

The best noodle for this dish is the ½-inch wide "broad" egg noodle. Of course, you can make it from other types just as well. The important thing is that you use the very same noodles crushed as boiled.

The oil swimming on the top of the boiling water will coat the noodles with a very thin layer of fat molecules as you drop them in. The outside surface will start to cook and firm up while the fat molecules are still adhering to it. As the noodles that have sunk to the bottom of the pot start to heat up, the oil will coat them so that they will not stick to each other; but they won't become greasy either.

Egg "Barley"

8 servings

4 slices finely chopped bacon
4 tablespoons oil or other
    shortening
½ cup very finely minced
    onions
salt and pepper to taste

1 tablespoon Hungarian
    paprika
1 pound egg barley (or farfel or
    similar pasta)
2 cups chicken broth
2 cups water

1.   In a heavy saucepan over medium heat, render bacon in other shortening. When hot, add onions, distribute evenly over

the bottom, increase heat, and keep stirring until onions turn glossy and translucent. Stir in the salt, black pepper (about ½ teaspoon or so), and paprika. Add egg barley.

2.   Stir with a wooden spoon every 2 to 3 minutes and toast the egg "barley" until it turns brown and some starts to fry. Slowly pour in chicken broth and water, stirring constantly. When all liquid is added and it comes to a boil, lower heat and simmer under cover for approximately 20 minutes. Remove lid and stir. If barley is too moist, increase heat and keep stirring until liquid evaporates. The consistency of this pasta should be fluffy, with each little barley being separate.

CHEF'S SECRET: Every country in Middle Europe has a pasta similar to this. If you wish, just before serving you may add some finely chopped green parsley, minced chives, or snipped dill weed. Instead of bacon you can use butter and oil or any other combination of shortening, and you can replace the chicken broth with a light beef or veal stock.

Napkin Dumplings

8 servings

8 day-old hard rolls
1 to 1½ cups milk
4 strips bacon cut into small
   squares
¾ cup butter
3 egg yolks plus 1 whole egg

1 tablespoon chopped parsley
¼ teaspoon black pepper
1 cup flour
2 tablespoons soft butter
salt

1.   Cut rolls into cubes ½ to ¾ inch. Pour the milk over the cubes.

2.   Fry bacon until glossy. Discard drippings.

3.   Mix butter with egg yolks and whole egg in an electric mixer until fluffy and light lemon colored.

4.   Add soaked cubes, parsley, and pepper to the butter-egg mixture. Add bacon and fold ingredients together, sprinkling the flour on as you fold. The dough should be loose but not runny.

5.   Wet a large cloth napkin or kitchen towel, wring it dry, and brush it very lightly with soft butter. Pour the dough on the

napkin, fashioning it into a roll (long enough to make two 8-inch loaves, 2 to 2½ inches wide). Tie the two ends with a string and boil in salted water for 1 hour. Remove from napkin and, with a very sharp knife, cut into slices.

6.   Serve with roast duck, roast pork, or any other Bohemian meat dish.

CHEF'S SECRET: It is important that the napkin be spread well with the soft butter; otherwise the dumpling will absorb too much of the boiling water.

If you wish, use a large piece of aluminum foil instead of a napkin. Butter the foil, roll the dough in it, and boil the dumpling in it. I tried this with very good results.

Pinched Dumplings or Csipetke

8 servings

2 cups flour
1 teaspoon salt
½ teaspoon baking powder
1 egg
2 tablespoons ice water

1 tablespoon salt
2 quarts water
2 tablespoons butter or
   shortening

1.   Sift together twice the flour, salt, and baking powder.

2.   Beat egg with ice water until frothy. Pour into flour mixture and mix with your hands, using all ten fingers and pressing the flour and liquid firmly together. It will not be easy, because this dough, when it is ready, must be extremely hard (harder than modeling clay). If you just can't manage it, add another tablespoon water, but definitely no more. When the mixture turns into a very firm ball, remove from bowl and keep kneading with the heels of your palms until it turns into an elastic, firm dough.

3.   Bring the salted water to a boil in a pot that has at least another quart capacity. With your thumb and index finger, pinch off pieces of dough the size of raisins, and drop them one by one into the water. Continue until about ⅓ of the dough is in the pot. Stir with a wooden spoon. Repeat with remaining dough. Wait until the water boils again before each addition.

Lower heat and simmer for 10 to 15 minutes, or until the chewy little dumplings no longer have a raw center.

4.   Strain, rinse quickly, fold in butter or shortening, and serve with any of the following soups: Oven Baked Beef, Oxtail, Transylvanian Beef, Cream of Potato, Sauerkraut, Wax Bean, Serbian Chicken, or other soup of your choice.

CHEF'S SECRET: After the dough is ready, you can do the pinching and spread out the little pieces of dough on a kitchen towel or paper towel, then cook when you are ready. You can keep the dough covered with a cloth for 2 to 3 days at room temperature.

Crêpes

8 to 12 crepes

4 eggs
1 cup flour
½ teaspoon salt
1⅓ cups milk

½ cup club soda (plain carbonated water)
½ cup butter
½ cup oil

1.   Break the 4 eggs into a bowl; add the flour and salt and vigorously mix with a wire whip until the mixture is smooth.

2.   Slowly add the milk and keep stirring until all has been added. Let it stand in a covered bowl at room temperature for at least 30 minutes.

3.   Add club soda and stir.

4.   In a small pan, over medium heat, heat together the butter and oil.

5.   Place an empty 8-inch-diameter heavy-aluminum frying pan (the bottom will be 6 inches in diameter) over medium heat. When it is hot, pour in the whole amount of melted shortening and heat it over medium heat for about 5 minutes or more. Pour shortening back into the small pan.

6.   Heat the heavy-aluminum pan for another 2 or 3 minutes and then start to make the crêpes as follows: Place a scant tablespoon of shortening in the pan and swirl pan with a circular motion. Holding the pan in the air, with one hand, pour into it a scant ¼ cup of the batter, swirling it until batter covers entire bottom.

7.   Place pan over medium heat and cook until batter firms up and edges start to look cooked.

8.   Dip the edge of a metal spatula into the hot shortening and loosen the edges all around. Ease the spatula with a wiggling motion under the crêpe and turn it over. Finish cooking. The crêpe should be creamy yellow, with very light brown areas on it. Holding the handle, shake the pan with a back and forth motion and if the crêpe moves, lift it out to a plate covered with an absorbent paper.

9.   Repeat until all batter is used. This recipe will make at least 12, but under the right conditions 13 to 14, crêpes.

CHEF'S SECRET: This is really a dish in which the most important part is the cook's skill and not the ingredients.

In mixing the crêpe batter, don't hesitate to make any small necessary adjustments in the amounts of flour or liquid used to compensate for the fact that flour is not as consistent as salt, sugar or shortening.

For frying crêpes, a mixture of lard and oil is, in my opinion, the very best. If you keep the shortening hot and maintain a very hot, even pan temperature throughout the preparation, you will need very little shortening, and the crêpes won't be greasy.

Deep-Fried Ham Crêpes with Mushroom Sauce

8 servings

8 unsweetened crêpes (see index)

Ham filling:

4 to 6 ounces of ham, ground twice	**¼ teaspoon freshly ground black pepper**
1 egg	**1 teaspoon sifted bread crumbs**
½ cup sour cream	

Breading:

1½ to 2 cups sifted bread crumbs	**2 eggs, beaten with 2 tablespoons of cold water until frothy**
shortening for frying	

Mushroom sauce:

5 to 6 ounces firm, small white
   button mushrooms
4 tablespoons butter
2 tablespoons finely chopped
   parsley
¼ teaspoon freshly ground
   black pepper
½ teaspoon salt

2 tablespoons flour
2 tablespoons cornstarch
2 cups milk
1 cup chicken broth or ½
   chicken bouillon cube dissolved in one cup
   warm water

1.   Prepare crêpes according to directions. Keep warm.

2.   In a bowl, combine ground ham, egg, sour cream, black pepper, and sifted bread crumbs, and mix gently until well blended. Taste and add a little more salt if needed (this will depend on the saltiness of the ham). Divide filling into eight portions and place a portion on each crêpe (see illustration).

3.   Fold the part of the crêpe closest to you over the filling. Fold up first the left then the right sides, covering the filling. Then roll the crêpe away from you so that after rolling it twice the edge farthest from you will be the bottom of the roll. Gently press so it turns into a flat rectangle. Chill for one hour.

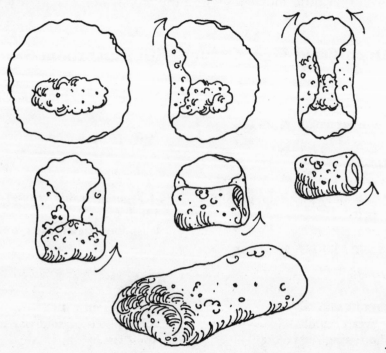

4. Spread the bread crumbs in a pie tin and pour the beaten eggs with the water into another pie tin. Roll the crêpe gently in the bread crumbs; then dip in the egg mixture and roll in the bread crumbs again.

5. When all are breaded, heat the shortening—preferably half lard, half oil—until a bread crumb dropped into it immediately jumps to the surface and bubbles. Fry the crêpes, not more than 2 or 3 at a time, until both sides are golden brown, turning just once. You may have to keep adjusting the heat as you do this in order to make the crêpes come out perfectly. Place the crêpes on absorbent paper towels and keep warm.

To make the sauce:

Cut off and discard stem ends of the mushrooms. To wash the mushrooms, sprinkle a tablespoon of flour on top of one quart of water, plunge in the mushrooms 4 or 5 at a time, and gently, quickly wash them. Lift out and pat dry immediately. Don't allow the mushrooms to remain in the water for more than a minute.

Slice mushrooms. In a sauté pan over moderate heat, melt the butter and add the parsley, mushrooms, salt, and pepper. Mix the flour and cornstarch with the milk and chicken broth. Lower the heat and cover. Bring gently to a boil, which will take not more than 2 or 3 minutes. Uncover, stir for a minute or so, then remove from heat and let stand for at least one hour.

Reheat immediately before serving. If you wish, stir in ½ cup sour cream or heavy cream.

Serve the crêpes on a platter decorated with fresh parsley, with the sauce in a small bowl on the side.

CHEF'S SECRET: This dish may seem complicated, but it is not. You can easily make the crêpes a day ahead of time, filling them with the ham mixture and leaving the breading for the day you serve them. You can also make the sauce a day ahead, mixing in the cream just after reheating and just before serving.

Don't try to add cold sour cream or heavy cream at once. Warm it first by stirring in some of the hot sauce; then stir the cream into the rest of the sauce.

Most cookbooks will tell you never to wash mushrooms. I strongly disagree with most authorities. Mushrooms are dirty and should be washed. The important thing is that they be washed properly and quickly. Sprinkling flour on the surface of the water before plunging in the mushrooms seems to help carry off the dirt and perhaps also coats the mushrooms so that they don't get water-soaked.

If you like a tangy mushroom sauce, add a good squeezing of lemon juice when you start to sauté the mushrooms.

8

Salads

In my library I have an Italian book from 1627. It has 428 pages and contains nothing' but salad recipes, salad dressings, and hints, advice, and stories about salads. The consumption of raw vegetables with some kind of liquid flavoring is, of course, much older than the book. In an ancient medical oath, the good doctor had to swear by all the Gods of Greece to feed his patients every day with onions and garlic. This prescription was always consumed after dipping in a mixture of salt, liquid, and oil, or vinegar and oil, or sprinkled with salt. Although it may seem otherwise, there has been little difference in basic salads for the last couple of thousand years. Fresh, crisp, tender greens, leaves, roots, fruits, and berries made more palatable with the juice of citrus fruits or vinegar, herbs, spices, and salt, enriched with oil, and consumed with crusty bread or with plain starch dishes or legumes are still the rule. True, there was a time when salads were distorted into very elaborate concoctions, but now we have brought back simplicity.

Crispness, freshness, and cold temperature are the main points in preparing salads. And remember color combinations. The vivid red of tomato, the deep green of spinach, or the light pastel hues of asparagus or avocado can beautifully complement the color scheme of a meal.

Not only the color but also the texture, shape, and temperature of the salad play a leading role in the meal. The salad is the perfect course to counteract the monotony of other dishes. In fact, the salad today is often the main attraction. A liquid starter, a main-course salad, and a light dessert can be a satisfying and festive lunch; a large salad as a starter, a hot fish or meat main course, and a dessert make a satisfying and elegant dinner for family and company alike.

Limestone Lettuce with Tomato Vinaigrette

8 servings

2 large ripe tomatoes
1½ tablespoons sugar
2 teaspoons salt
⅛ teaspoon freshly ground
   white pepper
⅛ teaspoon garlic salt

2 to 3 tablespoons chopped
   green parsley or dill, or a
   mixture of the two
⅔ cup oil
⅓ cup white vinegar
8 small or 4 large heads
   limestone lettuce, washed
   and trimmed

1.   Spear one tomato at a time on a fork and dip into boiling water for about 30 seconds. Remove and hold under cold running water or plunge it into ice water. Peel, quarter, and discard seeds and liquid.

2.   Cut tomatoes into small cubes. Place in a bowl and sprinkle with sugar, salt, pepper, garlic salt, and chopped parsley or dill. Gently toss and chill.

3.   In an electric mixer add alternately, drop by drop, oil and vinegar, beating constantly at highest speed until blended. Pour over marinated tomato cubes.

4.   Spoon over lettuce and serve.

CHEF'S SECRET: Adding the vinegar and oil drop by drop while beating at highest speed will bring the two ingredients into suspension. The dressing will be creamy and won't separate. This thick, opaque mixture with the tomato cubes folded in gives a beautiful appearance to the lettuce. It coats every leaf. The soft texture of the tomatoes, the creaminess of the dressing, and the fresh crunchiness of the lettuce will provide three very desirable textures.

Spinach and Apple Salad with Sweet and Sour Bacon Dressing

8 servings

2 medium-sized red apples,
   cored but not peeled,
   sliced wafer thin

1 to 1½ pounds fresh spinach,
   picked and washed,
   stems discarded

Dressing:

2 eggs   6 tablespoons bacon drippings
4 tablespoons sugar   ¼ cup vinegar
8 tablespoons corn oil
1 teaspoon salt

1.   In a large wooden salad bowl place all ingredients for the dressing except the vinegar. Stir vigorously, then beat for 5 minutes with a wire whip until the dressing turns pale yellow and has the consistency of honey. Slowly blend in vinegar.

2.   Fold in the apple slices, then the spinach. Chill for a few minutes; then serve.

CHEF'S SECRET: This is a "showmanship salad" that you can make beautifully in front of guests. Be sure that the wooden salad bowl, the wire whip, the eggs, and the corn oil have been chilled for at least 2 to 3 hours in the refrigerator. Have only the bacon drippings at room temperature, and if possible use the bottom part of the bacon drippings from the container, where the small bacon bits accumulate. This will enhance the flavor.

Core and slice the apples wafer thin at the very last minute. If you have a good, sharp cucumber slicer or other vegetable slicer, use it instead of a knife.

If spinach leaves are too large, break into bite-sized pieces.

Tomato-Green Pepper Salad

8 servings

4 to 6 medium-sized ripe   1 teaspoon salt
   tomatoes   ¼ cup vinegar
4 large bell peppers or, if a-   2 cups water
   vailable, 6 to 8 sweet, light   4 tablespoons oil
   green peppers (also called   freshly ground black pepper
   Hungarian or Cuban   1 teaspoon Spanish or
   peppers)   Hungarian paprika
1 medium-sized red onion   1 tablespoon fresh parsley,
3 tablespoons sugar   chopped

1.   Remove the stem end of the tomatoes. Cut each in half and then slice into ⅛-inch-thick slices. Lay the sliced tomatoes in a deep salad bowl or glass dish.

2.   Core the peppers. Cut out the inside, soft, light-colored veins. Split each in half and then cut crosswise into ⅛-inch strips.

3.   Split the onion in half lengthwise, cutting from the root to the leaf end. Remove the skin, then slice into ⅛-inch-thick slices.

4.   Cover the tomato slices alternately with onion slices and green pepper strips.

5.   Combine the sugar, salt, vinegar, and water and pour over the salad. Let stand at room temperature for only 30 minutes; then chill.

6.   Before serving, pour off almost all the marinade. Sprinkle the oil over the salad and sprinkle with the freshly ground pepper, paprika, and chopped parsley. Serve.

CHEF'S SECRET: This is an Eastern European salad, very popular in Hungary, Yugoslavia, and Rumania. It is a very pleasant accompaniment to Chicken Paprikash, Veal Goulash, or other summer dishes. You will notice that we do not keep the salad in the marinade for more than 30 minutes at room temperature. The flavor of the tomatoes, onion, and peppers improves if they stay in the marinade in the refrigerator for a few hours.

The red onions are milder and tastier than white or yellow onions.

The taste of the Hungarian or Cuban peppers, or sweet banana peppers, is very different from bell peppers, although all are closely related. If your grocery has none of them, try a Latin or Hungarian neighborhood store.

Tomato-Avocado Salad with Walnut Dressing

8 servings

4 firm tomatoes, approximately 2½ inches in diameter	¼ teaspoon freshly ground black pepper
1 teaspoon sugar	2 or 3 cups finely shredded lettuce
1 teaspoon salt	
4 very ripe avocados	1 cup Italian-style salad dressing

½ cup finely minced onions or scallions
juice of 1 lemon
½ teaspoon salt

1 tablespoon brandy or cognac
3 or 4 tablespoons chopped walnuts
4 black olives, cut in half

1.   Cut each tomato in half crosswise, as you would a grapefruit; remove seeds and liquid surrounding seeds. Carefully cut out flesh and chop it fine. Sprinkle a little sugar and salt on the inside of the tomato halves and turn them upside down to drain.

2.   Make a pulp from the ripe avocados. Blend in the minced onions and lemon juice. Add salt and pepper and the chopped flesh of the tomatoes.

3.   Heap the mixture into the 8 tomato halves. Arrange the tomato halves on the shredded lettuce. Chill for an hour.

4.   Mix Italian dressing with brandy and chopped walnuts and spoon over the tomato halves. Decorate each with a black olive half and serve.

CHEF'S SECRET: When you mash the avocados and add the lemon juice, onions, and tomato flesh, leave the avocado pits in the mixture until you heap it into the tomato crowns. They will keep it from turning dark.

Don't mix the walnuts into the dressing too far in advance of serving. Add at the last minute. This will keep the salad crunchy and give it an important third texture.

This salad is especially good with chicken or other fowl, or as a luncheon main course with cold meat or fish.

Hungarian Mixed Vegetable Salad

8 servings

2 cups cucumbers, sliced
2 cups firm tomatoes, sliced
2 cups onions, sliced
2 cups green pepper rings, sliced
1 clove garlic

3 cups water
2 teaspoons salt
½ teaspoon white pepper
3 tablespoons sugar
½ cup white vinegar

1.   Slice all vegetables into ¼-inch slices. Lay half the sliced cucumbers in the bottom of a large glass bowl. Put on top of them half the tomatoes, then half the onions, then half the green peppers. Repeat so that the peppers are on top again.

2.   Slice the garlic thin and drop into the water. Stir in salt, pepper, sugar, and vinegar. When sugar is dissolved, pour the mixture through a fine sieve onto the salad. Discard garlic and let the salad stand at room temperature for about an hour. Pour off this liquid twice and pour back again. Then chill the salad for a couple of hours in the liquid and serve, or, if you wish, pour off the liquid and serve.

CHEF'S SECRET: Sweet banana peppers are much tastier for this salad than bell peppers. If you use bell peppers, soak them after slicing in 2 cups tepid water; then rinse and pat dry.

Black Radish Salad

4 servings

2 cups shredded black radishes (approximately 10 to 12 ounces or 2 black radishes)	4 tablespoons oil
	1 tablespoon vinegar
	freshly ground black pepper to taste
1 tablespoon salt	

1.   Wash and peel black radishes and grate through the largest holes of a four-sided kitchen grater. Sprinkle with salt and mix it in with your fingers. Cover the bowl and let stand at room temperature for about 2 hours.

2.   Fill the bowl with ice-cold water, rinse radish by moving it back and forth with your fingers, then lift out in small amounts. Press radish gently to remove water, place on a kitchen towel, and gently pat dry. Refrigerate in a covered bowl.

3.   Just before serving, mix the vinegar into the oil with a wire whip and pour the mixture immediately over the chilled black radish. Grind a generous amount of fresh pepper over it and serve with dark bread, fresh butter, and beer.

CHEF'S SECRET: According to an old European saying, the radish is poison in the morning, food at noon, and medicine at night. This simple black radish salad goes best with good frankfurters, knackwurst, or cold cuts, and is an ideal accompaniment for certain types of cheese, such as brick, beer, and limburger.

The black radish you buy in the market may be limp and wrinkled, because it dehydrates fast. To restore it to life, place as much black radish as you want to use in a plastic container, fill it with water, weight the top so the radish won't float, and refrigerate overnight. The radish will be jet black, firm, and juicy.

Don't refrigerate black radishes if you have a lot of them. Wrap each piece individually in paper and keep in a brown bag.

Potato Salad Normandy

8 servings

2 pounds small new potatoes, boiled in jackets

2 cups celery, sliced very fine

1 teaspoon salt

¼ teaspoon or more freshly ground black pepper

1 cup finely diced ham

½ cup black olives, or, if available, 2 or 3 tablespoons chopped black truffles

1½ cups sour cream mixed with ½ cup light cream or half-and-half

4 teaspoons apple vinegar

2 teaspoons Calvados, apple-jack, or apple brandy (optional)

1. Boil potatoes, drain, and let cool until easy to handle. Peel and slice into thin slices.

2. Slice celery on a bias for diagonal thin slices.

3. In a bowl, blend potatoes and celery by hand or with a soft rubber spatula. Add salt, pepper, ham, and olives or truffles.

4. Gently stir together sour cream and light cream. Add vinegar drop by drop, and, if you wish, the Calvados or other apple brandy. Fold this mixture into the salad.

5. Chill and serve with additional sour cream, if desired.

CHEF'S SECRET: I learned this recipe many years ago from one of the chefs I admired most, Jean Conil, who at the time was chef at one of the great private clubs of London. One day we talked about what interesting twists might be given to ordinary dishes. To prove a point he fixed for me this salad (I must admit, not with black olives but with black truffles). Served with cold roast veal it was divine. I have tried it several times since with truffles and with olives, revising the recipe for American ingredients.

When you mix the potatoes and celery, the potatoes should not be quite cold. And the vinegar goes literally drop by drop into the mixture of sour cream and light cream; otherwise it will curdle. If it does curdle, bring some water to a boil and gently stir one or two tablespoons of boiling water into the curdled mixture with a wire whip. Then let stand for a couple of minutes and add 2 more tablespoons of sour cream. It will become smooth. This salad is excellent with poultry, cold veal, or cold fish.

Eli's Shrimp Salad

4 servings

16 large shrimp, ready-to-eat
2 tablespoons vinegar
½ cup water
1 teaspoon sugar
1 medium onion
1 cup sour cream

½ cup mayonnaise
1 tablespoon rinsed capers
juice of ½ lemon
8 lettuce leaves
4 sprigs fresh green parsley
1 lemon cut into 4 wedges

1.   Put shrimp in a clean plastic bag and submerge the bag in a container of ice water. Be sure no water touches the shrimp. Refrigerate.

2.   In a bowl, mix vinegar, water, and sugar and place in a shallow container. (The best is a glass pie dish.) Peel the onion, cut it into ¼-inch-thick rings, and marinate the rings in the vinegar mixture for about 30 minutes. Then cover and chill.

3.   Mix sour cream, mayonnaise, and capers. Add lemon juice.

4.   Before serving, place lettuce leaves, 4 shrimp, and several onion rings on each plate. Cover generously with the sour cream-mayonnaise mixture. Decorate with parsley and serve with lemon wedges.

CHEF'S SECRET: This is the only stolen property in this book. I ate this excellent salad at Eli's, that "place for steak" in Chicago, and I could not resist stealing it. The secret of this dish is that the shrimp keeps its identity and does not lose the typical shrimp taste. The onion rings, because no salt is added, remain very crisp, and the vinegar solution and the little sugar in it take away enough of the rawness of the onion to make it very pleasant. The difference between the texture and chewability of shrimp and the crunchiness of the onion, both covered with the smoothness of the sour cream-mayonnaise dressing with the little added surprises of the capers, make the dish a true adventure in eating.

I have tried many ways to refresh limp, wilted parsley, and of all methods the one that I find best is to submerge the parsley sprigs in tap water and cut the stems with a kitchen scissors or knife under water, keeping all stems submerged for about a minute or so after cutting. Then refrigerate the parsley in a bowl with the tap water for about an hour. Remove, shake off excess water, put the parsley in a bowl, cover with a wet towel, and place a handful of ice cubes on the top of the wet towel. Refrigerate for several hours or overnight. The parsley will be greener, crispier, and more fragrant than ever.

The type of large shrimp this dish needs is usually sold cooked, ready-to-eat, at the delicatessen counter of supermarkets or in fish stores. If you can obtain only medium or small shrimp, you will need more than 16.

Fresh Pineapple and Shrimp Salad

8 servings

2 pineapples, approximately 1½ to 2 pounds each	½ teaspoon salt
12 to 16 ounces cooked small shrimp or shrimp bits	⅛ teaspoon white pepper, or ¼ teaspoon freshly ground black pepper
1 cup mayonnaise (see index)	juice of 1 large lemon

1.   Split pineapples in half. Remove cores and cut flesh into small cubes.

2.   In a large bowl, toss together pineapple cubes, shrimp, mayonnaise, salt, pepper, and lemon juice.

3.   Arrange in pineapple shells, chill for at least an hour, and serve.

CHEF'S SECRET: The easiest way to find out if a pineapple is ripe or not is to try to lift it by one of the leaves in the very center of the green top. If the leaf comes out without the pineapple being lifted from the table, the pineapple is ready to eat.

Never store pineapple in the refrigerator. Keep it at room temperature in a brown paper bag, laying it on its side and turning it at least once a day. If you let pineapple stand upright, all its taste and juiciness will disappear.

Sometimes the price of shrimp is extremely high. You may substitute 8 ounces of shrimp and 8 ounces of inexpensive skinless, boneless fish fillet, poached according to package directions, then broken up into small pieces and mixed with the shrimp. For a special Oriental flavor add 1 teaspoon soy sauce to the mayonnaise and sprinkle the salad with toasted sesame seeds.

Carrot Blueberry Salad

8 servings

2 cups carrots, cubed to the size
  of blueberries
2 tablespoons vinegar
1 pint fresh blueberries
1 egg yolk
1 teaspoon prepared mustard
juice of ½ lemon
1 teaspoon sugar

½ teaspoon salt
1 cup sour cream
1 tablespoon snipped dill weed
  or chopped fresh parsley
lettuce leaves
2 slices whole wheat bread,
  toasted
2 tablespoons butter

1.   Wash and scrape carrots. Cut lengthwise into ⅓-inch slices; then cut slices lengthwise into ⅓-inch strips. Crosscut strips into small cubes approximately the size of blueberries. Place in a small saucepan, cover with water, and bring to a boil over high heat. Remove; let stand for 5 minutes. Discard water. Add

vinegar. Shake carrot cubes under cover and let cool in the vinegar.

2.   Wash, pick over, and chill blueberries. In the bowl of an electric mixer, blend egg yolk, mustard, lemon juice, sugar, and salt. Fold in sour cream by hand.

3.   Gently fold drained carrot cubes into the sour cream mixture. Then fold in blueberries, being careful not to break them. Arrange lettuce leaves in a salad bowl and place carrot-blueberry mixture on top. Sprinkle with snipped dill. Chill.

4.   Trim crust from the toast. Cut into small cubes. Heat butter in a small skillet over medium heat. Add toast cubes, increase heat, and turn with a spatula or slotted spoon until cubes turn deep brown. Stay with it; don't let them burn. Sprinkle cubes on top of the salad and serve, if possible, while the bread cubes are still warm.

CHEF'S SECRET: As the carrot cubes cool in the vinegar, they will acquire a pleasant flavor that will make an excellent contrast with the mild fragrance of the fresh blueberries. If you like your salads more on the tart side, add more vinegar to the carrots or sprinkle some on the blueberries before chilling.

To make the salad more colorful, save 10 to 20 blueberries and the same number of carrot cubes and sprinkle them on top of the toast cubes.

Avocado Christmas Trees

8 servings

8 avocados, not too ripe
1 small carrot, blanched
8 olives stuffed with pimiento
4 black olives
1 tablespoon minced onion
1 sweet pickle
1½ to 2 cups Italian-type salad dressing

8 lettuce leaves or 2 cups finely shredded lettuce
8 parsley sprigs
1 teaspoon small silver or gold nonpareils (used for cake decorating)

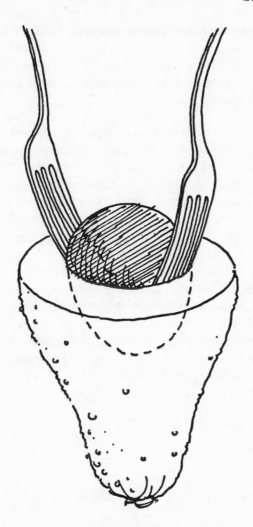

1.   Cut off bottom part of avocados. Lay them in front of you with the pits toward you. Press two forks into each pit (see illustration). Holding the forks, gently lift off the avocado. Peel and chill.

2.   Cut carrot, olives, onions and pickle into very small even dice or tiny shapes, depending on your artistic ability. Mix with Italian dressing. Leave dressing at room temperature, stirring occasionally.

3.   Arrange lettuce leaves or shredded lettuce on individual salad plates and place an avocado on each. Just before serving, spoon dressing over avocados and stick a parsley sprig into the top of each. If you wish, sprinkle with silver or gold nonpareils and serve at once.

CHEF'S SECRET: These little Christmas trees look beautiful and festive, and they can be served on many other occasions. If you wish, you can insert a small candle in the top of each instead of the parsley sprig, and light it at time of serving.

The Italian dressing with the colorful chopped vegetables in it can be replaced with a few tablespoons of the dressing gently folded into sour cream and spooned over the avocados, resembling snow.

Removing the avocado pit in this way, as shown in the illustration, is a method that can be applied to many other dishes made from whole avocado. You can cut off the narrow end, turn the avocado with the cavity up, and fill it with your choice of filling, surrounding it with slices or cubes of the cut-off part.

Always remove the pit first; then do the peeling. This way you will be sure not to ruin the flesh.

9

Sauces

In few departments of gastronomy have the changes been as dramatic as in the domain of the *saucier*. The man who made the sauces was once second in command in a great kitchen, and his work was extremely important. Then, slowly, sauces and gravies fell into disfavor and disappeared as chapter headings in cookbooks. In the United States there was a time when they were ignored, if not forbidden. Now they are slowly making a comeback, though they are quite different than they used to be.

Except in a few very special dishes, a *roux* is no longer used. Most homemakers don't even know (thank goodness) what it is. Before the invention of the refrigerator, shortenings turned rancid quickly; and before government controls, flour contained a much higher percentage of moisture than it does now, so it had a tendency to grow musty. Then a culinary genius discovered that if he cooked flour and shortening together very slowly, stirring constantly until they were golden brown and thoroughly cooked, they would keep for a longer time without turning rancid or moldy. This slowly cooked mixture of flour and shortening was called roux.

Today, when modern mills make excellent flour, and when oil, butter, and lard are thoroughly processed and refrigerated, it is absolutely unnecessary to spend hours and hours making *roux* as a base for sauces and gravies. When I read modern recipes with *roux* as an ingredient, I feel that we are back in Victorian times, when children of ten or twelve would stand for hours in front of a coal stove stirring *roux* with three-foot-long wooden spoons. I always thought that if I ever found the time I would write a book about sauce and call it *The Funeral of the Roux.*

Aioli (Garlic sauce)

8 servings

1 large boiled potato
1 slice day-old (or older) white
   bread
4 to 6 cloves garlic, chopped
4 tablespoons finely chopped
   flat-leaf parsley
¼ cup blanched crushed
   almonds

3 to 4 tablespoons red wine
   vinegar
1½ to 2 cups oil
1 teaspoon salt
¼ teaspoon freshly ground
   black pepper

1.   Peel and mash boiled potato. Place ⅔ cup mashed potato in a bowl. Tear the bread into pieces and add to the potato.

2.   Place the garlic, parsley, almonds, and part of the potato mixture in a blender. Add vinegar and ½ cup of oil and blend to a paste. Slowly add the rest of the potato mixture and blend again, alternating with the remaining oil until the mixture is the consistency of a thick mayonnaise.

3.   Add salt and pepper to taste, and, if you like, a few more drops of wine vinegar.

CHEF'S SECRET: This recipe sounds horrible but tastes heaven-, ly. A "large" potato is a U.S. Grade A, No. 1 baking potato, and this is the best kind for this sauce. (Incidentally, you can use a baked potato just as well as a boiled.) The sauce will keep in the refrigerator in a tight-fitting jar for as long as 2 weeks.

This sauce is excellent with roast, braised, boiled, or grilled meats, especially lamb, beef, and pork. It is also good with plain boiled or broiled fish, and with cold meats.

Tony's Barbecue Sauce

5 cups

16-ounce can tomato purée
3½ cups sugar
1 teaspoon salt
¼ teaspoon white pepper
¼ teaspoon garlic salt
⅓ cup prepared mustard
¼ cup vinegar

2 tablespoons lemon juice
2 tablespoons soy sauce
1 tablespoon Worcestershire
   sauce
3 to 4 drops Tabasco
3 to 4 drops red food coloring

1.   Blend all ingredients together.
2.   In a saucepan, warm the mixture over low heat, stirring constantly, for 2 to 3 minutes. Cover, adjust heat to medium, and bring to a boil. When it starts to boil, stir vigorously. Adjust heat to high and boil for 2 to 3 minutes. Adjust heat to lowest point and stir until boil subsides. Simmer gently for at least 2 hours.
3.   Let sauce cool and use as needed. You may refrigerate for 2 to 3 weeks or freeze for 3 months.

CHEF'S SECRET: This recipe was developed by The Bakery's Executive Chef Anthony Kowalczyk. When you read it, no doubt it will sound too sweet with 3½ cups of sugar. But when it is ready to use and you brush it on the meat, the sweetness will be gone—or at least much less than you expected.

The best way to use this sauce is to spice the meat you want to barbecue as you would for roasting. Place it in the oven with onions, carrots, celery, etc., and some moisture (stock or water), and moist roast at 350° F. for about 30 minutes.

Then brush each piece generously with barbecue sauce and continue the moist roasting for another 30 minutes. Turn the meat, brush again, and roast until done.

If you want to finish it on charcoal, brush again with sauce before putting it on the grill. Be sure that the coals are well burned and only glowing ashes are in the pit.

If you prefer a lingering sauce with more bite to it, add a couple tablespoons of prepared horseradish or increase the amount of Tabasco. For an Oriental flavor, replace the Worcestershire sauce with ½ tablespoon soy sauce and ¼ teaspoon powdered ginger.

Quick Cold Stroganoff Sauce

approximately 3 cups

1 teaspoon mushroom powder
1 teaspoon Spanish or
   Hungarian paprika
½ teaspoon salt
⅛ teaspoon freshly ground
   black pepper
1 teaspoon Gravy Master
½ teaspoon mustard
   (preferably Dijon)

¼ cup port wine or sherry
1 pint sour cream
1 cup thinly sliced or chopped
   mushrooms (you may use
   canned, but without the
   liquid)
1 tablespoon butter
1 tablespoon oil

1.   In a small bowl mix mushroom powder, paprika, salt, and pepper. As a rule, mushroom powder is lumpy, so be sure to smooth out lumps.

2.   Add Gravy Master and mustard; then slowly stir in wine. Be sure that the mixture is free of lumps. Gently fold in sour cream with a rubber spatula.

3.   If you use fresh mushrooms, sauté quickly in butter and oil, let cool, then fold into the sauce. Canned mushrooms may be drained and folded in at once.

4.   If the sauce is too thick for your purpose, add a few tablespoons of water, more of the wine, or a few spoonfuls of beef stock.

CHEF'S SECRET: The best way to eliminate small lumps in the mushroom powder is to mix the dry ingredients with the tip of your index finger in the bowl, or put all of the spices with the salt into a fine sieve and gently keep stirring with a small spoon until it all falls into the bowl.

Sour cream should never be handled with a wire whip or stirred vigorously if you wish to preserve its consistency. Fold it gently.

This sauce is excellent on cold meats and is also very good on a hamburger instead of ketchup. It is also excellent on fish and seafood.

Hungarian Style Gravy

2 cups

4 tablespoons lard	¼ cup finely chopped green
¼ cup finely minced onions	peppers
1 tablespoon paprika	¼ teaspoon bruised caraway
1 teaspoon Chef's Salt (see	seed
index)	1 cup water
2 tablespoons tomato purée (or	3 tablespoons flour
4 to 5 tablespoons tomato	2 cups hot water
juice)	

1.   In a heavy saucepan over medium heat, stir lard with onions until they start to brown (6 to 8 minutes, depending on thickness of pan).

2. Add paprika, Chef's Salt, tomato purée, green peppers, and caraway seed, stirring constantly until the mixture heats through.

3. Add 1 cup water, scrape bottom of saucepan, adjust heat to high, and cover. Cook on high heat for 10 to 15 minutes or until all water evaporates and minced onions and peppers start to stick to the bottom of the pan. The mixture should be orange-colored, from the paprika, with brown residues.

4. Sprinkle flour into mixture, stirring constantly for 3 to 4 minutes.

5. Remove from heat and slowly stir in hot water, first ½ cup to form a thick paste, then 2 to 3 tablespoons at a time to thin the paste into a runny, smooth substance. Lower heat and simmer for 30 minutes.

6. Strain through a sieve, correct seasoning, and use as you would a brown sauce or gravy.

CHEF'S SECRET: The method, not the ingredients, makes this sauce what it is. Be sure that the first cup of water evaporates completely. This is the point at which the taste of each ingredient loses its identity and they all combine into a new taste.

If you want more of a "paprika" character and color, add one more tablespoon of paprika before simmering.

You may substitute some of the water with white wine, red wine, or stock.

Onion Sauce

2 cups

2 tablespoons sugar
4 tablespoons shortening
2 cups chopped onions
2 tablespoons vinegar
1 teaspoon Chef's Salt (see index)

¼ teaspoon black pepper
3 tablespoons flour
1¼ cups beef consommé
¾ cup water

1. In a heavy saucepan over high heat, heat sugar until it turns yellow. Add shortening and stir with a wooden spoon. Add onions and cook 4 to 5 minutes, or until onions start to brown.

2.   Lower heat to medium. Add vinegar, Chef's Salt, pepper, and flour. Stir with a wooden spoon for 1 to 2 minutes.

3.   Stir in liquids, mixed. Scrape bottom, bring to a boil. Simmer for 30 minutes on lowest heat.

4.   Press through a fine wire sieve and serve.

CHEF'S SECRET: In Europe this is one of the most popular sauces with boiled beef, boiled pork, or fowl. If you like it sweet and sour, finish with 1 to 2 tablespoons sugar and 1 to 2 tablespoons vinegar.

The beef consommé can be replaced with many other liquids—water, white wine, apple cider or juice, milk, or light cream.

Wild Onion Sauce

2 cups

2 tablespoons bacon drippings
2 tablespoons oil
½ cup finely minced wild
   onion, including green parts
1 teaspoon salt
1 teaspoon sugar

1½ cups red wine
1 cup beef consommé or beef
   stock
2 tablespoons flour mixed with
   1 tablespoon Kitchen
   Bouquet

1.   In a heavy saucepan over high heat, heat bacon drippings and oil until smoking hot. Add wild onion and stir for 2 to 3 minutes.

2.   Lower heat to medium, add salt, sugar, and 1 cup red wine. Stir, cover, and cook over medium heat for 30 minutes, lowering the heat if liquid evaporates too fast.

3.   After 30 minutes add consommé and flour mixed with Kitchen Bouquet. Bring to a boil over medium heat; then simmer the sauce over very low heat, uncovered, for at least 45 minutes.

4.   Press through a fine sieve, stir in the last ½ cup of red wine, and serve with steaks or barbecued, broiled, or grilled meats.

CHEF'S SECRET: Wild onion is much more common in the United States than one would think. If you cannot find it, you can substitute half shallots and half chives, adding ⅛ teaspoon garlic salt—*not* garlic powder. If you cannot get shallots, substitute the white parts of scallions.

Burgundy Sauce

2 cups

1 tablespoon sugar	1½ teaspoons Chef's Salt (see
4 tablespoons shortening	index)
2 tablespoons grated onion	1 tablespoon Kitchen Bouquet
1½ cups beef consommé	1 cup red wine
2 tablespoons flour	red food coloring (optional)
1 tablespoon cornstarch	1 tablespoon butter

1. In a saucepan, melt sugar over medium heat until it starts to brown and bubble.

2. Add shortening and onions, stir, and cook for 5 minutes.

3. Stir flour, cornstarch, and Chef's Salt into 1 cup beef consommé. Slowly pour into onions and shortening, stirring constantly with a wire whip. Cook until it thickens.

4. Combine Kitchen Bouquet, red wine, and ½ cup consommé. Stir into sauce. Adjust heat to low and simmer, under cover, for 30 minutes, stirring occasionally.

5. Add a few drops of red food coloring, if you wish, then strain through a fine sieve into a water-rinsed pan. Add butter, bit by bit, stirring. Correct seasoning with Chef's Salt or a pinch of sugar. If needed, thin with 1 to 2 tablespoons red wine.

CHEF'S SECRET: The caramelized sugar will help to caramelize the onion quickly and will also counteract the acidity of the wine.

Some flour thickens much more than others, varying in the same brand from store to store and different brands from the same place. So be careful. Measure the flour exactly.

You can, if you wish, add to the sauce: 1 to 2 tablespoons tomato purée, or ½ teaspoon mustard, or 1 to 2 teaspoons

Worcestershire sauce, or less consommé and more red wine, or 1 to 2 teaspoons red currant jelly, or 1 to 2 tablespoons commercial barbecue sauce.

For Italian-style dishes, add ¼ cup minced green peppers and ¼ cup minced mushrooms cooked with the onions.

Red Wine Sauce

approximately 3 cups

Stock:

1 medium onion, finely minced
1 clove garlic, finely minced
2 pounds beef scraps, fat and lean
1 carrot cut into half-inch dice
2 stalks celery, diced into ½-inch pieces
1 tablespoon salt
1 pound marrow bones
1 tablespoon flour
1 whole bay leaf

Roux:

⅓ cup flour
⅓ cup shortening

Sauce:

½ cup red wine
¼ cup currant jelly
1 cup sauce base (stock and roux mixture)
¼ cup dry red currants
additional salt, if needed
Kitchen Bouquet (optional)
red food coloring (optional)

1. In a heavy saucepan, sauté the minced onion and garlic with the fat parts from the scraps. When the onions become translucent, add the carrots, celery, salt, and enough water to cover mixture. Cover the pan and cook rapidly until all the liquid evaporates.

2. Add remaining meat scraps and bones. Sprinkle with flour, and keep stirring over medium heat, until all particles get brown. Transfer to a soup kettle. Add bay leaf, peppercorns, and 1 gallon water. Bring to a rapid boil, then lower heat and simmer for 3 to 4 hours, skimming frequently. Strain liquid and skim again. Discard all solids. Allow to cool.

3. Make a roux by mixing the flour and shortening and stir over medium heat. When it starts to brown, remove the roux

from heat and slowly add the cooled liquid. Strain and return to a medium-sized saucepan. Bring to a boil, then lower heat and keep cooking until it becomes clear and glossy, skimming frequently. The amount will reduce to approximately 6 cups. This mixture can be refrigerated for up to a week, or frozen for two to three months.

4. To finish the wine sauce, combine the red wine and currant jelly. Stir this into the sauce base. Add the currants, bring to a boil, and simmer 10 to 15 minutes. Correct the seasoning and, if you wish, add some Kitchen Bouquet and a few drops of red food coloring.

CHEF'S SECRET: This is how the sauce for the Beef Wellington should be made if you use the whole tenderloin and either have the butcher trim it and give you all the scraps, or do the trimming at home.

Making the red wine sauce is time consuming, and it needs care and watching. A big part of its success depends on how quickly you can adapt this method to your own cooking utensils. The pot itself is important. A heavy aluminum, cast iron, or enamel-coated pot will bring much better results than a thin, light utensil.

Also, it is important for the bottom to be straight and flat, and it must be very clean. If the outside bottom, in direct contact with the heat, is dirty, the flour-sprinkled bones and scraps will burn down because any dirt and grease on the bottom will act as a much faster and higher heat conductor than the clean area.

White Wine Sauce Polonaise

2 cups

4 tablespoons butter
2 tablespoons shortening
2 tablespoons grated or very finely minced onion
2 tablespoons sifted bread crumbs
1 tablespoon finely chopped green parsley

1 clove garlic
1 teaspoon Chef's Salt (see index)
1 cup hot stock or water
1 cup dry or medium-dry white wine
1 tablespoon lemon juice
½ teaspoon sugar

1.   In a heavy saucepan over medium heat, heat together butter and shortening. When it starts to foam and the butter starts to brown, add onions, bread crumbs, parsley, and garlic mashed to a pulp with the Chef's Salt. Stir for 2 to 3 minutes. Lower heat and add stock and white wine. Cover and simmer for about 30 minutes, stirring occasionally.

2.   Remove from heat and cool. When lukewarm, strain through a fine sieve, pressing through the solids remaining in the strainer. Heat to serving temperature, add lemon juice and sugar if necessary, and serve.

CHEF'S SECRET: Sausages of Middle and East European nations are very popular in France. If there is a Polish, Hungarian, or German sausage-maker in the town, many local restaurants will purchase and offer such sausage on the menu. As a rule, the hot stock used in a white wine sauce made for Polish sausage is the stock in which the sausage was simmered. Two cups of sauce are enough for 8 portions.

If you want to serve this white wine sauce on Polish sausage, figure approximately 4 to 6 ounces of sausage per portion. Heat the sausage over very low heat, without boiling, for 10 to 15 minutes. Then cut the sausage into serving pieces and quickly fry in 2 or 3 tablespoons hot shortening, turning frequently. Serve with white wine sauce and plain boiled potatoes.

Of course, you can use this sauce with many other meats. It tastes very good on mildly cured ham steaks, pan-fried or broiled pork chops, or broiled or fried fish.

Sauce Louis

2½ cups

2 eggs
3 tablespoons prepared
    mustard
3 tablespoons light brown
    sugar
½ teaspoon salt

⅛ teaspoon ground white
    pepper
juice of 1 lemon
1 teaspoon vinegar
1 pint sour cream or sour
    half-and-half

1.   Blend eggs, mustard, sugar, salt, pepper, lemon juice, and vinegar in a medium-sized bowl, stirring them vigorously together with a wire whip.

2.   Gently fold in sour cream. Keep refrigerated.

CHEF'S SECRET: This is probably the simplest and quickest, yet most elegant, sauce. It can be made in 20 seconds, without cooking or even getting near the stove.

All the ingredients except the sour cream should be blended vigorously with a wire whip or in an electric mixer at the highest speed. But the sour cream must be gently folded into the sauce with a rubber spatula. If commercial sour cream is beaten it will become runny and will separate, and you will not get the proper silky texture and consistency.

Try it with yogurt!

Mushroom Sauce

2 cups

2 cups (8 ounces) mushrooms
3 tablespoons butter
2 slices finely chopped bacon
½ cup finely chopped onions
½ teaspoon Chef's Salt (see index)
2 tablespoons flour
10½-ounce can chicken broth
½ cup white wine
1 teaspoon Worcestershire sauce
1 teaspoon catsup or tomato purée
2 tablespoons freshly chopped parsley

1. Quickly wash, towel dry, and slice mushrooms thin.
2. In a heavy saucepan, melt butter, add bacon and onions, and cook over high heat until onions and bacon bits brown. Through a sieve, stir in Chef's Salt mixed with flour. Keep turning onions with a spatula; then add all mushrooms at once and keep turning the whole mixture until the mushrooms brown.
3. Combine chicken broth, white wine, Worcestershire sauce, and catsup. Stir into the saucepan at once.
4. Adjust heat to low and simmer for 15 minutes. Cool until lukewarm. Blend smooth in electric blender. Reheat and add parsley. Serve as is, or with some cream or sour cream added.

CHEF'S SECRET: This is a different kind of mushroom sauce, excellent on quickly sautéed thin slices of veal, or on pork, boiled beef, roast poultry, or fish.

Orange Sauce for Poultry

8 servings

1 cup chicken stock or canned
    chicken broth
1 envelope unflavored gelatin
3 or 4 tablespoons orange peel,
    cut in long, thin strips

2 cups boiling water
3 tablespoons sugar
juice of 2 oranges
juice of 1 lemon
4 tablespoons butter mixed
    with 3 tablespoons flour

1.   Set the stock to boil. Add gelatin when stock starts to warm. When it boils, adjust heat to simmer.

2.   Cut enough orange peel (the skin only, without the white pulp) into very thin strips 1 to 1½ inches long. Drop into boiling water and boil for 5 minutes. Drain and discard boiling water. Rinse boiled orange rind in cold water and let drip dry in a sieve.

3.   Place sugar in a large saucepan and brown it over medium heat until it melts and turns the color of yellow straw.

4.   Add to the sugar the orange juice, lemon juice, and simmered stock.

5.   In a saucer or small bowl, mix with your fingertips the butter and flour. Drop hazelnut-sized pellets into the sauce, stirring it constantly until all the butter and flour mixture is used. Adjust heat to low and simmer the sauce for another 10 to 15 minutes over low heat.

6.   Add orange peel and let stand in a warm place until serving.

CHEF'S SECRET: This is a basic, versatile sauce that may be used for duckling, squab, guinea hen, or other fowl. Of course, if you wish, you can use it just as well on chicken, capon, or turkey.

If you like a darker brown color, add a teaspoon or so of Kitchen Bouquet. Or if you want the color to be more orange, grate into the simmering stock about ½ tablespoon or so of carrots.

If you don't want the sauce to be too rich, or if you use a natural stock from the poultry you roast yourself, omit the butter-flour mixture and stir into the boiling stock 2 tablespoons cornstarch diluted in ½ cup cold water.

The gelatin won't jell, but it will give a "heavy" texture to the consistency of the sauce without enriching it.

If you wish to glaze the poultry, reduce ½ cup of this sauce over high heat to one-half its volume and spoon the thickened sauce over the bird.

Mock Venison Sauce

4 cups

1 cup vinegar
2 cups water
1 tablespoon salt
1 clove garlic
1 cup sliced onions
1 cup sliced carrots
½ cup sliced parsnips
6 to 8 peppercorns, bruised
1 bay leaf
4 tablespoons sugar
4 tablespoons lard or bacon
   drippings

4 tablespoons flour
2 tablespoons cornstarch
½ teaspoon crushed juniper
   berries
½ teaspoon lemon zest
juice of 1 lemon
1 tablespoon rinsed capers
2 tablespoons lingonberries (or
   red currants)
½ cup whipping cream
½ cup sour cream
1 egg

1.   Place vinegar, water, salt, garlic, onions, carrots, parsnips, peppercorns, and bay leaf in a large pot (not aluminum). Simmer over medium heat for 1 hour.

2.   Remove from heat and strain. Discard bay leaf, peppercorns and garlic. Blend remaining vegetables in an electric blender with some of the marinade liquid.

3.   In a heavy saucepan over medium heat, brown the sugar until it starts to melt and bubble.

4.   Add bacon drippings; heat.

5.   Mix flour and cornstarch into the marinade. With a wire whip, stir the mixture into the sugar and bacon drippings until it starts to boil. Reduce heat to low and simmer under cover.

6.   After 10 minutes add juniper berries, lemon zest, lemon juice, capers, and lingonberries. Simmer and stir for another 10 minutes.

7.   Blend whipping cream, sour cream, and egg. Spoon some of the hot sauce into it to warm, then gradually add to the sauce. Heat and serve.

CHEF'S SECRET: This is a very useful sauce that makes a plain piece of boiled beef into a great dish. It is also good with venison, pork, and fowl.

You can freeze half the sauce, if you wish.

Instead of water, you can use 1 cup beef or chicken stock and 1 cup red wine.

Hot Herb Butter for Fish

1 cup

1 cup butter
1 lemon
2 tablespoons cold water
1 teaspoon dried tarragon
1 teaspoon rosemary

1 teaspoon basil
4 or 5 sprigs fresh parsley, dried
2 to 4 tablespoons cognac or brandy

1. Heat butter in a small saucepan.
2. With a lemon zester or with a small grater, scrape off about ½ teaspoon lemon zest. Add to butter and stir.
3. Cut lemon, squeeze juice through a sieve into a cup. Put 1 tablespoon water in each lemon half; stir it with a spoon to scrape off all the flesh of the lemon. Press through a sieve.
4. Add tarragon, rosemary, and basil to lemon juice. Stir. Spoon mixture into the butter. Stir and keep herb butter hot.
5. Dip dried parsley sprigs into the cognac or brandy and place the sprigs on the fish. Heat remaining cognac and ignite it in the pan. Ladle flaming cognac all over the fish, being careful that the cognac-dipped dry herbs ignite and burn to ashes. Wait until the flames die, then spoon the hot herb butter over the fish, stirring constantly to distribute the herbs evenly.

CHEF'S SECRET: Buy some fresh green parsley, with long stems if possible. Tie the stems about 3 inches from each other on a piece of yarn. Hang the yarn in a dry place in the kitchen. In 2 to 3 days the parsley will wilt. The sprigs should then be wrapped in aluminum foil and kept for 3 or 4 hours in a 200° F. oven. (The best time to do this is after you have used the oven for baking and the heat is off.) Or, if you used the oven on the day the parsley is ready, place the foil with the parsley in the oven, leave the door open for 4 or 5 minutes, then close it and leave overnight.

You can keep the parsley in the kitchen, in a place where it won't break, for as long as two months. When needed, the sprigs will be bone dry. They will soak up the cognac very quickly and will burn into ashes with a pleasant aromatic smoke in a few seconds. This ash is very tasty on the fish. You can also do this with branches of tarragon, basil, rosemary, or any other herb.

If you are not sure whether your herbs are dry enough before dipping into the brandy, keep as many as you will need in a small dry pot or pan somewhere on or above the stove when you start to prepare the fish. If the cognac or brandy won't ignite, warm it up and try again. If it still won't light, someone may be watering your brandy.

Cheese Sauce

2 cups

4 tablespoons butter
1 cup chicken broth
1 cup warm milk
2 tablespoons flour
2 tablespoons cornstarch
½ teaspoon Chef's Salt (see index)
⅛ teaspoon white pepper

¼ cup grated American cheese
¼ cup grated Swiss cheese
2 tablespoons grated Parmesan cheese
2 to 3 dashes Worcestershire sauce
1 to 2 dashes Tabasco

1. In a heavy saucepan over medium heat, melt butter.
2. In a bowl, combine chicken broth, milk, flour, cornstarch, Chef's Salt, and pepper. Beat with a wire whip or electric beater until smooth.
3. Slowly add mixture to hot butter, stirring constantly.
4. Bring to a boil, stirring. Gradually add cheeses, Worcestershire, and Tabasco. Blend.
5. Remove from heat, cover, and keep warm until serving time. Correct seasoning.

CHEF'S SECRET: If you wish, you can substitute different cheeses. The amount should be ½ cup or more.

If you like a thicker sauce, add 1 tablespoon more flour.

Salsa

2 cups

1 cup peeled, seeded, and
   chopped tomatoes
   (approximately 3 medium)
1 tablespoon or more very
   finely chopped hot fresh chili
   pepper
¼ cup chopped onions

½ cup chopped bell peppers
½ cup chopped celery tops
¼ cup fresh cilantra (Mexican
   parsley)
1 cup water
1 teaspoon sugar
1 teaspoon salt

Combine all ingredients. Stir and let stand for at least 2 hours at room temperature. Chill overnight in a closed plastic or glass container. Serve on tacos, tortillas, or other Mexican dishes.

CHEF'S SECRET: This is one of millions of versions of this Mexican staple. You can adjust it to your own taste. The only important part is the Mexican parsley, or cilantra, which should not be replaced. It is available fresh throughout the year in Spanish markets, but also in many American supermarkets catering to Spanish-speaking Americans. If it is not available in the store where you shop, just ask the produce manager to get cilantra for you.

Cilantra is among the very few herbs that defy drying, freezing, or any other way of preservation. It loses its incomparable fragrance when it is not fresh, and its volatile oils can not be imitated by any chemical process.

You can keep fresh cilantra at room temperature in water for about two weeks and in the refrigerator for 3 or 4 days. (Cold destroys its fragrance.) But it is worth the bother to keep it. Change the water and snip the ends of the stems every two days.

Dill Pickle Sauce

2 cups

4 tablespoons bacon drippings
1 cup dill pickle, peeled and
   chopped
3 tablespoons flour
1 cup hot milk
1 teaspoon salt

2 tablespoons vinegar
1 tablespoon dry dill weed (or 3
   tablespoons fresh)
⅔ cup pickle liquid
1 cup sour cream

1.   In a saucepan over medium heat, bring bacon drippings to the smoking point. Carefully add chopped pickles (don't burn yourself with splattering fat).

2.   Stir until pickles heat through. Mix flour with milk, pour into pan, and stir until it thickens.

3.   Add salt, vinegar, and dill weed to pickle liquid. Add gradually to the hot sauce.

4.   Warm sour cream by adding 1 to 2 tablespoons of hot sauce; then gently fold heated sour cream into sauce. Serve with boiled meat, fowl, or fried or boiled fish.

CHEF'S SECRET: If you don't peel the pickles, the skin will be tough and chewy. If you wish, you can make the same sauce from garlic pickles or even sweet gherkins.

Lemon Sauce

2 cups

2 lemons
2 tablespoons butter
1 tablespoon chopped parsley
1 tablespoon plus 1 teaspoon sugar
1 teaspoon salt
¼ teaspoon white pepper
½ teaspoon dry tarragon

1 cup white wine
1 cup water
2 tablespoons cornstarch
1 tablespoon butter
1 tablespoon flour
1 tablespoon capers, rinsed and chopped

1.   Scrape enough zest from the lemons to have 2 tablespoons.

2.   Roll lemons with your palm on table top to soften. Cut in half and press out juice from 1 whole and ½ lemon.

3.   With a grapefruit knife, carefully cut lemon flesh out of remaining ½ lemon. Discard skins and save juice and flesh for later use.

4.   In a heavy saucepan over medium heat, bring butter to foaming. Add lemon zest, parsley, sugar, salt, and white pepper. Stir, lower heat, cover, and simmer 10 to 15 minutes.

5.   Crumble tarragon into white wine; bring to a boil in a small pan. Let stand under cover, off the heat, for 10 minutes; then strain wine into 1 cup water. Discard tarragon.

6. Mix cornstarch into wine-water mixture and slowly stir into butter-lemon mixture. Increase heat to medium, and when it starts to boil, add bit by bit the butter and flour mixed into a paste.

7. When it reboils, remove from heat. Add capers and lemon flesh removed from ½ lemon, stir in lemon juice, and serve with fish.

CHEF'S SECRET: If the sauce is too tart because of the size of the lemon, add a little more sugar. If the sauce is not tart enough, add more lemon juice.

It is important for the texture of the sauce to have the flesh of the lemon mixed in. If you can't get enough out with the grapefruit knife, peel a lemon completely, removing all the white pulp and yellow skin, then cut out the fruit with a small sharp paring knife.

As in all other recipes that use capers, it is very important to rinse the capers in cold water before you use them.

Hungarian Mustard Sauce

approximately 5 cups

1 quart water	⅓ cup cornstarch
½ cup prepared mustard	1 cup water
⅓ cup vinegar	½ cup prepared mustard
½ cup sugar	¼ cup port, Madeira, or cream
⅛ teaspoon white pepper	sherry
¼ teaspoon salt	

1. Combine first six ingredients in a saucepan and bring to a vigorous boil over high heat. Stir with a wire whisk when it starts to boil, and keep stirring for a minute or so.

2. Mix ⅓ cup cornstarch into 1 cup water and slowly pour mixture into boiling liquid, stirring constantly. Adjust heat to medium and continue to cook until mixture is thick, smooth, and opaque.

3. Remove from heat, cool 10 to 15 minutes, stirring occasionally; then stir in mustard and wine. Cool to room temperature; then chill. It keeps refrigerated for two to three weeks.

CHEF'S SECRET: This sauce is popular with the different kinds of Hungarian fresh sausages that are simmered in water or heated in a frying pan and eaten hot. It also makes an excellent sandwich spread instead of mayonnaise or butter.

If you wish, use a Bavarian-type mustard that has a pale gray color with small dark specks in it for at least half the mustard required by the recipe. It will give an excellent flavor.

If you don't wish to use an alcoholic beverage, add ¼ cup orange juice or other fruit juice.

Hungarian Paprika Catsup

2 cups

½ cup dry white wine
¼ cup plus 1 teaspoon sugar
2 tablespoons salt

¼ cup Hungarian paprika
2 tablespoons cognac
½ cup tomato purée

Stir all ingredients together. When well blended, add enough boiling water to yield 2 cups. Cool and chill. It will keep refrigerated for several weeks.

CHEF'S SECRET: The amount of salt and sugar will depend on the wine you use. Leave out some of both and taste 2 to 3 hours after preparing.

The Bakery's Boiled Salad Dressing

2 quarts

2 cups water
1 cup white vinegar
2 tablespoons prepared
   mustard
⅛ teaspoon freshly ground
   black pepper
⅛ teaspoon freshly ground
   white pepper
2 teaspoons salt
½ cup sugar

6 tablespoons cornstarch mixed
   with 1 cup cold water
1 cup oil
4 cups ice cubes
any 4 or 5, or all of the
   following herbs—2 to 3
   tablespoons of each, according to your taste: tarragon,
   dill, scallions, rosemary,
   parsley (curly or flat),
   watercress, marjoram, sage,
   chervil, celery tops

1.   Bring to a boil 2 cups water with vinegar, mustard, black and white pepper, salt, and sugar. When it comes to a boil, gently stir in cornstarch-water mixture. Bring to a boil, adjust heat to medium, and cook, stirring, until it thickens and becomes opaque.

2.   Remove from heat and pour into a large bowl. Add half the oil, stirring constantly. Then add half the ice cubes, half the oil again, and the second half of ice cubes. Keep stirring until ice cubes are melted. Refrigerate.

3.   Add herbs of your choice and mix when ready to serve.

CHEF'S SECRET: This dressing will keep for two to three weeks in the refrigerator. If you were to add the herbs before storing, the dressing would keep for three to four days at the most.

It is hard to get fresh herbs all the time. Therefore, at The Bakery we add some fresh and some dry herbs, depending on season and availability. If we add dry herbs, we always moisten them first with a few drops of vinegar and water and wait for a couple of minutes until they absorb the liquid.

This recipe is from a very old American cookbook which calls it "Another Dressing." At The Bakery we sprinkle over this. dressing some finely chopped hard-boiled eggs and grated Feta cheese. *Warning:* Once the cheese and eggs are mixed into the dressing it should not be kept more than one day.

10

Desserts & Bakery

My first kitchen job in the United States was in a Jesuit monastery. I had no trouble with my cooking but plenty of trouble with my complete lack of English.

On days when the janitor of the monastery was on duty, I had help. Tom, a red-headed Irishman, had married a Connecticut-born Hungarian girl; so if I couldn't understand what I had to do, she was on the phone in a second and explained it to me sweetly. But when Tom was off with his wife on a weekend trip, that was something else.

I'll never forget the day when the Jesuit Father in charge, discussing the menu, told me to make "something for dessert." I walked up and down in the storeroom among the shelves looking at every can, jar, box, and container, looking for "Something." But I couldn't find it. When one of the lay Brothers came to the kitchen for a cup of coffee, I asked him, "Please, what is

Something?" He told me, "Something is everything or any-thing." Back to the storeroom I went looking for Anything or Everything. Time was growing short and I was growing desperate when finally my brother, who had been in America longer and spoke much better English, telephoned and calmed me down.

I guess that was the only day during my career as a chef that the "Something" I served for dessert was canned peaches *au naturel*—just as they came from the can. I am still ashamed when I recall how much the good Fathers resented the canned peaches, mainly because before that I had really spoiled them with desserts.

Whatever it may be, I feel that a good dessert is extremely important. Fruit and cheese, a light pastry, rich cake, a smooth cream, or a complicated soufflé—it should be truly the climax of the meal.

Apfelkuchen

8 servings

1 cup butter or margarine	2 cups flour
¾ cup sugar	¾ cup milk
2 eggs	1½ pounds apples
1 teaspoon vanilla	⅓ cup raisins (soaked in warm
pinch of salt	water for 2 hours, then
1 teaspoon baking powder	patted dry)

1. Preheat oven to 350° F.
2. Cream butter or margarine in an electric mixer, using a paddle or dough hook if you have it.
3. Add sugar, eggs, vanilla, and salt.
4. Add baking powder to sifted flour.
5. Alternately add flour mixture and milk to sugar-egg mixture.
6. Pour dough into a buttered 10-inch pie tin.
7. Slice apples and arrange them on the dough. Sprinkle with raisins.
8. Bake for 30 to 40 minutes.

CHEF'S SECRET: This is an old and simple but very good recipe. Instead of apples and raisins you can use apricots, peaches, plums, or other fruits. Of course, fruits that turn acidic in baking, such as plums and apricots, need additional sugar. A good way is to mix 1 cup of granulated sugar with ½ teaspoon of cinnamon and dip the cut flesh side of the fruit into this mixture before placing it on top of the kuchen.

Woven Pastry Basket

1 package commercial pie-dough mix, or pastry for a 2-crust pie	2 to 3 tablespoons oil
	1 egg, beaten

1. Prepare pie dough according to package directions.
2. Oil the outside of a stainless steel bowl. Cover the outside with aluminum foil and oil the foil.
3. Roll out half the dough to form a circle large enough to cover the outside of the bowl.

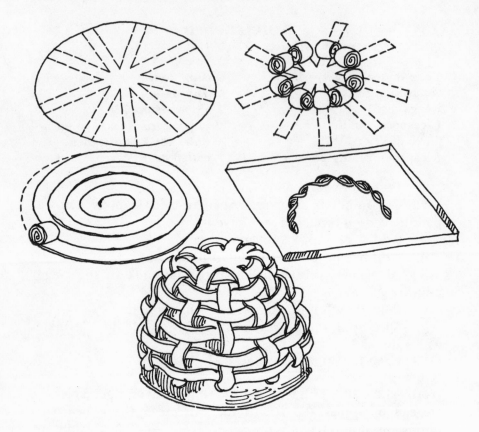

4.   With a pastry wheel, cut the circle according to the illustration, being sure that you end up with 9 strips approximately ¾ inch wide.

5.   Remove the triangles from between the strips. Fold the strips to the middle. Lift the dough and place it on the top of the bowl.

6.   Roll out the remaining half of dough. With a pastry wheel, start to cut the circle of dough in ½-inch strips, going around in circles, working from the outer edge toward the middle (pinwheel fashion).

7.   Roll up the strips to make them easier to handle.

8.   With one of the rolled strips, start to weave the basket, going around the bowl and weaving the pastry first under one strip, then over the next, continuing in a circle and covering the bowl.

9.   Brush the edge with beaten egg. Roll the dough back to form the edge, pinching it so that the dough sticks together.

10.   Brush the entire surface of the basket with beaten egg, and chill in freezer for at least 3 hours.

11.   With the leftover dough, roll a strip and twist it to resemble a rope. Shape it like an arch, place it on a cookie sheet, with the two ends the same distance apart as the circumference of the bowl. Brush with egg and chill. This will be the handle of the basket.

12.   Bake basket and handle in a preheated 425°F. oven for 15 to 20 minutes, or until golden brown.

13.   Cool before removing basket from bowl. Use round toothpicks to attach handle to basket. Insert toothpicks as follows: Touch the pastry with the tip of the round toothpick and twirl it rapidly back and forth between thumb and index finger, holding the pastry with the other hand and slowly increasing pressure on the toothpick.

CHEF'S SECRET: At The Bakery, one of the favorite special desserts that we prepare on festival occasions or for very honored guests is a basket made from pie dough, filled with large fresh strawberries, whipped cream, or some other fresh fruit and whipped cream, or just simply with a large assortment of fresh seasonal fruit.

The most important step in making the basket is to chill it for at least an hour before baking. If the pie dough goes from room temperature into the hot oven, instead of baking it starts to melt, and as it melts it falls off the bowl.

It is important to oil the bowl before you press on the aluminum foil, and it is just as important to oil the foil.

The easiest and most successful way to remove the pastry basket from the bowl is first to let it cool completely after baking. Then carefully remove the aluminum foil from the bowl so that the basket remains on the foil. Gently hold the basket turned upside down in the palm of one hand; then remove the foil from the inside. If the foil is not well oiled, the dough will stick to it and will be difficult to remove.

If, after removing the foil, you notice that inside the basket the dough is not completely baked (which may happen if the dough is thicker in some places than in others), don't worry. Simply put the aluminum foil back on the bowl, put the basket on again, and bake in a preheated 425° F. oven for an additional 5 minutes.

European Milk Bread

1 large loaf

½ cup white raisins	2 eggs
4 cups all-purpose flour	1 package dry yeast
1½ cups milk	½ cup warm water
pinch salt	4 to 6 tablespoons melted butter
4 tablespoons sugar	sugar crystals (optional)

1.   Soak the raisins in lukewarm water for 1 hour. Drain and dry them in a towel. Sift the flour and set in a warm place.

2.   Scald the milk; add the salt and 3 tablespoons of the sugar. Cool to room temperature.

3.   Separate 1 egg and set the white aside. Beat the other whole egg and the egg yolk lightly and add to the cooled milk.

4.   Dissolve the yeast in the warm water; then add the milk-egg mixture.

5.   Place the flour in a large bowl. Mixing with a wooden spoon, add the yeast mixture.

6.   Stir with the wooden spoon until the ingredients are combined; then turn the dough out onto a floured pastry board and knead until the dough is smooth and begins to blister.

7.   Press 4 to 5 holes into the dough with your fingers and distribute 1 tablespoon of the warm butter in the holes. Knead again until the butter is thoroughly mixed in. Repeat this procedure until all the butter is incorporated.

8.   Place the dough in a greased bowl, cover with a towel, and let it rise in a warm place. As it starts to rise, sprinkle ½ to ¾ tablespoon of flour over the top. Let the dough rise until it has doubled in size.

9.   Turn the dough out onto a lightly floured board. Sprinkle the entire surface with the raisins; then roll the dough jelly-roll fashion. Fold the two ends to the middle; then start to knead again.

10.   Once the dough is smooth again, form into a ball. Divide the ball into 3 pieces. Roll the pieces into even-sized ropes, using the palms of your hands.

11.   Secure the 3 ropes together on one end and then braid them together. When the braiding is finished, press the ends together, then tuck under the dough to secure it.

12. Brush a baking dish with shortening and place the braided milk bread in the dish. Dust the surface with flour and let it rise again.

13. Preheat the oven to 400° F.

14. Bake the bread in the preheated oven for 15 minutes.

15. With a fork, beat the remaining egg white with the remaining tablespoon sugar. Brush the top of the bread with this mixture and, if desired, sprinkle sugar crystals over it. Reduce the heat to 350° F. and bake for an additional 30 to 35 minutes.

16. Let the bread cool on a rack for 2 to 3 hours before slicing.

CHEF'S SECRET: Warming the flour for this dough will improve the texture of the bread. Adding the butter in small amounts and kneading after each addition will help to distribute the butter evenly throughout the dough and will also improve the texture.

This is a soft dough. The raisins not only add to the flavor but they also absorb a part of the moisture in the dough during baking.

Do not cut this bread while it is warm or the texture will be rubbery.

Salt Sticks

approximately 60 sticks

1 cup (2 sticks) salted butter	dash of salt
3 egg yolks	⅓ cup warm water
6 cups flour	1 egg
½ package dry yeast	3 teaspoons caraway seeds
5 tablespoons warm milk	½ cup coarse salt (Kosher)
dash of sugar	

1. Mix the butter and egg yolks in an electric mixer equipped with a paddle or dough hook.

2. Slowly incorporate all but a few tablespoons of the flour.

3. Dissolve the yeast in the warm milk.

4. Add the yeast mixture to the flour mixture along with the sugar, salt, and water.

5.   Keep mixing until the dough no longer sticks to the sides of the bowl. The dough will be somewhat crumbly, not very moist.

6.   Roll the dough out on a floured board to approximately ¼ inch thick.

7.   With a pastry wheel, cut pieces ⅓ by 3 inches.

8.   By hand, shape both ends of each piece of dough to form a point. Place the pieces on a lightly greased baking sheet. Cover with a towel and let them rest in a warm place 15 to 20 minutes.

9.   Preheat the oven to 350° F. or 375° F.

10.   Beat the egg; then run it through a sieve.

11.   Brush the top of each salt stick with egg and sprinkle generously with coarse salt and caraway seeds.

12.   Bake the salt sticks for approximately 12 minutes or until the points are browned.

CHEF'S SECRET: It is hard to give an exact baking time or temperature for this simple recipe. Only your own experience will teach you how hot an oven you should have, or how long you should bake, or how long you should mix the dough before rolling it out. But if you master this dough, you will be very proud of it.

These salt sticks are versatile—they can be served with scrambled eggs for breakfast, with soup and a salad at lunch, as an appetizer, or with cheese for dessert.

If you cannot get any salt but regular table salt, mix it with a little water so that it gets very thick, like a syrup. Dribble some of the mixture over the salt sticks after they have baked for 2 to 3 minutes. They will have little white salt dribblings resembling small pieces of popcorn, as sometimes seen on a professional baker's salt sticks.

Lemon Sour-Cream Pie

8 servings

1 cup sugar	grated rind of 1 lemon
3 tablespoons cornstarch	1 cup milk
¼ cup butter	1 cup sour cream
¼ cup lemon juice	Baked 9-inch pie shell
3 egg yolks	½ cup heavy cream, whipped

1.   Combine sugar and cornstarch in a saucepan. Add butter, lemon juice, egg yolks, lemon rind, and milk.

2.   Cook over medium heat, stirring constantly, until thickened and smooth. Chill.

3.   Fold the sour cream into the chilled mixture and spoon into the baked pie shell. Chill well and serve topped with whipped cream.

CHEFS SECRET: If you wish a much lighter consistency, leave 3 egg whites at room temperature for at least two hours and beat until stiff with 3 scant tablespoons sugar added slowly during the beating process. After the sour cream is folded into the cooked and chilled lemon mixture, add some of the mixture to the egg whites, folding it in gently; then fold the egg whites into the filling and spoon it into the pie shell. In this case, if you wish, you can omit the whipped cream topping.

Baklava

approximately 32 pieces

½ cup unsalted butter
¼ cup vegetable oil
10 filo leaves
1 cup ground walnuts
½ cup chopped walnuts
⅓ cup sugar

Syrup:

½ cup sugar
¾ cup water
3 tablespoons fresh lemon juice
   **(more may be needed to
   adjust sweetness)**
¾ cup honey

1.   Preheat oven to 350° F. Brush a 9 by 12-inch shallow pan with a mixture of the butter and oil melted together. Place in the pan one filo leaf so that half the leaf hangs out of the pan. Brush again with the mixture of butter and oil, and fold over the half hanging out of the pan. Brush again and add another leaf, alternating the placement of the leaves around each side of the pan (see illustration) and covering the sides of the pan as well. Sprinkle 3 to 4 tablespoons of the nuts mixed with the sugar on the two filo-leaf layers. Place on two more layers of the leaves, being sure to brush between each layer with the butter mixture;

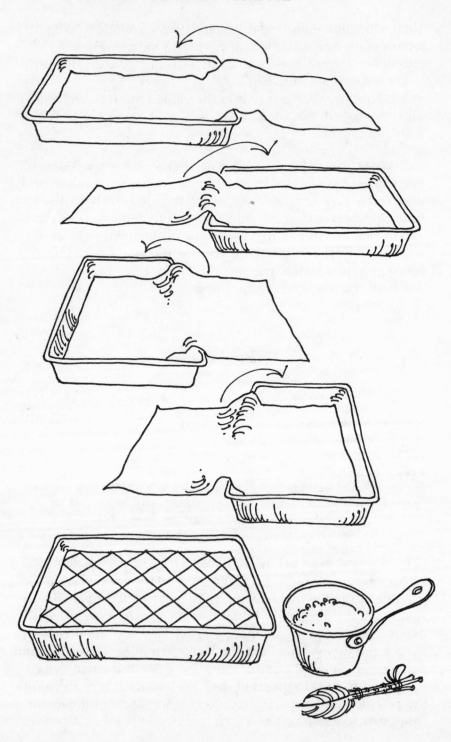

then add more of the nuts. Continue to layer in the same manner until all the nuts and leaves are used, making sure there is one nice leaf left for the top.

2.   Mark the top gently with a dull knife or the back of a spatula, pressing gently to make 1-inch squares or diamonds. Bake for 15 minutes. Lower the heat to 300° F. and continue to bake for an additional 20 minutes. Remove and cool slightly.

3.   Meanwhile, prepare syrup by placing ingredients in a saucepan, bringing the mixture to a boil, and boiling vigorously for 5 minutes. Adjust sweetness by adding more lemon juice if necessary. Pour syrup over partially cooled Baklava. Cool to room temperature and cut just before serving.

CHEF'S SECRET: This Baklava recipe is very basic, without any spices, without grated lemon rind or lemon zest, and with only one kind of nut. You can vary the results by mixing pecans, black walnuts, almonds, or filberts with the walnuts.

Use more sugar for a sweeter Baklava or more water for a juicier one. If you wish, you can add 2 to 3 drops of rosewater to the syrup.

Filo leaves are available in Greek stores. Strudel leaves (identical or almost identical to filo leaves) are obtainable in German, Austrian, and Hungarian stores, or you can order through the mail from my price list (see index).

Nut Crescents

approximately 4 dozen

2½ cups flour
1½ cups (8 ounces) ground walnuts or pecans (ground through a European-type grinder)

1¼ cups powdered sugar
1 cup plus 2 tablespoons unsalted butter
½ cup melted bittersweet chocolate

1.   Preheat oven to 325° F. Mix thoroughly flour, nuts, and sugar.

2.   Add cold butter as you would with a pie dough, working it in fast and gently until the dough forms a ball. Refrigerate for at least ½ hour.

3.   Form small crescents by rolling out dough ½ inch thick, cutting strips 2 inches long, and bending them into a crescent shape.

4.   Bake for 12 to 15 minutes or until pale brown. When cool, dip the two ends of each crescent into melted chocolate and dry on a rack.

5.   Store in a cookie jar or metal box with waxed paper between layers.

CHEF'S SECRET: This is a simple cookie with excellent flavor. The easiest way to cut the dough is with a pastry wheel. If your hands are warm, dip them into ice water and wipe them dry once in a while during the forming of the cookies, so as not to "burn" the dough.

Almond Crescents

approximately 4 dozen cookies

3 cups flour
8 ounces ground almonds
   (approximately 2½ cups)
1 cup powdered sugar
1 cup unsalted butter

2 egg yolks
2 cups or more powdered sugar,
   kept in a jar with a vanilla
   bean for a week or longer, for
   dusting cookies

1.   In a bowl, combine flour, almonds, and powdered sugar. Blend in butter as you would with pie pastry.

2.   Beat egg yolks with a fork and slowly work them into the mixture. Don't overwork. Let the dough rest in the refrigerator at least 30 minutes. Preheat oven to 325° F.

3.   Form small crescents and bake until they dry out, about 15 minutes.

4.   Remove cookies from cookie sheet and sprinkle very generously with vanilla sugar while hot.

CHEF'S SECRET: This is a very fine cookie—a bit time consuming, especially the first time you make it, but very rewarding.

The best way to form the crescents is to divide the dough into four equal parts and then pat out each part with a light hand into strips approximately 2 inches wide by 6 inches long. Divide the strip in half, then each half into half, continuing until you have approximately 12 to 14 small strips about ½ inch wide and 1½ to 2 inches long. Gently blend the strips one by one into crescent shapes right on the cookie sheet.

In many specialty stores you can buy vanilla beans (5 to 6 inches long, ¼ inch thick) and keep them in a tight fitting screwtop jar filled with powdered sugar. Fresh beans are moist, pliable, and fragrant; old ones are dry, dark gray, and brittle.

Store the cookies in a metal cookie jar with a waxed paper liner between each layer of cookies. They will keep for 3 to 4 weeks in a cool place.

Choco-Cookies

4 to 6 dozen cookies

1 cup butter
1 cup sugar
2 eggs
4 ounces melted baking
  chocolate

3½ cups flour
1 teaspoon baking powder
½ teaspoon salt
6 tablespoons milk

1.   Preheat oven to 400° F. With mixer at low speed, cream butter with sugar. Add eggs and chocolate; blend.
2.   Sift together flour, baking powder, and salt. Add alternately with milk, mixing until blended after each addition.
3.   Roll in 2-inch rolls; chill. Then cut into $^1/_{16}$-inch-thick slices.
4.   Bake 7 to 8 minutes on greased cookie sheets. Don't bake too many ahead of time; they are best right out of the oven.

CHEF'S SECRET: Nothing makes the home as friendly as the fragrance of something baking. With this recipe a busy cook can create an inviting home atmosphere for a last-minute date.

The dough can be kept in the refrigerator in roll form, wrapped in plastic and then in aluminum foil, for as long as 3 to 4 weeks. Then, just before the V.I.P. arrives, preheat the oven, cut the slices, and in 10 minutes the home will be filled with the heavenly fragrance of freshly baked cookies.

Apple Charlotte with Apricot Sauce

8 servings

½ cup plus 4 tablespoons
  unsalted butter, melted
8 slices French-style bread,
  crusts removed
2 pounds tart apples, peeled,
  cored, and thinly sliced
½ cup sugar
1 envelope unflavored gelatin,
  softened in 2 tablespoons
  water

1 cup applesauce
½ teaspoon cinnamon
8 ounces apricot preserves
2 tablespoons water
¼ cup brandy or applejack
  (optional)

1.   Preheat oven to 375° F. Lightly coat the bottom and sides of a small charlotte mold (or any small mold at least 3 inches deep) with butter. Cut 3 of the bread slices in half, and then each half on a diagonal, into a triangle. Quickly dip the triangles into the melted butter and lay them side by side in the bottom of the mold. With a small sharp knife, trim the triangles so that their points meet in the middle and no space shows between the slices. Cut another 3 bread slices in half, dip each quickly into the butter and place side by side around the edges of the mold.

2.   Cut the remaining 2 slices of bread into small cubes and sauté in 2 tablespoons of the remaining butter until lightly browned and crisp. Remove the toasted bread cubes from the skillet, and add the remaining 2 tablespoons butter, apple slices, and sugar. Gently sauté until apples are tender. Remove from heat.

3.   Soften the gelatin in 2 tablespoons water; then add to the applesauce. Combine applesauce and cooked apples. Add cinnamon. Cool slightly, then stir in the browned bread cubes. Pour the mixture into the lined mold and bake for 1 hour or until golden brown. Cool to room temperature; then refrigerate overnight.

4.   Next day, melt the apricot preserves with the water over medium heat. Add brandy if desired. Unmold the Apple Charlotte onto a serving platter, pour the sauce over the top, and serve at once.

CHEF'S SECRET: When you make this dessert for the first time, be sure you have more than the needed amount of bread on hand. You may ruin a few slices by cutting them incorrectly. If the bread isn't stale, let it stand at room temperature for a couple of hours, turning it every 30 minutes.

After you bake the charlotte and remove it from the oven, you may be frightened: it will look like a mess and you will think you can never unmold it. Don't worry. After chilling it overnight and loosening the edges with a knife dipped in very hot water, it will be easy to unmold the charlotte, and the glazing will make it beautiful. If you wish, serve it with very stiff whipped cream flavored with a small sprinkling of cinnamon.

Brandy Balls

approximately 60 pieces

2½ cups vanilla wafer crumbs
5½ cups (1 pound) ground
   walnuts, loosely packed
1 cup honey

¼ cup brandy
¼ cup rum
1½ cups powdered sugar

Mix vanilla wafer crumbs well with remaining ingredients, except powdered sugar. Form in balls; roll in sugar. Store in tightly covered containers.

CHEF'S SECRET: If you don't have a grinder to make vanilla wafer crumbs, put the wafers in two to three batches in plastic bags and gently break them with a rolling pin.

The easiest way to make 60 balls the same size is to spread out an even, thick layer of the whole mixture in a rectangle twice as long as it is wide. Divide the rectangle into 60 equal-sized squares and then roll the squares into balls. Have a wet cloth on hand and wet your palms from time to time so that the mixture won't stick to your hands but will roll easily.

Brownie Bottom Bourbon Pie

8 servings

5 egg yolks
¾ cup sugar
1 envelope unflavored gelatin
¼ cup cold water
½ cup bourbon

3 cups heavy cream
1 brownie baked in a 10-inch
   pie pan, from a brownie mix
   or your own recipe (don't
   overbake)

1.   Beat egg yolks until thick and lemon-colored. Slowly beat in the sugar.

2.   Soften the gelatin in cold water and add ⅓ of the bourbon.

3.   Heat this mixture of water, bourbon, and gelatin over boiling water until the gelatin dissolves. Then pour it into the yolks and stir briskly.

4.   Stir in remaining bourbon. Whip 1 cup heavy cream and fold into the mixture.

5.   Pour the filling into the pie pan over the brownie and chill at least 4 hours.

6.   Top the pie with the remaining heavy cream whipped with a few grains of salt and just a pinch of sugar. If you wish, sprinkle on top about 2 tablespoons of shaved chocolate.

CHEF'S SECRET: This is one of the most American of American pies. Brownies as we know them are the most American cookies, and bourbon is indeed the American whiskey.

After you have made this dish once or twice you may find you wish to use more sugar in the heavy cream or less bourbon in the filling. If you cut down on the bourbon, be sure to make up the difference in quantity with cold water, because the half-cup of liquid is necessary.

Cold Marble-Bavarian Soufflé

16 servings

3 envelopes unflavored gelatin
1 cup cold water
8 eggs, separated
1 cup granulated sugar
1 teaspoon vanilla extract
¼ cup flour

1 quart milk
4 squares semisweet chocolate
4 tablespoons cocoa
about 6 drops yellow food
   coloring
2 cups whipping cream
¼ teaspoon salt

1.   In a small bowl, sprinkle gelatin over cold water to soften.

2.   In large saucepan, combine egg yolks with ¾ cup sugar and add vanilla. Blend in flour, stirring until smooth. Add milk

and blend well. Cook over low to medium heat, stirring constantly, until custard coats back of spoon. Remove from heat.

3. Add gelatin mixture and stir until completely dissolved. Refrigerate, stirring occasionally, until a small amount mounds when dropped from a spoon.

4. Meanwhile, fold a 35-inch length of foil, 12 inches wide, in half lengthwise. Wrap it around the outside of a china soufflé dish so that a collar 3 inches high stands above the rim. Fasten it with cellophane tape.

5. Melt semisweet chocolate in small saucepan over hot, not boiling, water.

6. Divide cooled custard mixture in half, placing each half in a bowl. Into one half stir melted semisweet chocolate and cocoa, until smooth. Into the other half stir yellow food coloring.

7. Whip cream. Beat egg whites with salt until soft peaks form; gradually add ¼ cup sugar and beat until stiff. Fold half of whipped cream and half of beaten egg whites into chocolate mixture; fold remainder of cream and egg whites into yellow mixture. Alternately spoon yellow and chocolate mixtures into soufflé dish.

8. With rubber spatula, gently cut through mixtures several times, swirling light and dark batters. Freeze several hours or overnight.

9. Before serving, carefully remove foil from soufflé. (For 6 to 8 servings, make half the above recipe, using a 5-cup china soufflé dish with foil collar. Or use an 8-cup glass serving dish, omitting the foil collar.)

CHEF'S SECRET: The third step in the preparation reads "until a small amount mounds when dropped from a spoon." This means that when you stir the custard in the refrigerator, you should drop some onto a small plate or saucer. If it doesn't run like liquid but stands up in a little mound, it is ready.

You don't have to fold in the egg whites and the whipped cream completely. If both have some white streaks, the soufflé will have a nice third color, which will improve the marble effect.

The aluminum-foil collar makes the cold soufflé look like a hot soufflé that has risen in the oven several inches above the rim of the dish. This is the effect you want. If you wish, you can sprinkle the top of the cold soufflé with a generous amount of powdered sugar before removing the collar.

Chocolate Nut Roll

8 to 16 servings

6 eggs
6 heaping tablespoons sugar
6 tablespoons finely ground
  walnuts
1 tablespoon fine white crushed
  bread crumbs (store-bought
  commercial bread crumbs
  won't do)
¼ teaspoon baking powder

Icing:
1 cup unsalted butter
1 egg
8 to 10 tablespoons powdered
  sugar
8 to 10 tablespoons Dutch
  cocoa
1 tablespoon boiling water
1 to 2 tablespoons brandy
  or rum (optional)

1. Preheat oven to 375° F. Beat eggs with sugar on high speed in an electric mixer for 15 to 20 minutes, or until they are light, fluffy, and lemon-colored, resembling whipped cream just before it starts to form peaks.

2. By hand, gently fold in the nuts (sprinkled spoonful by spoonful over the surface), then the bread crumbs combined with the baking powder.

3. Grease a 10 by 15-inch jelly roll pan and line it with waxed paper. Pour in batter and bake 12 to 14 minutes. Remove from oven, invert on a clean kitchen towel, and roll it up with the towel jelly-roll fashion. Leave it rolled up and let it cool.

4. Make your favorite chocolate icing or make the following one. In an electric mixer, beat to a light, fluffy consistency 1 cup unsalted butter with 1 egg. Gradually add 8 to 10 tablespoons powdered sugar sifted together with the same amount of imported Dutch cocoa. Add 1 tablespoon boiling water and blend. Spread this icing over the surface of the cake; roll it up and frost the outside. If you wish, add 1 or 2 tablespoons brandy or rum to the icing.

CHEF'S SECRET: Don't start to make this recipe if you don't have the most important item—a European-style hand grinder that grinds the nuts into a fine nut flour without pressing the oil from them. You can buy this nut grinder in Chicago at Kuhn's Delicatessen, 3053 North Lincoln Avenue. Or you can order it from H. Roth & Son, Lekvar by the Barrel, 1577 First Avenue, New York, New York 10028. Incidentally, if you are serious about baking, it is worthwhile to get their lovely catalog listing all the European imports a fine baker needs.

You can bake this same batter in two 8- or 9-inch round cake pans and make a two-layer chocolate nut torte. You can also omit the cocoa in the frosting; add 6 tablespoons ground walnuts and 2 tablespoons rum, and decorate the slices with nut halves.

Peach Melba

4 servings

**2 tablespoons red raspberry
  jelly**
1 teaspoon sugar

3 or 4 tablespoons water
1 tablespoon bourbon or brandy
2 fresh peaches
½ pint vanilla ice cream

1.   Combine raspberry jelly, sugar, water, and bourbon or brandy in a small saucepan. Stirring with a wire whip, slowly heat the mixture until it comes to a boil and the jelly dissolves. Simmer over low heat for 2 to 3 minutes; then remove and let cool at room temperature. The sauce will thicken slightly as it cools.

2.   With a small, sharp paring knife, cut around each peach, dividing it in half. With a grapefruit knife, remove the pits from the peaches. Remove all but one strip of peel from each peach half.

3.   Divide the ice cream into four equal portions, placing one portion in each of four stemmed dessert dishes. Chill in freezer until serving time.

4.   To serve, place a peach half, cut side down, on top of the ice cream, and pour the sauce on top.

CHEF'S SECRET: The instructions suggest removing all but one strip of peel from each peach half. It looks pretty and natural if you leave some of the peel in the middle of the peach half, especially after you pour the sauce on, because the sauce will adhere to the part where the skin is left on.

To prevent the peaches from turning brown after cutting, sprinkle them with lemon juice or with water with some lemon juice added.

Never peel a peach first and then try to halve it. The flesh of peaches is very tender, and you will have a mess before you remove the pit even from the freestone varieties.

If you wish, decorate the rim of the peach with some whipped cream.

Hungarian Chocolate Bars

16 to 24 pieces

First Mixture:

½ cup butter
1¾ cups powdered sugar
3 egg yolks
1 teaspoon vanilla
2½ cups ground walnuts
4 tablespoons bread crumbs
3 tablespoons cocoa
7 egg whites

Second Mixture:

4 egg yolks
1 cup powdered sugar

Third Mixture:

1 cup sugar
2 tablespoons cocoa
¼ cup water
5 tablespoons butter

1.   Preheat oven to 375° F.

2.   For the first mixture, cream together the butter and half the powdered sugar. Add egg yolks and vanilla.

3.   In a separate bowl, mix together the ground nuts, bread crumbs, and cocoa.

4.   Whip egg whites and remaining powdered sugar until stiff peaks form.

5.   Alternately fold the butter-egg mixture and the nut-cocoa mixture into the egg whites.

6.   Pour batter into a 9 by 13-inch pan which has been greased and lined with waxed paper. Bake 15 to 20 minutes.

7.   Raise oven temperature to 425° F. Whip the egg yolks from the second mixture with the powdered sugar until lemon-colored and light. Pour over the baked layer and bake for an additional 15 minutes. Cool.

8.   Prepare a chocolate glaze as follows from the third

mixture: Combine sugar, cocoa, and water and cook over low heat for 5 to 6 minutes.

9.   Remove from heat and keep stirring for 2 to 3 minutes, then add the butter.

10.   Pour the glaze over the top of the baked chocolate bars.

11.   When cool, cut into squares or rectangles.

CHEF'S SECRET: I'll admit that many small pastries and cookies are much easier to prepare, but this is so good and so very different from any other pastry you have ever tasted that it is worth trying.

When the bars are cut into pieces, they freeze extremely well wrapped first in plastic wrap, then in aluminum foil, or wrapped in plastic wrap and then placed in a tight-fitting plastic container. They defrost in about an hour at room temperature if cut into 1½ to 2-inch squares.

The ground walnuts should be a fine bread-crumb or flour-like substance, the same type of nut flour mentioned in other recipes. For this you need a European-type nut grinder that grinds the nuts into a fine powder without pressing the oils out of the nutmeats (see index for price list, which will tell you where you can order such a grinder).

Hungarian Cheese Palacsintas

8 servings

2 cups baker's cheese
2 eggs, separated
¼ cup sugar
1 tablespoon lemon zest
½ cup seedless white raisins, soaked in hot water for one hour

8 palacsintas or crêpes (see index)
1 tablespoon butter
1 cup sour cream
¼ cup sugar

1.   Preheat oven to 350° F. In a large bowl, mix baker's cheese with egg yolks, sugar, lemon zest, and raisins.

2.   Beat egg whites until stiff. Gently fold a small portion of the egg whites into the cheese mixture. Then fold in remaining egg whites.

3.   Lightly butter an ovenproof dish, approximately 9 by 6 by 2 inches. Divide the filling into 8 portions and place one portion on each palacsinta. Roll up jelly-roll fashion and place the rolls next to each other in ovenproof dish.

4.   Heat sour cream in a small saucepan, gently stirring it with a wire whip until it liquefies. Pour half of it over the palacsintas. Spread it evenly and sprinkle with sugar.

5.   Bake for 20 minutes. Cover with remaining sour cream and serve at once.

CHEF'S SECRET: If you can't get baker's cheese, buy 1 pint of cottage cheese and press it through a fine sieve. If the consistency is too loose, add 1 tablespoon fine bread crumbs.

The lemon zest is the very outside yellow, thin skin of the lemon, which contains the lemon oils. If you don't have a lemon zester, you can replace a part of the ¼ cup sugar with 3 to 4 sugar cubes; rub the sugar cubes on the outside of the lemon until the sugar cubes turn yellow and have a lemon oil taste.

Basic Butter Cream

approximately 6 cups

1 pound butter, slightly colder than room temperature

6 cups powdered sugar
1 egg

1.   Use an electric mixer with a wire whip or paddle. Beating at high speed, add ⅓ of the butter, bit by bit. Stop the mixer and add about 2 cups of the powdered sugar. Very slowly start to beat again, and beat slowly until the sugar is incorporated. Then increase the speed to high. Add another third of butter, again bit by bit.

2.   Add the egg and beat until smooth. Stop the mixer, add more of the powdered sugar, then slowly start to beat again, increasing the speed as the sugar is incorporated. Add the remaining butter, stop the mixer, and add the remaining powdered sugar.

3.   Once the sugar is incorporated at low speed, increase the speed to high and beat until the butter cream is very fluffy. This basic butter cream can be flavored with bourbon, rum, brandy, or any imitation flavorings.

CHEF'S SECRET: To make a good, fluffy, smooth butter cream, you must start with a very clean, empty container. The electric mixer should run at the highest possible speed before you add the first small piece of butter. Do not add more than the size of an almond at once, and keep adding these small pieces every 15 to 20 seconds until you have about 1½ sticks or ⅓ of a pound in the mixer. All this time the beater should be at the highest possible speed. Then stop and add 2 cups sugar at once and incorporate it at the lowest possible speed before you beat it again.

I judge when the mixture is ready for the next addition by the sound of the cream in the bowl. As the mixture gets closer and closer to perfection, the sound of the beater will get a higher pitch and sound rather hollow. That's when you should make the next addition.

Be sure to scrape the sides of the bowl after stopping the machine during each step, otherwise the mixture won't be even. Be careful not to overmix, and in the summer chill the butter, the bowl, and the beater before starting.

Whipped Cream Frosting

4 cups

1 quart whipping cream
½ to ¾ cup powdered sugar, depending on taste

1 envelope unflavored gelatin
3 tablespoons plus ½ cup water

1. In an electric mixer, using a wire whip, start to beat the cream. As soon as it begins to stiffen, slowly add the powdered sugar. Beat until stiff but do not overbeat.
2. Dissolve the gelatin in the 3 tablespoons water. Bring the ½ cup water to a boil; then add the softened gelatin.
3. Cool the gelatin in an ice water bath until it becomes syrupy and is cooler than the temperature of your hand. Gently fold the gelatin, in a thin, threadlike stream, into the whipped cream. Chill before starting to frost a cake.

CHEF'S SECRET: If you use only 1 pint of whipping cream, be careful to divide the gelatin mixture only after the whole amount (1 envelope of gelatin with the 3 tablespoons plus ½ cup of water) is made according to directions. It is very difficult to make a decent gelatin mixture from half the amount given here, and it never comes out right. It costs much less to discard half an envelope of gelatin than a pint of whipping cream.

Chocolate Mousse

8 servings

1½ cups canned Hershey
  Chocolate Syrup
2 tablespoons brandy
2 envelopes gelatin dissolved
  in ⅓ cup water

1 cup boiling water
3 egg whites
2 cups whipping cream
2 tablespoons cocoa

1.   Pour chocolate syrup into a mixing bowl. Stir in brandy.
2.   Mix the dissolved gelatin into boiling water in a saucepan. Cool saucepan by dipping it into a larger pan of cold water. Keep stirring until syrupy.
3.   Stir gelatin into chocolate syrup. Whip egg whites until they form soft peaks and gently fold into the chocolate mixture.
4.   Whip the cream stiff. Sprinkle the cocoa through a fine sieve into the whipped cream and then fold it in. Whip again for a few seconds. Do not overbeat; otherwise it will collapse. Fold in whipped cream with cocoa into the other ingredients. Transfer to individual serving dishes. Chill and serve.

CHEF'S SECRET: In my lifetime I have been served the strangest and most diverse desserts called Chocolate Mousse. But I think that this recipe is closest to the genuine texture and flavor of the "real" chocolate mousse. Of course, I could give you a recipe where everything starts "from scratch," but I feel that the exact consistency and flavor of the commercial Hershey chocolate syrup is very hard to duplicate at home. And if you *are* able to duplicate it, what do you achieve by duplication?

The cocoa whipped into the heavy cream fortifies the chocolatey "mouth feel." The cocoa will dissolve in your mouth during eating, and your taste buds will convey a much more chocolatey feeling than they would without it.

Hungarian Christmas Balls

30 small pieces

1 cup sugar
2 tablespoons grated orange
 rind
2 tablespoons orange juice
2 tablespoons lemon juice

1 cup finely ground walnuts
½ cup finely chopped candied
 fruits
½ cup cocoa

1. In a saucepan over low heat, melt sugar with grated orange rind, orange juice, and lemon juice. Cool.
2. Add walnuts and fruit and work with hands until well mixed.
3. Pinch off pieces of dough and roll into ¾-inch balls. Roll in cocoa until coated.
4. Freeze balls for an hour for easier handling. Place each ball in a small paper candy cup or wrap each in foil. Store covered in a cool place.

CHEF'S SECRET: Be sure not to grate the bitter, white pulp of the orange rind into the mixture.

To make these balls, dip your index finger into a little oil or butter and rub the oil or butter on your palm. If your hands are oily, the rolling will go very fast. If the mixture is too dry, add a couple more spoonfuls of either the orange or lemon juice, according to your taste.

Prunes Frederick

8 servings

1 tablespoon butter
1 pound pitted prunes
1 cup (3½ to 4 ounces) pecan
 halves

1 cup brown sugar
1 cup water
1 lemon, thinly sliced
¼ to ⅓ cup bourbon

1. Preheat oven to 350° F. Coat a pie dish with the butter.
2. Stuff the pitted prunes with the pecans and place in the

dish. If you have any pecan pieces left, chop them coarsely and sprinkle over the prunes.

3.   In a small saucepan, bring to a boil the brown sugar, water, and sliced lemon. Boil for a minute or so; then strain the syrup over the prunes.

4.   Bake the prunes for about 20 minutes; then cover with the lemon slices. Bake for another 10 minutes.

5.   Remove. Bring to the table. Warm the bourbon in a small saucepan, ignite it, and pour over the prunes. Let it burn until all flame dies.

6.   Serve the prunes with some of the remaining thick syrup but without the lemon slices. Serve it as a side dish with any poultry or game, or serve it as a dessert with a scoop of vanilla ice cream on each serving.

CHEF'S SECRET: A tablespoon of butter may seem like too much for coating the pie dish, but you will need it. As soon as you pour the boiling liquid over the prunes, some of the butter will melt and will cover the surface of the liquid, preventing or slowing down evaporation of the syrup.

The lemon will give the dish a pleasant, slightly tart taste. But if you don't like this taste, simply peel the lemon before slicing and add just a small piece of the rind.

Index